The Global Turn:
Six Journeys of Architecture and the City, 1945–1989

Tom Avermaete
Michelangelo Sabatino

With a foreword by Mark Jarzombek

nai010 publishers

One's destination is never a place but rather a new way of looking at things.
— Henry Miller, *Big Sur and the Oranges of Hieronymus Bosch*

Passports thus recite the seeming imperative that we must be 'attached' to one place and only 'allowed' to enter into others. They tell stories about some of the most consequential ideas of our time, such as 'modernity', 'nation', and 'globalization', though the narratives they offer are far more intimate than these lofty abstractions suggest.
— Patrick Bixby, *A Cultural History of the Passport*

Foreword
Global History: in Progress   6
Mark Jarzombek

Introduction
Toward a New Road Map: Six Journeys
on the Global Turn   10

An Incomplete Conclusion:
Towards Other Times and Geographies   216

Coda
The Global Turn:
Perspectives from a Personal Journey   220
Leonardo Zuccaro Marchi

Acknowledgements   227
Authors and Contributors   230
Index   233
Image Credits   239
Colophon   240

1 Collaboration:
  Competitions, Workshops,
  and Transcultural Classrooms 36

2 Goods:
  Distribution Centres, Shopping Malls,
  and Trade Fairs 72

3 Mobility:
  Automobiles, Trains, Airplanes,
  and New Building Types 100

4 Knowledge:
  Journals, Manuals, and Mass Media 136

5 Construction:
  New Materials, Methods, and Systems
  for Building 164

6 Labour:
  From *Bidonville* to *Ville Nouvelle* 192

Foreword
Global History: in Progress

Mark Jarzombek
Professor of the History and Theory
of Architecture, MIT

Young scholars of architectural history might think that the word 'global' has always been part of the vocabulary of the field. But its use as a way to avoid the word 'world' — as in 'World History' — only began after the start of the new millennium. World History seemed at the time still too tied to its Eurocentric ideologies. But Global History was hardly a coherent thing. Advocates developed divergent methodological and philosophical directions. In architectural history the main purpose of this term was not just to challenge the deep roots of Eurocentrism but also to open the field to areas and subject matters that were understudied and underrepresented. Some of the issues were downright prosaic. When Vikramāditya Prakāsh and I were preparing the manuscript for the first edition of *A Global History of Architecture*,[1] we were astonished how few plans there were of South Asian buildings, of stave churches, and of buildings in Africa and China. Site plans were almost non-existent. Compared to what has been published on medieval cathedrals, for example, Borobudur, which is most certainly one of the most amazing buildings on the planet, had a bibliography with only a few meagre references and, at that time, there was still no overall plan or detailed study for it. If you multiply that problem by 1000, you come to the scale of the issue that we faced. Then, of course, there were — and remain — the problems associated with language, cost of travel, and the lack of archives, not to mention the fact that in some places civil war or other political realities make it difficult to visit or do research. If 'global' was an aspiration for a new and more dynamic field, it was clear that it would require work from the most basic to the most critical, over many generations.

What Vikramāditya and I also discovered along the way was that this emerging term 'global' was not uncontested. Many universities in the US today still teach architectural history along lines set out in the nineteenth century. And in many parts of the world ethnocentric, nation-centric, and even religion-centric narratives have arisen to foreclose a broader, more inclusive notion of history. At a conference in 2008 a scholar from Canada told me: 'Why should I teach global when the students do not even know about Canada?' The assumption seems to have been that these were mutually exclusive interests. Also, because in many parts of the world architectural history is so intimately connected to preservation, it is difficult for local scholars to develop or defend research agendas that look across horizons.

When a publishing company in India wanted to print a cheaper version of our textbook, we found out that they had removed the pages dealing with China and pre-Columbian American history. Needless to say, we did not approve, and this particular edition was never printed.

The most unexpected problem Vikramāditya and I encountered after our book was published was that educators who wanted to embrace a global approach to their teaching confessed that they had difficulty with the challenge of living up to expectations. How can you teach something about which you might not know very much or which you have not had the time or finances to research through travel? Furthermore, since the burden of teaching global history has often fallen on young educators who have also had to worry about tenure and other things, researchers have not been able to find the time and resources, much less an intellectual environment, with and in which to develop new content. In other words it would take decades to develop a teaching horizon that would be adequate to the newly expanded field.

To address the problem, Vikram and I created the Global Architectural History Teaching Collaborative (GAHTC), which from 2013 to 2020 was generously funded by the Andrew Mellon Foundation. This served as a rapid-response mechanism to the problem of teaching global architectural history. GAHTC provided the funding for groups of teachers to get together to design their pedagogies, syllabi, readings, and assignments. They would not only create lecture material but also *share* it. In that way, if one person knew something about Japan, they would share their lecture material with someone who knew something about aboriginal life in Australia. It was teachers teaching teachers. GAHTC eventually amassed some 500 collaboratively produced, peer-reviewed lectures that its members freely shared and modified and that are still being used.[2]

The side benefit of this was that these GAHTC exchanges produced new ways of thinking and even new types of scholarship, of which this book, *The Global Turn: Six Journeys of Architecture and the City, 1945–1989*, is an excellent example. Instead of seeing teaching as a trickle-down from advanced research, GAHTC treated it as participating in and creating an expanding field. Even students could become foot soldiers in that effort. This is, of course, all a continually morphing process. The slow grind of the tenure system, the increasing stress put on the humanities by economic pragmatists, and the lack of adequate financial support for research and travel, not to mention that the field itself is too small to handle its load and ambition, all keep the promise of a vibrant and expanded field just that, a promise. But the arrows are pointing in the right direction.

---

1 Mark M. Jarzombek, Vikramāditya Prakāsh, Francis D. K. Ching (illustrator), *A Global History of Architecture* (J. Wiley & Sons, 2006).
2 See the website https://gahtc.org/.

Introduction
Toward a New Road Map:
Six Journeys on the Global Turn

Tom Avermaete
Michelangelo Sabatino

> A global history is not the history of all the modern
> nations added up like beads on an abacus. But neither
> is it a history that assumes a universal aspect to mankind
> and its productions. For a global history to be more
> than just dates and facts, it has to be rooted in the
> principle that each of us learns how he or she is indeed
> different in the eyes of others.
> — Mark Jarzombek and Vikramāditya Prakāsh,
> *A Global History of Architecture*[1]

Journeys are about the travel of people, things, and ideas that can lead to new ways of seeing and doing.[2] In this book 'journey' is used to suggest a somewhat open-ended experimental approach to the selection of six intertwined themes on architecture and urbanism: collaboration, goods, mobility, knowledge, construction, and labour. Our argument is that these six journeys capture the phenomenon of the Global Turn in relation to the built environment from the end of World War II on 2 September 1945 to the fall of the Berlin Wall on 9 November 1989. We selected these two significant historical events because they bookend a period of time that witnessed the dramatic rise and subsequent development of globalization.

We have not set out to write a definitive study of these phenomena nor to comprehensively examine all examples that could further illustrate them. Rather we view our six journeys as an initial cartography of thematic 'roads' that may enhance

Le Havre after the destruction of World War II, 1945.

Fall of the Berlin Wall, 1989.

Marshall Plan graphic, 1948.

our understanding of the Global Turn in the built environment during a period of time that witnessed an extraordinary shift in the identity and practice of the architect and the spaces of architectural practice. Having made clear the modest intent of our undertaking, we invite our readers to meander through these pages with a mind as open as this tentative road map with its six journeys. When we embarked on this book project in 2014 as an outgrowth of our participation in the Global Architectural History Teaching Collaborative (GAHTC), first launched at MIT in 2013, we could never have imagined that a single event might show the profound impact (both positive and negative) of globalization on our professional and personal lives. Naively, we did not anticipate the possibility of a global pandemic prolonging the completion of this book. The World Health Organization declared COVID-19 a global pandemic on 11 March 2020. The physical and virtual interconnectedness of our world and its dependence on rapid travel, trade, and information exchange became strikingly apparent as the COVID-19 virus spread across borders with a speed and on a scale never seen before.[3] Supply chains were disrupted, highlighting the vulnerability of our globalized economy. Nations around the globe collaborated on an unprecedented scale to develop vaccines and share vital medical knowledge, underscoring the necessity for cooperation when faced with global crises. The pandemic revealed the intertwined complexity of our earth and emphasized the importance of taking into account global implications in all endeavours, a lesson we could have hardly envisioned at the project's inception. It also confronted people with an urgent need to find alternatives to face-to-face communication that led to us using software such as Zoom. Now, as we have become reliant upon this and other software to communicate across time and space, we recognize this development as a silver lining to the disruption caused by the pandemic.

The collaborative research we present in the form of this book started with the intention of uncovering some of the visible and 'invisible' (invisible because concealed in process-oriented developments) ways in which architecture has both been informed by and contributed to the multifaceted processes of globalization from 1945 to 1989. From the outset, we aimed to explore how design practices and built environments have been affected by the forces of globalization while also examining the roles these practices and environments have played in shaping and facilitating global interactions. We seek to demonstrate the part that cultural, economic, and social changes during this period played in generating 'new' building types, including airports, tall buildings (i.e. skyscrapers), and shopping malls. 'Global' has gradually replaced adjectives and concepts such as 'modern' or 'international'. It has also, however, tended to absorb some of the meanings of both these concepts. For example, if it is true that the tall building is one of the most 'global' building types, such buildings inevitably deploy functional and aesthetic principles that can be traced back to modern and/or so-called 'International Style' architecture.

The primary title of our book, articulated in six different themes (journeys), deploys 'turn' in association with 'global' to imply a change of direction.[4] It suggests change in ways similar to Malcolm Gladwell's concept of the 'tipping point', understood as change that dramatically manifests itself after a series of more discrete developments.[5] To be sure, as the reader will soon discover in the pages of this book, the global turn did not happen all at once; it was a multifaceted phenomenon facilitated by a series of events and discoveries (at times coordinated and at others not) that took place at different times and in different cities of the world. Readers will notice that the examples discussed in our six journeys tend to be mostly limited to North America and Europe. This decision was driven by our desire to use examples drawn from our own research on the twentieth-century built environment. Nevertheless, we are confident that our road map can be successfully applied in other geographies as well by others (students or researchers) who might be interested in doing so.

While we have drawn on the work of scores of historians, economists, cultural theorists, and sociologists who have made concerted efforts to unpack the global phenomenon, here we write from the perspective of two architectural and urban historians. Both authors are contemporaries, and both were trained in Europe (Sabatino also trained in Canada and the US). Since GAHTC was born as a collaborative for teachers of architectural history, it stands to reason that we wrote this book with students of the built environment in mind. But we hope to extend the idea of 'student' beyond academia to include professionals from a range of related fields as well as members of the general public who are curious about the virtual and physical ways in which globalization has transformed the built environment during the period examined and vice versa.

Five Faces of Globalization
(as Seen in the Built Environment)

Globalization as a cultural condition

Although globalization is not a new cultural phenomenon, the period (1945 to 1989) examined in these pages clearly has its own specific characteristics. Increasingly global patterns of trade and consumption were undisputedly part of the early modern era. Recall, for example, the Silk Road(s).[6] With the circulation of goods came also the circulation of ideas and practices

Medieval trade routes connecting China to India.

across cultural boundaries.[7] Meanings, uses, and rituals were transmitted together with 'objects' (including edible commodities such as coffee, spices, rice, to name just a few), and, at the same time, objects were shorn of their original meanings and engendered reinterpretations and sometimes misunderstandings upon arrival in a new location.[8]

The world fairs (i.e. expositions) in the nineteenth and twentieth centuries provided opportunities to consume as well as learn about the global 'other'.[9] However, it was the years after World War II that saw a heightened awareness ('consciousness') of globalization as a cultural condition that operates simultaneously and interrelatedly in the political, economic, technological-communicational, and cultural spheres of human life. The British-American sociologist Roland Robertson has written:

> Globalization as a concept refers to both the compression of the world and the intensification of consciousness of the world as a whole ... both concrete global interdependence and consciousness of the global whole in the twentieth century.[10]

In this book we maintain that post-war globalization involved new forms of connectivity by way of collaboration and increased mobility; additionally, it fostered the emergence of new regimes of circulation of goods, knowledge, and construction-related materials and techniques, as well as new forms of labour — on unprecedented scales and at unprecedented speeds. The British sociologist Anthony Giddens offers us a clear definition of its impact:

> Globalization is really about the transformation of space and time. I define it as action at distance and relate its intensifying over recent years to the emergence of means of instantaneous global communication and mass transportation.[11]

Together, the new logics and regimes create a transformation in space and time in which events outside our immediate localities — what Giddens calls 'action at distance' — are increasingly consequential for our experience. Giddens claims that there is an 'intensification of worldwide social relations which link distant localities in such a way that local happenings are shaped by events occurring many miles away and vice versa.'[12]

Global forms of connectivity and regimes of circulation are sometimes paired with abstraction of social and cultural practices from contexts of local particularity. For example, the Australian sociologist Malcolm Waters has argued that this abstraction can bring a 'deterritorialization' that diminishes the significance of social-geographical location for the mundane flow of cultural experience; he describes this as 'a social process in which the constraints of geography on social and cultural arrangements recede and in which people become increasingly aware that they are receding.'[13]

Globalization does not, however, necessarily imply that localities are destroyed, as maintained by scholars who follow the perhaps overly negative thesis of homogenization in accordance with which all places become culturally uniform — but that places become increasingly affected by the global circulation of people, things, and ideas. While cities, neighbourhoods, and buildings may retain a high degree of distinctiveness, this particularity is no longer — as it may have been in the past — the sole most important determinant of our cultural experience.

This book also argues that the cultural condition of globalization is marked by significant inequalities. Participation in global exchanges requires access to transportation, technology, and, often, financial resources. In addition, people perform different roles at different times and places in the global regimes of circulation.[14] While some might be well-paid designers of a commodity and located in one part of the world, others might be low-wage producers at the other side of the globe. In this context globalization perpetuates economic, social, and other disparities between individuals, groups, nations, and regions.

Globalization as a working condition for architects

Architectural practice, like many other fields, is affected by and affects processes of globalization. In the twentieth century the practice of architecture became increasingly transcultural as a result, first, of access to affordable travel and, second, of the advent first of the internet and subsequently of the World Wide Web in 1989.[15] In the years after 1989, as interest and access expanded exponentially, the first and second digital turn in architecture enabled collaboration and the exchange of professional skills and expertise across time and space in ways that were never possible before.[16] It is tempting to regard architects and other designers as members of a global, cosmopolitan culture that transcends national boundaries and identities. Architectural approaches, technologies, drawings, buildings, and even workforces may seem to travel easily between cultures and continents.

The years after World War II generated a whole new set of opportunities for transcultural encounters, collaboration, and exchange — against the background of a nascent postcolonial world order in which new geopolitical alliances were being formed. Modern architects had already worked between countries and continents, but in the post-war period we see an increased globalization of professional practices which threw into question the role, approaches, and instruments of architects. This change was not immediate. The Congrès International d'Architecture

Group photograph of Congrès International d'Architecture Moderne (CIAM) at La Sarraz, Switzerland, 1928.

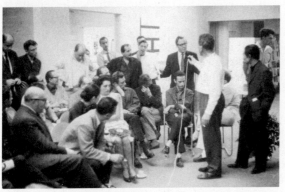

Meeting of Congrès International d'Architecture Moderne (CIAM) at the Kröller-Müller Museum in Otterlo, Netherlands, 1959.

Moderne (CIAM), for instance, founded in June 1928 in La Sarraz, Switzerland, had from its inception the ambition to become an international forum for discussion, but it was not until the post-war years, with the disbanding of CIAM in 1959 and the emergence of Team 10, that the nature of the exchange and collaboration became truly transcultural.

Our book presents new readings of well known and lesser-known events, works, and organizations that played key roles in shaping global architectural discourse and practice from 1945 to 1989. For example, an important role was played by shared conversations hosted by, for instance, the Institute for Architecture and Urban Studies (IAUS; spearheaded by Peter Eisenman in New York from the late 1960s), the International Laboratory of Architecture and Urban Design (ILAUD; founded by Giancarlo De Carlo in Urbino, Italy, in 1976), and the Delos Conferences (organized by Constantinos Doxiadis and Jacqueline Tyrwhitt and held on board ship in the Aegean Sea between 1963 and 1975). Additionally, the United Nations Technical Assistance Seminars, initiated by Ernest Weismann and Otto Koenigsberger, the American, German, and Spanish academies in Rome, the Aga Khan Award, founded in 1977, and the Pritzker Prize, established in Chicago in 1979, all provided important venues for global exchange of ideas and production of new discourse in and outside academia.[17] As did the rise of international cultural and research institutions such as the Canadian Centre for Architecture in Montréal (established in 1979 and opened to the public in 1989).[18] Additionally, in 1980 La Biennale di Venezia launched a separate section devoted to architecture: the Venice Biennale of Architecture (Mostra di Architettura di Venezia); this has since become an important venue of global exchange for a wide variety of architectural professionals and enthusiasts.[19]

Architects must nevertheless still confront the stubborn, sometimes intractable characteristics of local cultures. The organization of the construction industry, for instance, varies widely from country to country, with profound consequences for building design. National and local governments continue to define specific legal frameworks that are proper to their social and economic geographies and influence design methods. And value systems seem to aspire to global dwelling ideals while remaining profoundly culture-bound — with great consequences for the compositional, typological, and material characteristics of the built environment.

Technological globalization and homogenization

The globalization of architecture extends beyond the mere transnationalization of working conditions for architects; it encompasses the globalization of technologies used in the construction and operation of buildings as well. In the increasingly interconnected world of the twentieth century architects started to design with a wide array of construction technologies that transcended geographical boundaries. From innovative construction techniques, such as 3D space frames, to prefabricated building elements, architects gained unprecedented access to a global marketplace of technological solutions. They now appeared to be navigating a global landscape of construction methods and materials in which technological advances transcended geographical limitations to shape the way buildings were designed, constructed, and operated worldwide.

Mineral wool, a global insulation material, applied to the roofs of sheds.

Some authors in the field of architecture have maintained that the globalization of technologies, characterized by the application of similar building methods, materials, and styles across different regions, has resulted in a homogenization of built environments in different regions. This trend has raised concerns about loss of cultural authenticity and diversity in urban spaces, as distinctive architectural styles and vernacular traditions have been overshadowed by globally prevalent design standards.

In his seminal essay 'The Generic City' Dutch architect Rem Koolhaas tackled the question of urban homogenization as early as the 1990s. Koolhaas analyzed the rise of what he termed the 'generic city', characterized by standardized urban forms and architectural typologies that transcend cultural and geographical boundaries.[20] He argued that globalization and the increasing influence of capitalism were driving forces behind the emergence of these generic urban environments, which lack distinct identity and character. Koolhaas's critique highlighted the paradoxical nature of urban development, where the pursuit of efficiency and the use of global technologies have often resulted in the erasure of local specificity and cultural richness. Through his provocative analysis Koolhaas challenged architects and urban planners to reconsider their approaches to city-making and to grapple with the complexities of globalization in shaping contemporary urban landscapes.

Global commissioners, constructors, and users
In the twentieth century the globalization of architecture extended well beyond architects and technologies to encompass various stakeholders involved in the built environment, such as commissioners (i.e. clients), constructors, and users. Architects' clients played a crucial role in driving globalized processes by commissioning projects that transcended national boundaries. Private companies such as the Hilton Hotels Corporation (founded by Conrad Hilton in 1919) and public organizations such as the United Nations (established in 1945) exemplified this trend as they commissioned respectively hotels and housing worldwide. These globalized commissioners sought to establish landmarks that symbolized modernity and international cooperation. With their standardized luxury and global presence, Hilton hotels became synonymous with hospitality on a worldwide scale, while the United Nations' housing programmes were a monumental endeavour in disaster relief, diplomacy, and governance.

Hilton Hotel (Sedad Hakkı Eldem with Skidmore, Owings & Merrill, 1953–1955), Istanbul, Turkey, 1950s.

Similarly, constructors of buildings and neighbourhoods started to operate within globalized logics. Multinational engineering and architecture firms, such as Energoprojekt of Yugoslavia (founded in 1951 in Belgrade), Kampsax A/S of Denmark (founded in 1917; now COWI A/S), and Sweco of Sweden (originally established as FFNS in 1958), emerged as key players in shaping urban landscapes worldwide. From different political and ideological points of departure these globalized constructors brought expertise in diverse construction methodologies and techniques, facilitating the realization of ambitious architectural projects across continents. In a range of construction fields from highways and bridges to residential complexes and industrial facilities these firms spearheaded the development of infrastructure on a global scale, working across national borders but often within specific geopolitical frameworks. By leveraging their international reach and resources, they contributed to the standardization of construction practices and the homogenization of built environments, reflecting the interconnected nature of global markets and trade relations.

Users of architecture also became part of globalized processes in the twentieth century, driven by the rise of mass tourism, transnational companies, and the business traveller. Mass tourists sought immersive experiences in iconic destinations around the world, influencing the design and development of tourist-centric architecture and urban spaces. Transnational companies expanded their operations globally, necessitating the construction of corporate headquarters and office spaces that reflected their brand identity and corporate culture. Business travellers, meanwhile, demanded functional and well-designed accommodation and facilities in cities worldwide, leading to the proliferation of standardized hotel chains and corporate accommodation. These globalized users shaped architectural trends and preferences, driving the demand for standardized and globally recognizable built environments that catered to their needs and aspirations.

Globalization as frame, substance, and goal of architectural practice

In the second half of the twentieth century, particularly as globalization gained prominence, architects increasingly found themselves responding to its influence, either resisting or embracing its impacts. In his exploration of 'critical regionalism' from the early 1980s onwards the Anglo-American critic Kenneth

Frampton voiced concerns about the relentless and homogenizing changes in the built environment driven by advanced technologies in the production of building materials.[21] Frampton saw these changes as a consequence of time-space compression: as the movement of people, information, and goods accelerated, economic and social competition intensified, often leading to a decline in the quality of architectural outcomes.

The American architectural theorist Dana Cuff criticized Kenneth Frampton's concept of critical regionalism in an increasingly globalized architectural landscape.[22] Frampton argued that critical regionalism's core strategy was to balance universal elements with those specific to a particular locale, thereby creating architecture with a distinct and autonomous identity in a cost-effective way. Cuff, however, challenged this view, asserting that Frampton underestimated the significant influence of the global economy on local economies and architectural practices. She used Frank Gehry's Guggenheim Museum in Bilbao (inaugurated on 18 October 1997) as a case in point, comparing Gehry's iconic style to a designer's label on a handbag. According to Cuff, architectural branding has become deeply embedded in both the design and materials of our built environment. The Guggenheim Bilbao in Spain, affiliated with the Solomon R. Guggenheim Foundation in New York, exemplifies how Gehry's globally recognized architectural approach can transform an industrial wasteland into a worldwide tourist attraction. From this perspective Cuff sheds light on how globalization has simultaneously become the frame, the substance, and the goal of architectural practices.

Guggenheim Museum Bilbao (Frank Gehry, 1993–1997), Bilbao, Spain.

A Global History of Architecture?

In her book *Writing the History of the Global: Challenges for the Twenty-First Century* the historian Maxine Berg presents a compelling argument regarding the need to comprehend the impact of globalization on our lives.[23] She acknowledges that despite significant strides, there remains substantial work ahead if we are to fully grasp the multifaceted implications of global processes. Berg emphasizes that while globalization has undeniably reshaped societies, economies, and cultures worldwide, comprehensively documenting and understanding its effects poses formidable challenges. These challenges stem from the complex and interconnected nature of global phenomena which transcend traditional disciplinary boundaries and necessitate interdisciplinary approaches to research and analysis. We believe that Berg's arguments also hold true for twentieth-century architecture and urbanism.

A pedigree of global history writing in the field of architecture

The exploration of a 'global' history in the field of architecture has been a longstanding endeavour, evidenced by the works of scholars across different epochs. In the second half of the twentieth century writers such as Udo Kultermann, Jürgen Joedicke, and Erwin Anton Gutkind paved the way for understanding global architectural trends through their cross-cultural research and publications in books and renowned journals such as the British *Architectural Design* and the French *L'Architecture d'Aujourd'hui*. For example, the German-born American architectural historian Udo Kultermann wrote a number of English-language surveys of architecture in Africa, Japan, and the Middle East.[24] These scholars have contributed significantly to the discourse surrounding global architectural history, offering valuable insights into the interconnectedness of architectural practices in the twentieth century.

The architectural critics Sibyl Moholy-Nagy and Bernard Rudofsky, among others, have further expanded this discourse by exploring the concept of a 'global' vernacular in architecture, drawing upon structuralist anthropological assumptions.[25] Their works have not only broadened the understanding of global architectural practices but also highlighted the interconnectedness of architectural traditions across different cultures and geographies. Additionally, the debates surrounding critical regionalism in the 1980s, spearheaded by theorists such as Kenneth Frampton, Alexander Tzonis, and Liane Lefaivre, were instrumental in exploring the delicate balance between local identity and global influences in architectural design and discourse.[26] For these and other scholars, professorships at prominent universities in the US and Europe offered an additional platform, in addition to publications, from which to engage with students and future leaders of the profession.

Architectural historiographies rooted in Marxism have provided critical perspectives on the broader structural forces of capitalism that influence urban and architectural developments worldwide. The Italian historian Manfredo Tafuri's *Architecture and Utopia: Design and Capitalist Development* is a case in point.[27] This book discusses how the US stock market crash of 1929 triggered a reorganization of capitalism, altering people's perception of cities. No longer seen as productive structures, cities were now viewed as 'inevitable' superstructures rooted in capitalist principles of investment and speculation, with architecture reduced to a merely compliant role. Scholars from beyond the field of architecture, such as the sociologists Saskia Sassen and Manuel Castells, have shed further light on the complex history of the role played by neo-liberal logics in shaping urban practices and realities on a global scale.[28] Speaking respectively about 'global cities' and 'informational cities', they have illuminated how cities and regions across the world were transformed during the second half of the twentieth century under the combined impact of a restructuring of the capitalist system and technological revolution.

More recently, the emergence of postcolonial historiographic approaches has challenged traditional historical narratives, prompting a re-evaluation of the inequalities and dependencies of twentieth-century architectural practices within various global frameworks, including colonialism and coloniality. Mark Jarzombek and Vikramāditya Prakāsh led the way with *A Global History of Architecture*, first published in 2006 (second edition: 2011; third edition: 2017). A layer of scholarly complexity was added by *Architecture since 1400* (Kathleen James-Chakraborty, 2014). Other surveys have eschewed the adjective 'global' in favour of 'world': Spiro Kostof's *A History of Architecture: Setting and Rituals,* first published in 1985, was reconceptualized and republished long after the author's death by Richard Ingersoll with the title *World Architecture. A Cross-Cultural History* (2013). Additionally, Marian Moffet's popular *Buildings Across Time: An Introduction to World Architecture* (2004) continues to be revised and is currently in its sixth edition (2023).

A number of edited volumes with a focus on how global perspectives have informed historiography have been published in recent years. They include: *Terms of Appropriation. Modern Architecture and Global Exchange* (Amanda Reeser Lawrence and Ana Jiljacki, eds., 2018), *Rethinking Global Modernism. Architectural Historiography and the Postcolonial* (Vikramāditya Prakāsh, Maristella Casciato, Daniel E. Coslett, eds., 2022) and *Narrating the Globe. The Emergence of World Histories of Architecture* (Petra Brouwer, Martin Bressani, and Christopher Drew Armstrong, eds., 2023).[29] Through the contributions of these scholars and theorists the field of architectural history and criticism has continued to evolve, enriching our understanding of architecture's role in shaping and reflecting global dynamics.

Pitfalls of writing a global history

While invaluable in its attempt to provide an understanding of history on a global scale, global history writing is not without its pitfalls. One significant challenge arises from the tendency to regard the North American or European path of development as the norm. In the field of architecture one of the most outright visual expressions of this Eurocentric perspective, positioning Europe as the model for historical development and progress, was provided by the British architectural historian Sir Banister Fletcher. In his *A History of Architecture on the Comparative Method* (1896) Fletcher reproduced a so-called 'Tree of Architecture' showing 'the main growth or evolution of architectural styles'; this had Greek and Roman architecture at the stem of the tree and Peruvian, Egyptian, Assyrian, Chinese, and Japanese architecture relegated to the branches.[30] This Eurocentrism, which prides itself on being the default marker of historical development, was throughout the twentieth century a persistent trope in architectural historiography and too often denied the value of contributions made by non-European architects and cultures. The recent revision of Fletcher's history as *Sir Banister Fletcher's Global History of Architecture* under the editorial oversignt of Murray Fraser is accordingly to be warmly welcomed.[31]

Introduction

Tree of Architecture, showing 'the main growth or evolution of the various styles', from Sir Banister Fletcher, *A History of Architecture on the Comparative Method*, 6th edition, 1921.

Another pitfall of attempting to write a global history lies in the challenge of identifying and interpreting mutual influences without reinforcing or exaggerating the differences between the regions or units being compared. While we advocate for a 'global history' that emphasizes interconnectedness, there is a risk of oversimplifying or essentializing the diversity of historical experiences across various regions and cultures. This can obscure the complexities of historical processes, potentially perpetuating stereotypes or misconceptions, particularly with regard to non-western societies.

The issue of scale is another obstacle in any attempt to write a global history. An expansive scope that covers diverse geographies, time periods, and a wide array of cultural and social contexts inevitably makes it more difficult to effectively capture and analyze historical processes and events. Such a broad perspective risks overlooking local and regional dynamics as well as the agency of individuals and communities. Striking a balance between a macroscopic view of global processes and detailed examination of local and regional contexts remains a persistent challenge.

This survey of the pitfalls of attempting to write a global history makes it clear that the most audacious attempts at constructing a global historical narrative are not immune to biases or limitations. This is certainly also the case in the current book, which proposes to address the globalization-architecture nexus from the perspective of six journeys across space and time.

The Global Turn: Six Journeys of Architecture and the City, 1945–1989

How did the global simultaneously expand and shrink the world in which we live? To what extent did the circulation of people, things, and ideas transform the way architecture and the city were collaboratively designed, realized, and, finally, experienced during the second half of the twentieth century? In this book we propose that the core factor in globalization as a historical phenomenon has been dramatically increased mobility across place and time. Following developments in transport and media, the twentieth century saw a proliferation of new forms of connectivity as well as of new regimes of circulation of goods and commodities, knowledge, experts, techniques, people, and labour across geographies — on unprecedented scales and to unprecedented rhythms.

In this experimental roadmap we present architects, historians, students, and general readers with an analysis of the relationship between architecture and globalization through six 'journeys' across different cultural, political, and social geographies. The six journeys — exploring collaboration, goods, mobility, knowledge, construction, and labour — concretize and combine in various ways the so-called 'five faces of globalization' in architecture discussed above. They represent confrontations, engagements, and disengagements with, and effects of, these five faces of globalization in the built environment. Rather than offering a comprehensive survey, our six journeys represent specific perspectives on the architecture-globalization nexus that can also inform future analysis of other case studies not discussed here.

The first of our book's six journeys focuses upon tools and scenarios of *collaboration* as evidenced by architectural competitions and cross-cultural learning environments (e.g. classrooms) made possible by the new culture of exchange amongst universities following the end of World War II. Expanding upon the post-World-War-I experience of the competition for the Palace of Nations in Geneva, the framework deployed to design the United Nations Headquarters in New York offered a unique 'workshop' opportunity for a design team composed of members from different countries and continents. In parallel with this new form of collaboration that demanded an extraordinary synthesis of design, the emergence of an increasingly cross-cultural classroom facilitated shared educational experiences amongst students from different nations. Watershed pedagogical experiences — such as the summer schools held by the Congrès International d'Architecture Moderne (CIAM) in London and Venice from 1949 to 1957 and the International Laboratories of Architecture and Urban Design (ILAUD) from 1976 forwards — served as important catalysts in an increasingly mobile educational landscape.

Our second journey focuses on the heightened circulation of *goods* that characterized the post-war period under the influence of processes such as rising consumerism. In Western Europe, for instance, the welfare states became consumer societies after World War II, creating an unparalleled, demand-led economic upswing. This led to the emergence of new building types. Architects were commissioned to conceive so-called 'distribution centres' from which goods could be distributed, as can be seen in Egon Eiermann's distribution centre (Frankfurt, 1961) for Neckermann, one of the leading mail order firms in Germany, and James Stirling's headquarters and distribution centre for the Italian typewriter and office-equipment manufacturer Olivetti (Milton Keynes, 1971). The building type that embodied the new regimes of mass distribution and mass consumption par excellence was the shopping mall. Invented by the Austrian émigré architect Victor Gruen in the USA as a reaction to North American urban sprawl, the shopping mall travelled to Europe to become a key actor in post-war urban reconstruction, as was the case with De Lijnbaan in Rotterdam (Van den Broek and Bakema, 1953) and Frankfurt-Römerberg (Candilis-Josic-Woods, 1960), and in new urban development, such as Milton Keynes (Woodward et al., 1970). In all these cases the shopping mall was regarded by not just architects and urban planners but citizens as well as a new focus for urban collectivity.

The third of our six journeys reveals how dramatically increased *mobility* in the period following World War II generated and amplified global interconnectedness, prompting the design of new hybrid building types in response to new forms of transport and the widespread circulation of people for business, education, and leisure tourism. This phenomenon produced a number of new remarkable buildings in various cities and countries, including motels in America, airports in London and Paris, and train stations in Rome and Tokyo. Moreover, we argue that different forms of business, educational, and leisure travel and transport generated a global transfer of knowledge, a transformation of human settlements on a worldwide scale, as well as a different conception of architecture as a discipline itself. Architecture and architects reacted to an upsurge in mass mobility throughout the second half of the twentieth century by modifying the programmatic as well as experiential qualities of buildings.

The dissemination and circulation of architectural *knowledge* in different media is the topic of our fourth journey. Whereas travel remained an important source of direct learning about architecture during the second half of the twentieth century, the proliferation of printed matter and photography expanded possibilities for learning from afar — possibilities which were eventually even more radically transformed by film and television. The 1960s and 1970s were the heroic age of the architectural periodical. Following the universal spread of more inexpensive high-quality printing techniques (e.g. offset printing) as well as in response to the political, social, and artistic changes of this time, the post-war period saw a surge in the number of independent architectural periodicals; engines of an intensely creative period of architectural design, these also provided a space for architectural theory to flourish and an arena for critical discussion of the role of politics and new technologies in architecture. The dissemination of architectural periodicals such as *Architectural Design* (UK), *Architectural Review* (UK), *Domus* (Italy), *Casabella* (Italy), *Deutsche Bauzeitung* (Germany), *Revista Arquitectura* (Spain), *Arquitectura Bis* (Spain), and *Forum* (the Netherlands) established a global network of exchange in which the design thinking and practice of architects and urban designers in South America, Africa, and Asia was conceived as being in direct dialogue with that of their counterparts in Europe and North America. This idea of a modern architectural culture as being a more 'global phenomenon' would have lasting effects.

Our fifth journey addresses the increasingly complex *construction* process tied to both the design and construction phases (recall, for example, manufacturing companies such as

François Hennebique and Pilkington). The post-war period saw the widespread use of specific architectural elements (e.g. glass windows and glass curtain walls) and the emergence of new building typologies, such as the 'tall building' (the skyscraper), which has become a symbol of globalization and relentless homogenization. Additionally, it is worth noting that this dimension of construction did not exclusively concern physical movement of materials; it also involved a 'theorisation' in the form of growing awareness of intellectual property identified by technical and commercial patents and licences.

Our last journey focuses on the migration of construction *labour* in the post-war period. After World War II millions of people were displaced. As a result, internal migration increased within Europe as hundreds of thousands of people sought new lives and work opportunities after the war. The United Nations Refugee Convention of 1951 influenced many European countries to accept refugees and asylees from war-ravaged areas. The post-war period was also a period of decolonization: European colonists were encouraged to return home, and former colonial subjects moved to Europe for work and studies. This travelling construction labour was instrumental in post-war reconstruction and urban development in Europe. Migrant labour forces were crucial in constructing new housing estates, hospitals, administrative offices, and schools, thereby contributing substantially to housing in European welfare states. Simultaneously, however, these labour forces also had to be housed themselves. In France, for instance, the authorities had been relatively successful in creating housing and facilities for guest workers before the war but did not immediately undertake the infrastructural adjustments needed to cope with the rapid increase of immigrant workers in the late 1950s and early 1960s. As a result, the post-war period saw the emergence of a new territorial phenomenon: the *bidonville* or shanty town. In the vicinities of heroic construction sites in the European welfare states there emerged more prosaic urban settlements for the labour forces that were at work on these very construction sites. In 1960s Paris, for example, the *bidonville* next to a new housing estate (a *ville nouvelle* or a *habitation à loyer modéré*) became an omnipresent phenomenon that many people perceived as a 'black belt' surrounding the city.

As co-authors of *The Global Turn*, we hope that our book offers students, in academia and the profession, as well as a more general audience an opportunity to better understand the profoundly transformative period in the history of the built environment defined by the end of World War II and the fall of the Berlin Wall. During this period complex negotiations with new regimes of circulation posed creative challenges to 'modern' architectural discourse and practices while initiating substantial innovations in terms of process. Although we neither celebrate nor demonize globalization, it is hard not to see that, more often than not, globalization in architecture and the city during the nearly 50 years covered in our book fell short in terms of its potential to make the design and realization of the built environment more equitable and sustainable.[32] Even if one were to look beyond the fall of the Berlin Wall, which is where we end our book, we believe that globalization, while expanding educational borders and increasing business and leisure mobility, is continuing to generate inequities in the built environment that are proving increasingly difficult to eliminate.[33]

World Trade Center (architects: Minoru Yamasaki with Emery Roth, 1970–1972), photograph by G. E. Kidder Smith, 1975.

World Trade Center.

1   Francis D. K. Ching, Mark Jarzombek, Vikramāditya Prakāsh, *A Global History of Architecture* (Hoboken, NJ: John Wiley & Sons, Inc., 2011), p. 797.
2   See Giovanna Borasi (ed.), *Journeys. How Travelling Fruit, Ideas and Buildings Rearrange our Environment* (Montréal: Canadian Centre for Architecture, 2010).
3   Mohammad Gharipour and Caitlin DeClercq (eds.), Epidemic Urbanism. Contagious Diseases in Global Cities (Bristol: Intellect Books, 2021). Christopher Schaberg, *Grounded: Perpetual Flight ... and then the Pandemic* (Minneapolis: University of Minnesota Press, 2020).
4   'Turn' as a verb and a noun has also been used in the context of digital design. See Mario Carpo (ed.), *The Digital Turn in Architecture 1992–2012* (Chichester: Wiley, 2013).
5   Malcolm Gladwell, *The Tipping Point: How Little Things Can Make a Big Difference* (Boston: Little Brown, 2000).
6   Peter Frankopan, *The Silk Roads. A New History of the World* (London: Bloomsbury, 2015).
7   Timothy Brook, *Vermeer's Hat. The Seventeenth Century and the Dawn of the Global World* (London: Profile Books Ltd, 2008).
8   Neil MacGregor, *A History of the World in 100 Objects* (London; New York: Allen Lane, 2010); Edward S. Cooke, Jr., *Global Objects. Toward a Connected Art History* (Princeton and Oxford: Princeton University Press, 2022). See also the Edible series published by Reaktion Books: Fred Czarra, *Spices. A Global History* (London: Reaktion Books, 2009); Renee Marton, *Rice. A Global History* (London: Reaktion Books, 2014); Jonathan Morris, *Coffee. A Global History* (London: Reaktion Books, 2019).
9   For a brief history of the Bureau des Expositions see https://www.bie-paris.org/site/en/about-the-bie/history-of-the-bie (accessed 7 September 2024)
10   Roland Robertson, *Globalization: Social Theory and Global Culture* (London: Sage Publications, 1992), p. 8.
11   Anthony Giddens, *Beyond Left and Right: The Future of Radical Politics* (Stanford, CA: Stanford University Press, 1994), p. 5.
12   Anthony Giddens, *The Consequences of Modernity* (Stanford, CA: Stanford University Press, 1990), p. 64.
13   Malcolm Waters, *Globalization* (London: Routledge, 1995; 2nd ed.: 2001), p. 3.
14   E. Maskin, 'Why Haven't Global Markets Reduced Inequality in Emerging Economies?', *The World Bank Economic Review*, Vol. 29, no. suppl_1, 2015, pp. 48–52. Online. Available https: https://doi.org/10.1093/wber/lhv013 (accessed 20 August 2024).
15   James Gillies and Robert Cailliau, *How the Web was Born: The Story of the World Wide Web* (Oxford: Oxford University Press, 2000). Online. Available https: https://www.home.cern/science/computing/birth-web/short-historyweb#:~:text=Tim%20Berners%2DLee%2C%20a%20British,and%20institutes%20around%20the%20world (accessed 1 September 2024).
16   Mario Carpo (ed.), *The Digital Turn in Architecture 1992–2012* (Chichester: Wiley, 2013) and Mario Carpo, *The Second Digital Turn: Design Beyond Intelligence* (Cambridge, MA: The MIT Press, 2017).
17   Kim Förster, *Building Institution: The Institute for Architecture and Urban Studies, New York 1976–1985* (Bielefeld, Germany: Architekturen, 2024); Ashraf M. A. Salama, *Architectural Excellence in Islamic Societies: Distinction Through the Aga Khan Award for Architecture* (New York: Routledge, 2021); Ruth Peltason and Grace Ong Yan, *Architect. The Pritzker Prize Laureates in Their Own Words* (New York: Black Dog & Leventhal Publishers, 2017),
18   Larry Richards (ed.), *Canadian Centre for Architecture: Buildings and Gardens* (Montreal, CA and Cambridge, MA: MIT Press, 1989).
19   Online. Available https: https://www.labiennale.org/en/history-biennale-architettura#:~:text=The%20first%20exhibitions%20curated%20by%20Vittorio%20Gregotti&text=It%20was%20in%20fact%20within,exhibitions%20in%201976%20and%201978 (accessed 1 September 2024).
20   Rem Koolhaas, 'The Generic City', O.M.A., Rem Koolhaas, and Bruce Mau, *Small, Medium, Large, Extra-Large* (Rotterdam: 010 Publishers, 1995), pp. 1239–1264.
21   Kenneth Frampton, 'Prospects for a Critical Regionalism', *Perspecta* 20 (1983), pp. 147–162. Online. Available doi: 10.2307/1567071 (accessed 6 September 2024). Kenneth Frampton, 'Towards a Critical Regionalism: Six Points for an Architecture of Resistance', in: Hal Foster (ed.), *The Anti-Aesthetic: Essays on Postmodern Culture* (Washington: Bay Press, 1983), pp. 16–30.
22   Kirsten Walker, 'Architectures of Globalization', *Places*, 14 (2), 2000, pp. 70–73.
23   Maxine Berg (ed.), *Writing the History of the Global: Challenges for the Twenty-First Century* (Oxford: Oxford University Press, 2013).
24   Udo Kultermann, *Architecture of Today. A Survey of New Building*

Throughout the World (London: A. Zwemmer, 1958); Udo Kultermann, *New Japanese Architecture* (London: The Architectural Press, 1960); Udo Kultermann, *New Directions in African Architecture* (New York: G. Braziller, 1969); Udo Kultermann, *Contemporary Architecture in the Arab States: Renaissance of a Region* (New York: McGraw-Hill, 1989).

25 Architekturzentrum Wien (ed.), *Lessons from Bernard Rudofsky: Life as a Voyage* (Basel and Boston: Birkäuser, 2007). Hilde Heynen, *Sibyl Moholy-Nagy. Architecture, Modernism and its Discontents* (London: Bloomsbury Publishing, 2019), in particular Chapter 2, 'Vernacular architecture and the uses of the past'.

26 Alexander Tzonis and Liane Lefaivre, 'The Grid and the Pathway: An Introduction to the Work of Dimitris and Suzana Antonakakis, with Prolegomena to a History of the Culture of Modern Greek Architecture', *Architecture in Greece* 15 (1981), pp. 164–178; Vincent Canizaro (ed.), *Architectural Regionalism: Collected Writings on Place, Identity, Modernity, and Tradition* (New York: Princeton Architectural Press, 2007), p. 11. See also Michelangelo Sabatino, *Pride in Modesty: Modernist Architecture and the Vernacular Tradition in Italy* (Toronto–Buffalo: The University of Toronto Press, 2010) and M. Sabatino and Jean-François Lejeune (eds.), *Modern Architecture and the Mediterranean: Vernacular Dialogues and Contested Identities* (London: Routledge, 2010).

27 Manfredo Tafuri, *Architecture and Utopia: Design and Capitalist Development* (Cambridge, MA: MIT Press, 1976).

28 Saskia Sassen, *The Global City: New York, London, Tokyo* (New York: Princeton University Press, 2001); Manuel Castells, *The Informational City: Information Technology, Economic Restructuring, and the Urban Regional Process* (Oxford: Blackwell, 1989).

29 Kathleen James-Chakraborty, *Architecture since 1400* (Minneapolis: University of Minnesota Press, 2014); Vikramāditya Prakāsh, Maristella Casciato, Daniel E. Coslett (eds.), *Rethinking Global Modernism: Architectural Historiography and the Postcolonial* (London: Routledge, 2022); Petra Brouwer, Martin Bressani, and Christopher Drew Armstrong (eds.), *Narrating the Globe. The Emergence of World Histories of Architecture* (Cambridge, MA: The MIT Press, 2023).

30 Banister Fletcher, *A History of Architecture on the Comparative Method for Students, Craftsmen, and Amateurs*, 6th ed. (London: B. T. Batsford, 1921).

31 Murray Fraser, general editor, *Sir Banister Fletcher's Global History of Architecture*, 21st edition, 2 volumes (London-New York: Bloomsbury Visual Arts, 2020). See, in Volume 2, Rhodri Windsor Liscombe and Michelangelo Sabatino, 'Canada and the United States since 1914', pp. 1264–1320.

32 Tom Avermaete and Michelangelo Sabatino, 'About a global turn and lost opportunities,' *Domus*, n. 1073, November 2022, pp. 4–7.

33 Graham Owen (ed.), *Architecture, Ethics and Globalization* (New York: Routledge, 2009).

1 Collaboration: Competitions, Workshops, and Transcultural Classrooms

Michelangelo Sabatino

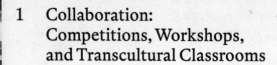

Fig. 1.1
John B. Parkin & Associates office at Don Mills, Canada, 1958.

Americans and Europeans are prone to thinking of their own societies as the center and source of world civilization, forgetting that the West is only one of the world's great cultures, and forgetting also that some of the most barbarous physical and intellectual slaughters of all history have taken place in the West within our lifetime.
— J. William Fulbright, in:
Walter Johnson and Francis J. Colligan, *The Fulbright Program. A History*[1]

Group practice, in its essence, depends on those in the group believing that they are within that compass. They must believe that their own contribution to the group is an active factor in its existence and that for them to leave it would reduce its effectiveness.
— Misha Black, in: Michael Middleton, *Group Practice in Design*[2]

In the realm of architecture and the city (i.e. urbanism), collaboration and its corollary, cooperation, are not a recent phenomenon: they can be traced back to societies and periods of time throughout history. Arguably, the world fairs (i.e. expositions) held in cities in the US and Europe in the late nineteenth and first half of the twentieth centuries were the first 'global' showcases in which architects and various other design professionals collaborated, even though in these cases each individual was ultimately responsible for the realization of their own project.[3] In the second half of the twentieth century, however, a new form of collaboration facilitated the emergence of a distinctly global mindset related to the design and transformation of the 'modern' built environment. This was characterized by an increased reliance upon multi-disciplinary practices (involving architects, artists, engineers, landscape architects, and urban planners) in place of dependence on the individual 'genius'.[4] Inevitably, this led, in many instances, to the creation of capacious 'open' offices in which this collaborative work could be carried out under the same roof.[5]

→ Fig. 1.1

'Collaboration' is an action noun that signifies diverse individuals creating and working together towards common objectives. Although collaboration should be understood here as a distinctive development defined by its own internal dynamics, it is nonetheless intertwined with the other five themes (journeys) discussed in this book, namely goods, mobility, knowledge, construction, and labour.

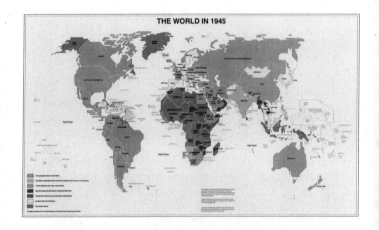

Fig. 1.2
The world in 1945 (founding UN member states).

1 Collaboration

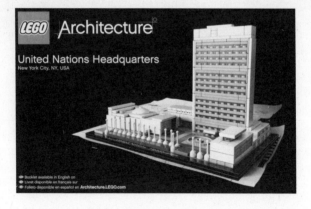

Fig. 1.3
Postcard, 'United Nations Headquarters on the East River, New York City'.
Fig. 1.4
LEGO architecture set, 'United Nations Headquarters, New York City, NY, USA'.

Fig. 1.5
CIAM III, Museum of Fine Arts, Horta Hall, Brussels, 1930.

1 Collaboration

Fig. 1.6
Toronto City Hall and Nathan Phillips Square competition entries on display at Horticultural Building, Exhibition Place, Toronto, 1958.

Fig. 1.7
Postcard, 'Palais des Nations Unies [The United Nations Office at Geneva, Switzerland]'.

Competitions, Workshops, and Transcultural Classrooms

Fig. 1.8
Palace of Nations jury (left to right): Victor Horta,
Attilio Muggia, Karl Moser, Charles Lemaresquier, Bernardo
Attolico (diplomat), Josef Hoffmann, John J. Burnet,
25 March 1927.

1 Collaboration

Fig. 1.9
Architectural planning of United Nations permanent headquarters: Markelius, Le Corbusier, Bodiansky (behind), Sicheng, Harrison (behind), Niemeyer, Soilleux (behind), Bassov, Abramovitz (behind), Cormier, Weissmann (behind), Antoniades (behind), Nowicki, 18 April 1947.

Competitions, Workshops, and Transcultural Classrooms

Fig. 1.10
Le Corbusier, New York, 1947.
Fig. 1.11
Oscar Niemeyer, New York, 1947.

Fig. 1.12
In the foreground: Franklin D. Roosevelt Four Freedoms Park (original design: Louis Kahn; design development: Mitchell/Giurgola Architects, 2010–2012), Roosevelt Island, 2013.

Competitions, Workshops, and Transcultural Classrooms

Fig. 1.13
CIAM Summer School, students and tutors in Piazza San Marco, Venice, 1956.

Fig. 1.14
ILAUD — Giancarlo De Carlo (second row, centre) with students, 1986.

1 Collaboration

Fig. 1.15
ILAUD (International Laboratory of Architecture and Urban Design), 1st residential course, Urbino, 1976.
Fig. 1.16
Spazio e Società, Rivista internazionale di architettura e urbanistica diretta da Giancarlo De Carlo, n. 10, 1980.

Collaboration in architecture and urbanism as it relates to the Global Turn is more concerned with process than with the aesthetic qualities of buildings understood in visual, spatial, and structural terms. The antagonistic and divisive events of the first and second world wars fuelled a desire for collaboration and cooperation that was strongly felt by a wide variety of academics and professionals in different countries around the globe. What emerged during the interwar years and after, as Mark Crinson has argued, was an 'international mindset' that was not just a formal engagement with the tenets of the 'International Style'.[6] For example, the urgent need for shared expertise in order to rebuild cities and countryside after the destruction wrought by World War II led to professionals in different nations putting aside their cultural differences in order to develop shared approaches as common ground.

Three key expressions of international collaboration emerged during the post-World-War-II years. Firstly, architectural competitions for high-profile institutions were awarded to cross-cultural teams of architects and urban planners. The mid-century modernist United Nations Headquarters complex of buildings, designed and built on New York's East River between 1947 and 1951 and inaugurated on 10 October 1952 under the presidency of Harry S. Truman, is perhaps the single most high-profile and consequential commission during those years. The United Nations was established with 51 founding members on 24 October 1945.[7] However, as attested by a group photo of architects representing member nations around the world ranging from Brazil and Australia to France and Canada, even though individual schemes were submitted, the final scheme for the headquarters complex was more the result of a collaborative workshop than of a competition won by a single architect.[8] The United Nations Headquarters became a favourite with the general public, as is clear from the proliferation of souvenir items on which it features, ranging from postcards to a LEGO set issued in 2013.

→ Figs. 1.2–4

Secondly, as a means of expanding the possibilities of dialogue inside and outside academia, architectural pedagogy during the period following World War II witnessed the rise of the transcultural classroom in the form of workshops that brought students from different institutions together in dialogue; these new educational opportunities facilitated an exchange of new forms of knowledge amongst practitioners, educators, and their students. Two consequential such examples are the summer schools of the Congrès International d'Architecture Moderne (CIAM), held in London and Venice from 1949 to 1957, and the establishment of the International Laboratory of Architecture and Urban Design (ILAUD) in Urbino (Italy) under Italian architect Giancarlo De Carlo in 1976. Both these schools and laboratories attracted a remarkably diverse group of international faculty members and students from a range of universities.

Thirdly, the second half of the twentieth century saw a series of collaborative initiatives amongst design professionals. CIAM was an association of mainly architects established in 1928 in La Sarraz, Switzerland, with the underlying assumption that it was to promote dialogue around issues concerning architecture and urban planning.[9] After meetings in La Sarraz, Frankfurt am Main, Brussels, Athens, Paris, Bridgwater, Bergamo, Hoddesdon, Aix-en-Provence, and Dubrovnik, CIAM was disbanded in Otterlo in 1959 due to challenges from Team 10, a group of architects who assembled in July 1953. Like CIAM, Team 10 eschews individuals' names in favour of collective identity; its use of the word 'team' in its name stresses collaboration.[10] ILAUD, which continues to function today, is an association with collaborative underpinnings aimed at promoting networking and shared knowledge with regard to the built environment.

→ Fig. 1.5

Other fora for collaboration and cooperation emerged in the years following World War II. Union internationale des architectes (the International Union of Architects), founded on 28 June 1948 in Lausanne (Switzerland), continues to operate to this day with members organized into five regions, including Western and Eastern Europe, the Americas, Asia, and Oceania.[11] Learned societies concerned with architecture are likewise based on an implicit collaboration through knowledge sharing amongst their members, who tend to be both academics and practising architects. Recall, for example, the Society of Architectural Historians (SAH), founded in America in 1940, and the Society of Architectural Historians of Great Britain (SAHGB), founded in 1956.[12] Much more recently, the Congress for the New Urbanism was founded in Alexandria (VA, US) in 1993 with the intention of critiquing anti-urban practices attributed to some members of the Congrès International d'Architecture Moderne (CIAM).[13]

One cannot speak of collaboration in architectural workshops and competitions and transcultural classrooms without understanding the degree to which significantly increased mobility during the post-war years by automobile, train, and air transport between various countries and geographic regions made these events more accessible to middle-class citizens. During the first decades following World War II face-to-face interactions increased significantly before the emergence of computer-aided design and digital platforms during 'the digital turn' allowed collaborators to convene in virtual workspaces.[14] As a result, the sharing of new tools and design approaches as well as knowledge about materials and modes of construction became part of a shared approach to practice in different countries and cities. A significant increase in travelling students led to shared educational experiences that brought cross-cultural knowledge into the field of architectural culture in ways that went beyond the cliché of an 'international style'. Thus 'modern' architectural practice benefitted from a broader field of references (both historical and contemporary) and experiences based on, for example, building for climate and culture.

International Competitions and Workshop Collaborations

The role of architectural competitions (whether open to everyone or restricted to a group of pre-selected architects) has deep roots in the history of architecture. At times such competitions have acquired mythological status as incubators of watershed experimental ideas which have transformed architectural practice or of architectural pioneers who have driven the profession forwards. Whether they were 'a sort of nightmare, as an incubus or vampire, stifling the breath of professional life, and draining its blood'[15] or 'the only door that can always be kept open to the unknown man who has something to give that the world of architecture needs',[16] architectural competitions gradually became an opportunity for blue-sky thinking and experimentation and occasionally for dissemination of the avant-garde in architecture and society. Especially when submissions are anonymous, competitions allow lesser-known architects to emerge through the sheer force of their ideas without the need for an already established reputation.

In the context of collaboration, competitions have facilitated dialogue amongst architects from different countries and with different perspectives. This has encouraged transcultural collaboration/cooperation/negotiation among new team members who, under the pressure of competition requirements and deadlines, embrace alternative ways of practising architecture. From this perspective, the 'workshop' for the United Nations Headquarters complex in New York, announced in 1947, like its precursor, the competition for the Palais des Nations (Palace of Nations/United Nations Office at Geneva), announced in 1926, is an important case study for rethinking how early forms of architecturally related political compromise have shaped modern and contemporary architectural practice. What made the design process for the United Nations Headquarters remarkable was not only the international identity of the architects but also its collective, collaborative character. Although two other post-World-War-II competitions — those for the Sydney Opera House (announced in 1956 and won by Danish architect Jørn Utzon), which received 200 entries from architects from around the world, and for Toronto City Hall (announced in 1958 and won by the Finnish architect Viljo Revell), which attracted 500 entries — attracted global attention, the winning schemes in both were realized by individual architects. The same is true of the Internationale Bauausstellung Berlin (International Building Exhibition Berlin/IBA), realized between 1979 and 1987 and curated by Josef Paul Kleihues (IBA Neubau) and Hardt Waltherr Hämer (IBA Altbau) in the years leading up to the fall of the Berlin Wall on 9 November 1989.

→ Fig. 1.6

A Pre-history of Global Collaboration:
the Palais des Nations (1926–1936)

The cross-cultural character of the competition to design the Palais des Nations in Geneva (Switzerland) mirrored the international and transcultural entity and destiny of the League of Nations (the predecessor of the United Nations) itself, which, according to the organizers, was to be represented by the new building.[17] The quest for balance between the institution's international character and the broader global provenance of the competition proposals reached an impasse: agreement could not be found between the multiplicity of political standpoints held by members of the League and the various architectural languages expressed in the 377 proposals submitted in 1927 to the competition. As a result, no final winner was selected. Criticized as a 'symbol of the crisis of judgement in the twentieth century',[18] the Palace of Nations competition failed to meet the initial expectations for it as envisaged, for instance, by Patrick Abercrombie who, as early as 1919, had advocated that 'the harmony of the world rather than its dissonances should influence the character of [the new building's] design, while its organic structure should reflect the emerging order of the new world.'[19] The competition became a symbol of an international multi-generational struggle between avant-garde practices and traditionalism and between modern architecture and historicism.

→ Fig. 1.7

In 1926 the League of Nations, whose primary political purpose was to ensure that disputes were settled by any means except war, decided to hold an international competition for its headquarters in Geneva. The new headquarters was meant to convey in spatial and visual terms 'the peaceful glory of the twentieth century, through the purity of its style and the harmony of its lines.'[20] The only restriction imposed by the competition was that it should be open only to professionals from the 55 member states of the League of Nations and not from around the world, as had initially been envisaged in order to ensure that the palace would have a 'truly universal' character.[21] The choice of the site itself reflected a transnational emphasis. Geneva was chosen primarily because of Switzerland's neutrality; this emphasized from the very beginning a sense of equality and impartiality among the member states.

The jury was an international committee, with each member coming from a different country and representing diverse architectural tastes, attitudes, and backgrounds. This group ranged from 'progressive avant-gardists', such as Victor Horta (Belgium), who was head of the jury, Hendrick Petrus Berlage (Netherlands), Josef Hoffmann (Austria), Karl Moser (Switzerland), and Ivar Tengbom (Sweden), to 'eclectic classicists', such as Carlos Gato (Spain), Charles Lemaresquier (France), Attilio Muggia (Italy), and Sir John J. Burnet (United Kingdom).[22]

→ Fig. 1.8

Despite these efforts to give the competition an international 'soul', based on a cross-section of political and architectural views and bolstered by the choice of a neutral site, the outcome was indecision and failure to assign an official first prize to any one of the 377 entries submitted, notwithstanding six weeks of deliberation and 64 meetings. The immense technical and bureaucratic machine assembled to identify a proposal that could symbolize the twentieth-century idea of freedom produced no certain result.[23] *Ex aequo* second prizes were awarded to nine projects, the same number as the jury members, mirroring the impasse into which the competition had fallen.[24]

As far as the submissions were concerned, they represented a broad spectrum of design approaches and references, from Étienne-Louis-Boulleè-inspired and neoclassical solutions to Gothic Revival, Beaux-Arts, constructivism, and modernism.[25] Within this jumble of different approaches and references there was a clear clash between experimental, modernist, and more tradition-inspired solutions. According to the jury, this conflict revealed 'the evolutionary phase through which contemporary architecture is now passing.'[26]

The modernist proposals submitted by Le Corbusier/Pierre Jeanneret and Hannes Meyer/Hans Wittwer remain groundbreaking projects in the history of architecture as both sophisticated examples of modernist avant-garde architecture and epitomes of 'the cooperative and social democratic idea behind the optimistically created League'.[27] More importantly, they embodied the new faith in and progressive spirit of an institution for the future, such as was the League of Nations, which deserved, in the words of Camille Marlin, neither 'a costume copy of old-fashioned engravings' nor 'to be buried in a cenotaph built by men who have no faith in the resources of the present and who have no hope for the future.'[28] 'A League of Nations building that ties itself to the ghosts of history,' warned Sigfried Giedion, writing in support of Le Corbusier in the German journal *Bauwelt*, 'is likely to become a haunt of ghosts.'[29]

Le Corbusier's project was disqualified for technical reasons: he had submitted blueprints instead of the original drawings specified in the rules. However, this disqualification was likely based upon more trivial and politically biased reasons. It was probably 'a result of conspiracy'[30] — a conspiracy cooked up by one of the jurors, Charles Lemaresquier, who, according to Giedion, was supported by the French president of the Council of the League of the Nations, Aristide Briand, 'an inflexible opponent of contemporary architecture'.[31]

Interestingly, this political-architectural sabotage was destined to have a greater impact than could have been foreseen. According to Giedion, the mean-spirited elimination of Le Corbusier's project even became one of the motivations for founding CIAM one year later, in 1928; CIAM was to become the most important collaborative group of prominent architects aimed at fostering transnational dissemination of modern architectural ideals.[32] The rejection of a 'modern' language in the Palais des Nations competition thus enabled and propelled broader global discussions and, probably also, a common feeling of urgency among modernists regarding the diffusion and institutionalization of modern architecture. The legacy of Le Corbusier's proposal also survived its rejection. In the end Le Corbusier's rivals embraced the rational organization of the site plan put forward in his proposal.[33] His solution became a prototype for future institutional buildings for world organizations that shared ideals similar to those of the League of Nations, such as the United Nations headquarters and UNESCO's headquarters in Paris.

Finally, the stalling, indecision, and ultimate failure of the League of Nations' international competition resulted in a compromise which was the opposite of confidence in the future, although it was based on the initial international aim of unity beyond national views. The League invited five architects with traditionalist visions, each from a different country, to collaborate in order to outline a plan: Henri-Paul Nénot (France), Julien Flegenheimer (Switzerland), Camille Lefèvre (France), Carlo Broggi (Italy), and József Vágó (Hungary).[34] The initial strivings to design a progressive expression of an emerging new world order as envisaged by Abercrombie — a symbol of Kantian 'perpetual peace'[35] — were flattened and 'normalized' into diplomatic-academic neutrality.[36] The new traditionalist building embodied a state of political stagnation between 'waning European imperialism and [the] latent prowess of the emerging Pax Americana' rather than a leap towards progress, the future, and a new political body of global peace.[37] The Palais des Nations opened in 1936, 10 years after the competition was launched in 1926. As Giedion said, 'Everyone, from typists to diplomats, agreed that it was a failure.'[38]

United Nations Headquarters

In the same way as the architectural competition to design the League of Nations headquarters failed, resulting in compromise and cross-cultural design collaboration, the political project of the League of Nations was itself aborted a few years later. The main factors in this failure were conflicts among some of the member states and a traditionalism that derived from nationalism. Although a pioneering example of an international institution of global welfare, the League had been unable to guarantee the promised global peace and collective security. Its legacy and principal aims, however, lived on in a newborn institution, the United Nations, which was established by the five permanent members of the Security Council on 24 October 1945. Lord Cecil, one of the League's founders, declared during its final assembly, held in Geneva on 8 April 1946, 'The League is dead, long live the United Nations!'[39]

The Palais des Nations became the UN's headquarters outside the US. In the same way as the UN replaced the League, broadened its scope, and improved its effectiveness in pursuing ultimate world peace, it was understood that the new UN headquarters to be built in New York needed to be an expression of a collaborative 'workshop of peace' rather than a pale compromise.[40] As a result, in a bid to speed up the process of choosing a design, collaboration between a team of 10 prominent international architects was preferred to selection of a project through an open competition; the general secretary of the new international organization was mindful of the failed evaluation process for the League's Palais des Nations building.[41] The team, which included Le Corbusier (France) and Oscar Niemeyer (Brazil), was composed of architects from different member countries of the UN; this too reflected the necessity for global participation and a deliberate neutrality in order to overcome any suggestion of nationalism or political preference as in the League competition.[42] This experimental collaboration was touchingly — and somehow speculatively — explained on 18 April 1947 in a speech by Le Corbusier in which he emphasized the importance of the anonymous work performed by the entire team in a modern global common effort:

> To those outside who question us we can reply: we are united, we are a team; the World Team of the United Nations laying down plans of a *world* architecture, world, not *international*, for therein we shall respect human, natural and cosmic laws. ... We are a homogeneous block. There are no names attached to this work. As in any human enterprise, there is simply discipline, which alone is capable of bringing order. Each of us can be legitimately proud of having been called upon to work in this team; that should be sufficient for us. ... Each of us can give to Mr. Harrison the assurance that all will work anonymously.[43]

The emphasis on the 'world team' as a 'homogeneous block' of modern architects mirrored the underlying purpose behind this workshop: the collaborative design of a building which could represent the global unity of the UN through a modern language that transcended any national and cultural specificity.

→ Figs. 1.9–11

This team was not, however, wholly self-managed: it worked under the guidance of an American architect who served as chief planning director, Wallace Harrison.[44] Harrison was known as 'a good administrator and a reliable architect: in addition, he was related to the Rockefeller family. What more could one want?'[45] — as Giedion provocatively put it. He assumed the challenging role of 'ambassador', mitigating and negotiating divergences among architects and projects so as to find compromises, common views, and agreements, a task which was made more difficult by the need to deal with the egos of famous architects, particularly that of Le Corbusier.

Le Corbusier was selected not only for his unquestioned importance in the history of modern architecture but also because of his preceding involvement and unfair — in his supporters' eyes — disqualification in the competition for the League of Nations building. The modern compositional principles in Le Corbusier's project for the League became the prototype for the UN building as well. The UN workshop was founded on common modern principles. As Le Corbusier emphasized, architecture had arrived at a moment of 'decisive fruition' in 'the land of applied modern technique', in contrast with 'the competition for the League of Nations Building in Geneva, where 380 [377] plans [had] all cried out for recognition.'[46]

Nevertheless, the workshop was anything but a peaceful collaboration. Although the important participating architects were motivated by common values and a common project of global organization, cooperation between them could not, according to architectural historian Kenneth Frampton, but run into friction between different viewpoints; this transformed the workshop into an 'intractable and demoralizing process'.[47] The collaboration ended with reconciliation of different versions, which were synthesized into a carefully adjusted compromise, in particular between Le Corbusier's blocklike solution and the visions of a great plaza and esplanade conjured up by Oscar Niemeyer, whom the French master harshly labelled 'just a young man', adding, 'That scheme isn't from a mature architect.'[48] The final project, unlike the result of the competition for the League of Nations building, bore no trace of the traditionalist Beaux-Arts approach or of political pressure but represented a middle ground between other more interesting and radical proposals, something which Niemeyer himself regretted.[49]

The final proposal was then developed further by Harrison on his own. Harrison's opening of his own 'UN Headquarters Planning Office' put an end to the international collaboration and 'the happy period of the affair, which had had,' Sigfried Giedion deploringly remarked, 'such a friendly and hopeful beginning.' All in all, if 'the erection of a building that should be the symbol of a future world government required the hand of a genius,' Giedion understood that this workshop was instead the result of a process of negotiation which, besides its architectural outcome, served as an unprecedented 'site of experimentation' for the formation of cross-cultural collaborations between international architects that would later continue to bear fruit in various transcultural experiments, competitions, and transfers of architectural knowledge.[50] Finally, whether or not one places a high value on the architectural results of the Palais of Nations and UN Headquarters competitions, both these processes encouraged exploration of forms of collaboration among architects under the auspices of global institutions of peace. We see a similar expression of the importance of collaborative creativity in FDR Four Freedoms Park, which, based on a design produced by Louis Kahn in 1973–1974, opened to the public on the southern tip of Roosevelt Island, just across from the UN, on 24 October 2012, almost 40 years after Kahn's death.

→ Fig. 1.12

The Global Classroom: International Pedagogical Collaboration

Besides international competitions and team partnerships, another form of ground-breaking international cooperation in the post-world-war era was the global classroom as a venue for pedagogical collaboration between young architects and students from around the world. Although they came from different backgrounds and brought with them different experiences, the collaborators shared a common purpose and the ambition to learn new methods of design that would advance their profession during the duration of their lives. Some of these classrooms were activated and organized by international organizations such as CIAM, which was willing to both educate the younger generations and to ensure the spread and 'continuing revolution' — as the Milan-based architect Ernesto Nathan Rogers put it[51] — of their theoretical/design principles, ideals, and visions.

Tellingly, the need for interactions among students and teachers from different universities in a worldwide flow of knowledge was highlighted by the youths themselves. It was a necessity that came directly from the bottom rung, from the younger and often scarcely visible group at the main congresses who, after finishing their studies, felt 'a great lack of understanding of human beings and of the society for which we must work', as the young Christian Norberg-Schulz put it at CIAM 8, held in 1951 in Hoddesdon, England.[52] Together with a diverse group of international students and young architects, Norberg-Schulz presented a sort of manifesto — the 'Ten Points'[53] — for a new educational programme with, as its last point, a global summer school of architecture that was a highly specific proposal for an architectural pedagogy based on an experimental laboratory.

Although these groups represented different and conflicting generations of architects, a remarkable line of continuity can be traced through the pedagogy of their global laboratories. Starting in 1949, CIAM organized summer schools in London and Venice, situating CIAM theories in real urban contexts through research carried out by students.[54] Subsequently, in the 1970s 'Team 10 was followed by ILAUD [the International Laboratory of Architecture and Urban Design]',[55] which revealed the importance that Team 10 members placed upon pedagogy in relationship to their professional practices.

Both schools and laboratories facilitated unprecedented debate between older and newer generations and interaction between abstract theories and concrete urban situations, with pedagogical collaboration and exchange serving as the main propellant of progressive thinking. More importantly, they facilitated experimentation with concepts and design approaches in medium-sized historical cities such as Venice and Urbino, both of which had a socio-spatial structure and a history that had been deeply influential through testing, negotiating, and questioning ideas and 'thinking tools' in previous centuries.[56]

Finally, both these modern pedagogical experiences fostered an active mode of knowledge formation and transmission that represented a particular viewpoint on modern urbanism, even becoming a 'precursor' of later urban design programmes. They remain a pivotal reference for our worldwide academic milieu to this day.[57]

CIAM Summer School

That several CIAM summer schools were organized in Venice was no coincidence. Venice and its lagoon are a unique place in which, as Italian historian Manfredo Tafuri has written, 'there is no contradiction between tradition and innovation, development and memory, continuity and renewal, sacred and mundane.'[58] This lack of antithesis and, at the same time, the place's great fragility in its continuous labile equilibrium between the artificial and the natural became fertile ground for testing CIAM's principles. Venice was an urban landscape in which modern principles could be tested through laboratories; as a continuous experiment, it was even, as Manfredo Tafuri and Vittorio Gregotti put it, 'a city of the new modernity'.[59]

After a first edition in London in 1949, in Venice (1952–1956, with the exception of 1955) the CIAM summer school became a platform for tackling CIAM's renewed interest in history and context.[60] It challenged students to analyse and rethink the peculiar social-urban tensions manifested in Venice between technological innovation and the historical built environment. These urban dualities were translated into design themes focused on: the link with the mainland (1952); the Biennale Gardens and the touristic city (1953); the mechanized bridgehead and the historical city (1954); and the expansion of the Venice mainland at Mestre and Marghera (1956).

→ Fig. 1.13

Faced with these design topics dealing with the rising role of history and its context in the modern project, students from different countries — mainly from Europe, USA, Australia, South Africa, Brazil, Argentina, Peru, and Colombia — were grouped into heterogeneous international teams which amalgamated and cooperated for a typical timespan of one month. This laboratory of teamwork encouraged the formation of networks of peers, and often friendships, among the young participants and influenced their practice in the following years in terms of collaboration and design thinking. Apart from CIAM's efforts to diffuse modern principles among the younger generations, the most important legacy of its summer schools was the personal relationships forged across nationalities in Venice while discussing and redesigning the city; these left their mark on the formation of the young participants, a few of whom, such as Vittorio Gregotti (Italy), Reima Pietilä (Finland), John Turner (US), and Denise Scott Brown (South Africa), would later become prominent architects on the world architectural scene.[61]

In parallel to these networks of contacts and friendships among peers, the visual, physical, and emotional bond with Venice also lived on as an important inheritance for at least some of these talented young students in the 1950s. For instance, Denise Scott Brown, who participated in the 1956 edition with her first husband, Robert Scott Brown, worked on the new plan for 'Mestre-Venice-industry-new settlements'.[62] The influence of the CIAM summer school was manifested throughout her career. From 'From Venice to Venice Beach',[63] the infrastructural study of the Venetian mainland resonated in her subsequent work in the US, while the symbolical and historical weight of Venice influenced both her thought and methods of analysis through the brand-new 'wayward eye' of photography.[64] All in all, Venice and its CIAM summer school paved the way for later watershed research and design proposals, even if the full extent of its complex legacy and influence is difficult to grasp.

Finally, after a rift led to CIAM's dissolution in 1956, the CIAM summer school suffered the same fate. The fifth and last edition of this international global classroom in 1957 was held not under the umbrella of CIAM but under the more neutral name 'International Summer Seminar of Architecture'. Nevertheless, the Italian CIAM members Franco Albini, Ignazio Gardella, Ernesto Rogers, and Giuseppe Samonà remained directors, as in the previous editions, and the city of Venice continued to be the primary research and design theme.[65]

ILAUD

A few years after the CIAM summer school ended, another global classroom emerged — ILAUD. Likewise held in Italy, ILAUD was founded by a Team 10 member, the Italian architect Giancarlo De Carlo. In the 1950s De Carlo had worked as an assistant at the CIAM summer school. His presence in both laboratories traced a line of continuity between the two global classrooms and between CIAM and Team 10 as well. According to Mirko Zardini, ILAUD was 'De Carlo's version of Team 10, enlarged to include new voices ... combining the moral legacy of CIAM and the energies of Team 10.'[66] However, this line of pedagogical continuity encompassed some important transformations, including a series of epistemological shifts. The CIAM summer school in London in 1949 had primarily been conceived as a design studio; the later editions in Venice had been an open urban-research laboratory aimed at situating the universal language of CIAM in the lagoon city. ILAUD, on the other hand, was not envisaged as a summer school. De Carlo stated that there was 'no need for one more institutional school of architecture and especially for one more summer school of architecture.'[67] Instead, ILAUD was an annual international laboratory organized around both permanent activities throughout the year and a workshop-laboratory during the summer. More importantly, it was, as De Carlo put it, 'a "place" where teachers and students from different countries meet, compare their views and the outcomes of their activity.'[68] In this evolution from design school to research laboratory to gathering 'place' the modern global classroom assumed a wide range of forms of 'radical pedagogies', whose legacy deserves to be taken into account in our contemporary educational system too.[69]

→ Fig. 1.14

The 'ILAUD-place' was based on the principle that urban and architectural design are a twofold unity and that participatory architecture is key in addressing the meaning and role of architecture in the global development of society.[70] These beliefs were experimented with at ILAUD and, at the same time, published in annual 'reports'. In 1978 De Carlo founded the journal *Spazio e Società* with the aim of reaching a broader readership beyond the attendees of the laboratory reports. Confronted with these aims and urgent ideas, the most important method stressed during the laboratory was 'reading', conceived as conjectural understanding, discovery, interpretation, and re-activation of observed forms and relations. Additional focuses of attention were interaction as a form of human action, structure in socio-spatial organization, and architectural presences within cities and their territories.[71] Reading is not an analytical activity *per se*. On the contrary, it is the first important step in a design process which, wrote De Carlo, also implies '[imagining], forming sequences of plausible hypothesis: and this means designing. So we can say that reading has to be carried out with an open mind oriented towards design, in order to disclose the past and foresee the future.'[72]

→ Figs. 1.15–16

This reading-design process — through diagramming, sketching, collages, and photographs — saw collaboration between international students, tutors, and professors from different universities around the world,[73] with a core group consisting of Team 10 members, including George Candilis (Greece/France), Ralph Erskine (United Kingdom), Aldo van Eyck (Netherlands), Jaap Bakema (Netherlands), Herman Hertzberger (Netherlands), and Reima Pietilä (Finland).[74] Participants took part in discussions and also situated ideas and topics previously introduced at the main congresses and meetings in the Italian territories of Urbino, Siena, San Marino, and, lastly, Venice again — as the CIAM summer school had done. For example, 'Janus-Thoughts for Siena' by Peter Smithson was a re-interpretation and reiteration in the historical Tuscan city of the 'in-between' theory discussed by Team 10.[75] Hence the distinctive and complex historical-cultural overlapping which characterizes this Italian territory — first studied by ILAUD as a historical centre and later subjected to a broader analysis which included the city's periphery and entire built environment — was seen once again as indicative of a place of cultural hybridization; (post)modern avant-garde theories were discussed through the global pedagogical experience of the younger generation.

Finally, this international collaborative reading process tackled a number of recurrent themes, such as reuse, territory, and participation, and compound topics, such as multiple language; multiplicity and complexity; place, memory, identity and environment; and language and modern architecture. The multiplicity of themes was brought together under ILAUD's central socio-spatial purpose — 'to nurture, to help create, an architecture that can be valuable to all people'[76] — in a reconsidering of the deep relationship between space and society — Henri Lefebvre's 'espaces et sociétés'[77] — through a brand-new form of global circulation and exchange of ideas among students, universities, and members of Team 10.

From the long process of negotiations and international collaboration for the United Nations Headquarters to the international laboratory and meeting 'place' that was the CIAM Summer School and ILAUD, the period following World War II saw increased cross-cultural mobility and cooperation in architecture and architectural education. This international collaboration and global knowledge transfer occurred among both established architects and young students and architects. To be sure, this transnational infrastructure was never exclusively framed for architecture. Recall for example, the Fulbright Program established by President Harry Truman in 1946. This was conceived as a form of cultural and educational diplomacy to promote the exchange of teachers, professors, and research scholars between the United States and participating countries.[78] The Erasmus Programme (the European Community Action Scheme for Mobility of University Students), established in 1987, did much to encourage exchanges amongst students studying the built environment in all its facets (architecture, landscape, urban design, and planning) and became an integral part of the pipeline of transnational cooperation in education.[79] The European Union was established on 1 November 1993 in Maastricht, Netherlands. Even before that, however, the Schengen Agreement had permitted 'check-free' travel across borders (between the Federal Republic of Germany, France, Belgium, Luxembourg, and the Netherlands), encouraging a greater mobility — with positive effects for educational collaboration.

Through new political global institutions and international schools, collaboration both challenged architectural practice with new global rivalry or cooperation and fostered the formation of young architects influenced by the emergence of networks of peers during their earlier pedagogical experience in transnational teams. These competitions and schools anticipated and prepared the ground for other, later, forms of collaborative architectural experience. In 1987 the biennial European Prize for Contemporary Architecture (Mies van der Rohe Award) was established as a partnership between the European Commission, the European Parliament, and the Fundació Mies van der Rohe in Barcelona. Europan, an international competition organized under the auspices of the European Union for architects under the age of 40, has since 1989 combined a transnational institutional competition with a platform for emerging young architects, fostering ongoing teamwork, exchanges through inter-session forums, and new forms of architectural collaboration.[80] The landscape of competitions has been further enhanced by competitions promoted over the years by the Venice Biennale di Architettura (Venice Biennale of Architecture), whose inauguration was jumpstarted by Paolo Portoghesi's provocative *The Presence of the Past* exhibition in 1980. Despite the subsequent proliferation of city-based architecture biennales, the Venice Biennale di Architettura remains the most prestigious of global venues for debates concerning the built environment, as a forum where, every two years, architects from all over the world are invited to collaborate in a collective dialogue about the state of architecture.[81]

1 Collaboration

1   J. William Fulbright, in: Walter Johnson and Francis J. Colligan, *The Fulbright Program. A History* (Chicago and London: University of Chicago Press, 1965), p. vii.
2   Misha Black, in: Michael Middleton, *Group Practice in Design* (London: Architectural Press, 1967), p. 285.
3   Erik Mattie, *World's Fairs* (New York: Princeton Architectural Press, 1998); Pieter van Wesemael, *Architecture of Instruction and Delight: A Socio-Historical Analysis of World Exhibitions as a Didactic Phenomenon (1798–1851–1970)* (Rotterdam: Uitgeverij 010, 2001).
4   Collaboration amongst artists as well as artists and architects is also not uncommon during this period. See, for example, Cynthia Jaffee McCabe, *Artistic Collaboration in the Twentieth Century* (Washington, D. C.: Smithsonian Institution Press, 1984); Barbara Diamonstein (ed.), *Collaboration: Artist and Architects* (New York: Watson-Guptill Publications, 1981).
5   Jennifer Kaufmann-Buhler, *Open Plan: A Design History of the American Office* (New York: Bloomsbury Publishing, 2021); Stephan Petermann and Ruth Baumeister (eds.), *Back to the Office: 50 revolutionary office buildings and how they sustained* (Rotterdam: Nai010 Publishers, 2022).
6   Mark Crinson, *Rebuilding Babel: Modern Architecture and Internationalism* (London: I. B. Tauris & Co Ltd, 2017).
7   Stephen C. Schlesinger, *Act of Creation: The Founding of the United Nations: A Story of Superpowers, Secret Agents, Wartime Allies and Enemies, and their Quest for a Peaceful World* (Boulder, Colo.: Westview Press, 2003). See also 'UN Membership'. Online. Available https: https://research.un.org/en/unmembers/founders#:~:text=Founding%20Member%20States,51%20Founding%20Members%20in%201945 (accessed 9 January 2024).
8   George A. Dudley, *A Workshop for Peace. Designing the United Nations Headquarters* (Cambridge: The MIT Press, 1994).
9   Eric Mumford, *The CIAM Discourse on Urbanism 1928–1960* (Cambridge, MA: The MIT Press, 2002).
10   Max Risselada and Dirk van den Heuvel (eds.), *Team 10: in search of a Utopia of the present 1953–1981* (Rotterdam: nai010, 2005).
11   'Members section'. Online. Available https: https://www.uia-architectes.org/en/ (accessed 9 January 2024).
12   The European Architectural History Network is a comparative newcomer on the scene, having only come into existence in 2005. See https://eahn.org (accessed 9 January 2024).
13   Peter Katz, *The New Urbanism: Toward an Architecture of Community* (New York: McGraw-Hill, 1994). Online. Available https: https://www.cnu.org/movement/cnu-history (accessed 16 June 2019).
14   Mario Carpo (ed.), *The Digital Turn in Architecture 1992–2012* (Chicester: Wiley, 2013).
15   William Robert Ware, *American Architect* (1899), p. 107. Quoted in: Hélène Lipstadt (ed.), *The Experimental Tradition* (New York: The Architectural League of New York, 1989), p. 15.
16   H.R. Goodhart-Rendel, *Journal of the RIBA* (21 November 1938), pp. 62–63. Quoted in: Barry Bergdoll, 'Competing in the Academy and the Marketplace: European Architecture Competitions 1401–1927', in: Hélène Lipstadt (ed.), *The Experimental Tradition* (New York: The Architectural League of New York, 1989), p. 45.
17   Ilia Delizia and Fabio Mangone, *Architettura e politica. Ginevra e la Società delle Nazioni, 1925–1929* (Rome: Officina Edizioni, 1992). See also Louis Cheronnet, *The Palace of the League of Nations* (Paris: L'Illustration, 1938).
18   Jean-Pierre Chupin, Carmela Cucuzzela, Bechara Helal, *Architecture Competitions and the Production of Culture, Quality and Knowledge* (Quebec: Potential Architecture Books, 2015), p. 15.
19   Patrick Abercrombie, 'Planning a City for the League of Nations', *The Architectural Review* 46, No. 12 (1919), p. 151. Quoted in: Carola Hein, *The Capital of Europe: Architecture and Urban Planning for the European Union* (London: Praeger, 2004), p. 28, note 39.
20   From the competition brief (April 1926). Quoted in: Joëlle Kuntz, 'Architectural Competitions: Imagining the City of Peace'. Online. Available http: http://www.geneve-int.ch/architectural-competitions-imagining-city-peace (accessed 7 May 2019).
21   Ibid.
22   Carola Hein, op. cit. (note 19), p. 224, note 42. For the division between avant-garde modernists and eclectic classicists, see Kenneth Frampton, 'Le Corbusier at Geneva: The debacle of the Société des Nations 1926–1939', in: Hilde de Hann, Ids Haagsma (eds.), *Architects in Competition. International Architectural Competitions of the Last 200 years* (London: Thames and Hudson, 1988), pp. 193–203.
23   Four million Swiss francs were paid so that technicians working at the competition could spend 'six months sorting through 10,000 blueprints', whereas the budget for the entire building was estimated at 13 million francs. See Joëlle Kuntz, op. cit. (note 20).

24 Carola Hein, op. cit. (note 17), p. 28. 165,000 Swiss francs were distributed among 27 projects, including nine prizes of 12.000 francs; nine honourable mentions, class 1, of 3800 francs each; nine honourable mentions, class 2, of 3500 francs each. See Dennis Sharp, 'Architectural Competitions: a watershed between old and new', in: Hilde de Hann, Ids Haagsma (eds.), op. cit. (note 22), pp. 181–192.
25 See Frampton, op. cit. (note 24), p. 201.
26 Dennis Sharp, op. cit. (note 24), p. 188.
27 Ibid., p. 191.
28 'A notre avis, ce serait un non-sens que de revêtir une Institution d'avenir, telle que la Société des Nations, d'un costume copié sur des gravures de mode d'autrefois. Ce serait même un aveu d'impuissance puisque l'esprit nouveau qui doit animer les peuples et l'organe international qu'ils ont créé, serait ainsi enseveli dans un cénotaphe construit par des hommes qui n'ont pas foi dans les ressources du présent et qui n'espèrent rien de l'avenir.' Camille Marlin, 'Le concours pour l'édification d'un palais de la Société des Nations à Genève, *Das Werk: Architektur und Kunst = L'oeuvre : architecture et art*, 14 (1927), p. 171. Online. Available http: http://doi.org/10.5169/seals-86274) (accessed 7 May 2019).
29 Sigfried Giedion, *Space, Time and Architecture: The Growth of a New Tradition* (Cambridge, MA: Harvard University Press, 1941; 5th edition: 2009), p. 538.
30 Online. Available https: https://www.unog.ch/virtual_tour/palais_des_nations.html (accessed 19 August 2024). Encyclopaedia Britannica says this was 'almost certainly a result of conspiracy on the part of conservative members of the jury'. Online. Available https: https://www.britannica.com/biography/Le-Corbusier (accessed 19 August 2024).
31 Giedion, op. cit. (note 29), p. 537.
32 'The elimination of Le Corbusier's project for the League of Nations was one of the reasons for founding the CIAM in 1928.' Giedion, op. cit. (note 29), p. 538.
33 'In the case of the League of Nations building in Geneva (1927), it was French political intrigues that annihilated [Le Corbusier's] scheme though, in the end, his rivals were obliged to imitate the organization of his site plan.' Giedion, op. cit. (note 29), p. 564.
34 Online. Available https: https://www.unog.ch/virtual_tour/palais_des_nations.html (accessed 14 May 2019).
35 Immanuel Kant, 'Perpetual Peace: A Philosophical Sketch' (1795). Online. Available https://web.archive.org/web/20080514211750/http://www.mtholyoke.edu/acad/intrel/kant/kant1.htm (accessed 14 May 2019).
36 '… a compromise made in terms of diplomatic prestige and ruling taste.' See Frampton, op. cit. (note 22), p. 202.
37 Ibid.
38 Giedion, op. cit. (note 29), p. 538, note 10.
39 See UNOG Library, Registry, Records and Archives Unit, 'History of the League of Nations (1919–1946)', pp. 13–14.
40 'And I feel that we have built not a symbol of peace but a workshop of peace.' Online. Available http: http://webtv.un.org/watch/a-workshop-for-peace/5240676028001 (1:21–1:31; accessed 15 May 2019). See George A. Dudley, op. cit. (note 8). Niemeyer said in 1947: 'When we make a building for the UN, we must have in mind what the UN is. It is an organization to set the nations of the world in a common direction and gives to the world security. I think it is difficult to get this into steel and stone. But if we make something representing the true spirit of our age, of comprehension and solidarity, it will by its own strength give the idea that that is the big political effort, too.' Online. Available https://archives.un.org/con10t/oscar-niemeyer-and-united-nations-headquarters (accessed 15 May 2019).
41 'The process [of the League of Nations competition] was lengthy; many years elapsed from the time of the decision on site location until buildings were available for occupancy. Determined to speed up the process this time, U.N. Secretary-General Trygve Lie decided an international board of design should be convened to carry out the initial design.' George A. Dudley, op. cit. (note 8), pp. 2, 4. See also Suzanne Frank, 'Reviewed Work(s): A Workshop for Peace: Designing the United Nations Headquarters by George Dudley', *Journal of Architectural Education (1984)*, Vol. 48, No. 4 (May 1995), pp. 274–275. Online. Available https://www.jstor.org/stable/1425392 (accessed 19 August 2024).
42 Under the direction of Wallace K. Harrison (United States) with Max Abramovitz (United States) and John Antoniades (Greece), the team consisted of Sven Markelius (Sweden), Le Corbusier (France), Liang Ssu-ch'eng (Sicheng) (China), G.A. 'Guy' Soilleux (Australia), Nikolai Bassov (Soviet Union), Vladimir Bodiansky (France), Ernest Cormier (Canada), Gaston Brunfaut (Belgium), Howard Robertson (United Kingdom), Julio Vilamajó (Uruguay), Matthew Nowicki (Poland), and Oscar Niemeyer (Brazil).
43 Le Corbusier, New York, 18 April 1947. In George A. Dudley, op. cit. (note 8), p. 213.

44 Victoria Newhouse, *Wallace K. Harrison, Architect* (New York: Rizzoli, 1989), in particular Chapter 12, 'The United Nations: the battle of designs', pp. 114–137; Chapter 13, 'The United Nations: the critics', pp. 138–143.
45 Giedion, op. cit. (note 29), p. 564.
46 'For the first time in history we meet with an overriding common idea, the realization of which will enable us to give the world a clear and optimistic architectural solution. ... A wonderful result has been achieved and one which is worth noting: we are all of the same opinion. Consider the competition for the League of Nations Building in Geneva, where 380 plans all cried out for recognition. Why are we so unanimous? Because after 100 years the evolution of architecture has today gradually reached decisive fruition. We are in the land of applied modern technique. We can, therefore, realize all modern ideas.' In: George A. Dudley, op. cit. (note 8), pp. 210–213.
47 Frampton, op. cit. (note 22), p. 203.
48 During meeting 33 on Monday, 28 April. George A. Dudley, op. cit. (note 8), p. 240.
49 The project was an anything but happy compromise, as later regretted by Niemeyer himself. Online. Available http: http://webtv.un.org/watch/a-workshop-for-peace/5240676028001 (minute 42:22; accessed 15 May 2019).
50 'Harrison alone was named Planning Director of Project 23 A. In the eyes of the client the ten had fulfilled their contract, and Harrison opened his own "UN Headquarters Planning Office". This marked the end of the happy period of the affair, which had such a friendly and hopeful beginning.' Giedion, op. cit. (note 29), p. 564.
51 Rogers, 'Architectural education, first session, CIAM 8, 1951', gta/ETH, 42-JT-7-473/475.
52 Norberg-Schulz, 'Commission 3A (Young Architects). Report on Architectural Education. CIAM 8', *Report of Hoddesdon Conference*, p. 113.
53 'CIAM 8, THE TEN POINTS', gta/ETH Archive, 42_JT_7_403. See Leonardo Zuccaro Marchi, 'CIAM Summer School in Venice. The Heart of the City as Continuity', in: Leonardo Zuccaro Marchi, *The Heart of the City. Legacy and Complexity of a Modern Design Idea* (Routledge, 2018), pp. 104–107.
54 For a complete description of the CIAM summer school, see Leonardo Zuccaro Marchi, ibid., pp. 98–148.
55 'For me, personally, Team 10 was followed by ILAUD. Ilaud was a completely different business, though when I founded it, I obviously carried over a lot of ideas from Team 10.' Clelia Tuscano, 'How can you do without history? Interview with Giancarlo De Carlo. Milan, Via Pier Capponi 13, 23 May 1990, 20 February 1995, and 24 November 1999', in: Max Risselada, Dirk van den Heuvel (eds.), op. cit. (note 10), p. 343.
56 A thinking tool was, for instance, the CIAM 'grid', the main analytical system for presenting all CIAM projects. See Le Corbusier, 'Description of the CIAM Grid, Bergamo 1949', in: J. Tyrwhitt, J.L. Sert, E.N. Rogers (eds.), *The Heart of the City: Towards the Humanisation of Urban Life* (London: Lund Humphries, 1952), pp. 171–176.
57 'In focusing on "architectural aspects of the central urban planning" this summer school [in London in 1949] served as precursor to the urban design program that Tyrwhitt assisted CIAM president Jose Luis Sert and Giedion to establish at Harvard a decade later'. In: Ellen Shoshkes, *Jaqueline Tyrwhitt: A Transnational Life in Urban Planning and Design* (New York: Routledge, 2013), p. 112. See also Eric Mumford, 'Sert and the CIAM "Heart of the City": Precursor to Urban Design, 1947–1952', in: Eric Mumford, *Defining Urban Design: CIAM Architects and the Formation of a Discipline, 1937–1969* (New Haven and London: Yale University Press, 2009), p. 80.
58 Manfredo Tafuri, *Venice and the Renaissance* (Cambridge: MIT Press, Cambridge, 1995), p. X. Originally published in Italian as *Venezia e il Rinascimento* (Torino: Einaudi, 1985).
59 Manfredo Tafuri, 'The Forms of the Time: Venice and Modernity', lecture for the start of the academic year (1993) (Italian title: 'Le forme del tempo: Venezia e la modernità'). The architect Vittorio Gregotti refers to Tafuri's lecture in his thesis that Venice is a city of a new modernity. Vittorio Gregotti, *Venezia Città della Nuova Modernità* (Venezia: Consorzio Venezia Nuova, 1999), p. 12. See also Leonardo Zuccaro Marchi, 'The Heart as Continuity', in: Marchi, op. cit. (note 48), pp. 14–15.
60 The CIAM summer school was held in Venice during the summers of 1952, 1953, 1954, and 1956. The 1955 edition was cancelled for organizational reasons, while in 1957 the summer school was renamed 'International Summer Seminar of Architecture' since it was no longer institutionally recognized by CIAM, reflecting the rift that had occurred within CIAM in 1956. See Leonardo Zuccaro Marchi, 'CIAM Summer School in Venice. The Heart of the City as Continuity', in: Marchi, op. cit. (note 53), pp. 98–148. See also: Herman van Bergeijk, 'CIAM Summer School 1956', *OverHolland*, No. 6, 2010, pp. 113–124; Lorenzo Mingardi, 'Reweaving the city: the CIAM summer schools from London to Venice (1949–1957)', in: Lorenzo

Ciccarelli, Clare Melhuish (eds.), *Post-war Architecture between Italy and the UK. Exchanges and transcultural influences* (London: UCL Press, 2021), pp.107–126; Franco Berlanda, 'La scuola estiva del CIAM', in: Franco Mancuso (ed.) *Lo Iuav di Giuseppe Samonà e l'insegnamento dell'architettura* (Roma, Fondazione Bruno Zevi, 2007), pp. 79–85; Ilhyun Kim, 'Alcuni episodi della biografia intellettuale di Samonà: dai rapporti con la scuola romana alla scuola estiva dei CIAM', in: Giuseppe Marras, Marco Pogačnik, *Giuseppe Samonà e la scuola di Architettura a Venezia* (Venezia: Il Poligrafo, 2006), pp. 61–92.

61   The importance of this network of peers at the CIAM Summer School was confirmed by Vittorio Gregotti during several personal discussions in 2012, 2013, and 2016 with Leonardo Zuccaro Marchi and at a conference held at IUAV on 2 September 2013 organized by Leonardo Zuccaro Marchi ('Il Cuore della Città — CIAM 8', participants: Gregotti, Rykwert, Secchi, Viganò, Avermaete, Zuccaro Marchi). See Zuccaro Marchi, 'Effects of the summer school', in: Leonardo Zuccaro Marchi, op. cit. (note 53), p. 108.

62   See Leonardo Zuccaro Marchi, 'Digression: Denise Scott Brown', in: Leonardo Zuccaro Marchi, op. cit. (note 53), pp. 136–137.

63   Denise Scott Brown, 'From Venice to Venice Beach: Denise Scott Brown's "Wayward" Eye', *Metropolis Magazine*, 13 July 2016. Online. Available http://www.metropolismag.com/July-August-2016/From-Venice-to-Venice-Beach-Denise-Scott-Browns-Wayward-Eye/ (accessed 28 July 2016).

64   Denise Scott Brown, op. cit. (note 63).

65   Mentioned in *Gazzettino di Venezia* and *Il Gazzettino* (4 September 1957).

66   Mirko Zardini, 'Urbino, Siena, San Marino and Venice (Taly) 1974–2004. Giancarlo De Carlo and the International Laboratory of Architecture and Urban Design'. Online. Available http: http://www.team10online.org/team10/meetings/1974–2004-ilaud.htm (accessed 4 June 2019). See also Ceccarelli, Paolo (ed.), *Giancarlo De Carlo and ILAUD. A movable frontier* (Milano: Fondazione OAMi, 2019).

67   Giancarlo De Carlo, letter to Peter Smithson about ILAUD, 12 December 1977, Biblioteca Civica d'arte Luigi Poletti, Fondo ILAUD, NOTE GDC, 1997. Published in: Giovanna Borasi (ed.), *The Other Architect. Another Way of Building Architecture* (Montreal: Canadian Centre for Architecture, Spector Books, 2015), p. 24.

68   Ibid.

69   Online. Available http: http://radical-pedagogies.com/ (accessed 4 June 2019).

70   See Lode Janssens, 'In order to discuss ILAUD', in *Architecture, multiple and complex* (Firenze: Sansoni, 1985), pp. 164–173.

71   Ibid., pp. 165–166.

72   '"Reading": for ILAUD this means identifying the signs of physical space, extracting them from the layers in which they are embedded, interpreting, ordering and recomposing them in systems that are meaningful for us also today. In the course of this process it is necessary to understand but also to imagine, forming sequences of plausible hypothesis: and this means designing. So we can say that reading has to be carried out with an open mind oriented towards design, in order to disclose the past and foresee the future.' Giancarlo De Carlo, 'Reading and Designing the Territory', in ILAUD, *Lettura e Progetto del territorio* (Rimini: Maggioli editore, 1996), p. 7.

73   For instance, in 1976: Escola Tecnica Superior de Arquitectura de Barcelona, Oslo School of Architecture, Katholieke Universiteit Leuven, Università degli Studi di Urbino, MIT, ETH Zurich.

74   See Mirko Zardini, 'Urbino, Siena, San Marino and Venice (Taly) 1974–2004. Giancarlo De Carlo and the International Laboratory of Architecture and Urban Design'. Online. Available http: http://www.team10online.org/team10/meetings/1974-2004-ilaud.htm (accessed 4 June 2019).

75   Peter Smithson, 'Janus-Thoughts for Siena', *Interpretations* (Genova: SAGEP, 1988), pp. 86–93.

76   Donlyn Lyndon, 'Architecture: A Complex Engagement', *Language of Architecture: Lectures, Seminars, and Projects, Urbino 1981* (Firenze: Sansoni, 1982), pp. 70–77.

77   *Espaces et Sociétés* was an interdisciplinary scientific journal of geography, architecture and urbanism, humanities, and social sciences founded by Henri Lefebvre and Anatole Kopp which influenced De Carlo's *Spazio e Società* magazine.

78   Walter Johnson and Francis J. Colligan, *The Fulbright Program. A History* (Chicago and London: University of Chicago Press, 1965; with a foreword by J. William Fulbright); Leonard R. Sussman, *The Culture of Freedom: The Small World of Fulbright Scholars* (Lanham, Md.: Rowman & Littlefield, 1992).

79   Alberto Amaral (ed.), *European Integration and the Governance of Higher Education and Research* (Dordrecht: Springer, 2009).

80   Online. Available https: https://www.europan-europe.eu / (accessed 6 June 2019).

81   William Menking and Aaron Levy (eds), *Architecture on Display: On the History of the Venice Biennale of Architecture* (London: Architectural Association, 2010).

2 Goods: Distribution Centres, Shopping Malls, and Trade Fairs

Tom Avermaete

Fig. 2.1
Advertisement by the mail-order company Sears, 1961. Neil Baylis.

In 1961 the Chicago-based mail-order company Sears published an advertisement for all the appliances it provided and serviced. The accompanying photograph offers a telling image of how consumer products that were produced in various geographies started to circulate in the American built environment. Mass goods entered the dwelling space in unprecedented quantities but also quickly left them again, to be replaced by new ones. In the post-war period circulation of goods increased under the influence of what Hungarian-born American psychologist George Katona called 'a new and unique phenomenon in human history, the mass consumption society'.[1]

The private house formed the bedrock of this post-war mass consumption economy in the United States, becoming not only an expensive commodity purchased by an unparalleled number of consumers but also the place par excellence where goods such as appliances, cars, and furnishings were accumulated. Residential construction experienced an unseen boom.[2] Twenty-five per cent of all homes in the United States were constructed during the 1950s. Homeownership reached over 60 per cent in 1960, a 20 per cent increase compared to 1940.

The American economist Walt Whitman Rostow wrote in 1960 that 'the age of high mass consumption' had arrived not only in the United States but also in Canada, Australia, Japan, and many Western European countries.[3] In Western Europe, American-style mass distribution and consumption spread rapidly, with the number of self-service stores increasing from 1200 to 45,500 between 1950 and 1960. By the early 1970s Germany, France, and several smaller nations, including the Netherlands, Switzerland, and the Scandinavian countries, were familiar with mass marketing, chain retailing, and the many other techniques and institutions of modern mass commerce.[4] The French economist Jean Fourastié coined the term 'Les Trente Glorieuses' (The Glorious Thirty Years) for the period between 1945 and 1975 that saw a revolution in mass consumption,[5] while many Japanese commentators spoke of a post-war economic boom based, unlike the pre-war booms that had mostly been driven by military demand, on consumer demand, particularly for home electronic appliances.[6]

→ Fig. 2.1

Fig. 2.2
Neckermann Distribution Centre (Egon Eiermann, 1961), Frankfurt, Germany. A 400,000-square-metre building surrounded by road and parking infrastructure.

Fig. 2.3
Neckermann Distribution Centre. Four towers, each with stairs, elevators, and service rooms arranged in front of the building.

2 Goods

Figs. 2.4–5
Olivetti Technical Centre and Distribution Centre
(Kenzo Tange, 1970), Yokohama, Japan.

Distribution Centres, Shopping Malls, and Trade Fairs

Fig. 2.6
Renault Parts Distribution Centre (Foster Associates, 1983), Swindon, United Kingdom.

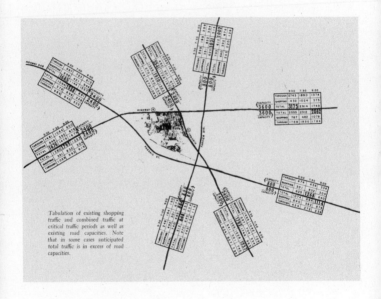

Fig. 2.7
Tabulation of existing shopping traffic and combined traffic at critical moments. Victor Gruen and Larry Smith, *Shopping Towns USA: The Planning of Shopping Centers* (New York: Reinhold publishing corporation, 1960), p. 119.

Distribution Centres, Shopping Malls, and Trade Fairs

Fig. 2.8
Southdale Shopping Center (Victor Gruen, 1976), Mineapolis, USA. A new shopping centre in the midst of road infrastructure and urban sprawl.
Fig. 2.9
The interior as a new and optimistic urban space for commercial and social gathering throughout the year.

Fig. 2.10
International Fair (Robert Maddalena and Raymond Lucaud, 1953–1960) and its entrance pavilion (Jean-François Zevaco), Casablanca, Morocco.

Fig. 2.11
International Fairground (Oscar Niemeyer, 1962–1975), Tripoli, Lebanon.

Fig. 2.12
International Trade Fair (Jacek Chyrosz and Stanisław Rymaszewski, Victor Adegbite, 1967), Accra, Ghana.

Several organizational and economic innovations accelerated consumerism. One of these was modern financing. People opened bank accounts, but their capacity to buy and thus to participate in consumer society was also fuelled by more easily accessible forms of personal and mortgage loans and the introduction of credit cards.[7] Another important accelerator of consumer culture was mass motorization, involving both professional and private vehicles.[8] For transporting raw materials as well as finished products, carriage by road became during the post-war period a faster, cheaper, and more flexible door-to-door alternative to traditional railways. Rail transport was increasingly considered incompatible with modern logistics and the time-based challenges of the new mass consumer culture. In a consumer-oriented society characterized by just-in-time delivery of consumption goods, truck transportation by road became the prevailing way to ship freight.

From the 1950s onwards, in many countries transportation by truck was supported by political decisions to consolidate, expand, or develop motorway networks. In the United States the Interstate Highway System provided a basis for transport networks between major cities. Highways were necessary for 'speedy, safe transcontinental travel' bypassing existing dangerous and inefficient routes, as claimed by President Dwight Eisenhower when he signed the Federal-Aid Highway Act in 1956 for the creation of a 41,000-mile 'National System of Interstate and Defense Highways.'[9] In Europe countries such as Italy and Germany took the lead in constructing motorway infrastructure during this period, offering an example that other European nations would follow during the 1960s.[10]

These motorway infrastructures were not only built to transport goods and appliances but also to promote private 'mass motorization', epitomized by the proliferation of the automobile. During the post-war period the private car became increasingly considered 'a harbinger of full mechanization', as the Swiss critic Sigfried Giedion labelled it in his 1948 book *Mechanization Takes Command*.[11] The lead in car ownership maintained by the US, where one quarter of the population already owned a car in the 1930s, over the rest of the world, where just one twentieth of the population of France and England had a car in the 1930s, slowly disappeared; the automobile peacefully conquered the whole world,[12] soon becoming domesticated as 'a personal appurtenance which comes to be understood as a movable part of the household'[13] or even a beloved 'family pet' to wash every weekend.[14] Its viral diffusion as a new domestic actor had a radical influence on people's everyday social life, on urban structure, and on the organization of entire territories.[15] The private car enabled remote areas to be developed into new residential neighbourhoods. It blurred the dividing line between urban and rural modes of living, changed forms of sociability, and turned driving into an activity associated with leisure and freedom.

Above all, mass motorization opened the way for a new system for circulating consumer goods across geographies. It fuelled new systems of mass distribution and mass consumption. From the perspective of producers and sellers, truck transport allowed for fast national and international shipping of goods, even to the most remote territories and places. From the consumer's viewpoint, the private car would not only become one of the most aspired to consumer products but also the vehicle that made it possible to transport everyday goods and appliances from sellers to the private home, where they could be accumulated, consumed, used, and disposed of. Mass motorization, in this sense, propelled consumer culture but also acted as a transformative agent in the built environment: it not only changed the architecture of the private house — introducing, for instance, new domestic spaces, such as the driveway and the garage — but also launched new building typologies in which mass consumer culture and mass motorization merged.

The Global Distribution Centre

One of these new building types was the so-called 'distribution centre'. As mass-produced goods circulated globally, they also had to be brought to the territories and houses of consumers. This called for the introduction of a new logic which may be summarized as 'mass distribution'. Processes of mass distribution took many urban and architectural forms, ranging, for instance, from large centralized warehouses to distribution centres. Avantgarde modern architects were often assigned the task of conceiving the character of this new architecture of mass distribution.
→ Figs. 2.2–3

The German architect Egon Eiermann was one of them. In the late 1950s he was contacted by Neckermann, a company which had ambitions to become a major player in one of these logics of mass distribution — mail order. Retail by mail order was not a new phenomenon. The Thonet brothers in France and the Sears Company in the US had been experimenting with it since the late nineteenth century, but in the mass consumer culture of the post-war period this commercial formula took on unprecedented importance.[16] The German entrepreneur Josef Neckermann had established his mail order business by merging several businesses that he had acquired from Jewish owners during the Nazi regime.[17] Neckermann built his distribution expertise as part of the economy of World War II in order to deliver clothes and bed linen for forced labourers and winter uniforms for the Wehrmacht, the armed forces of the Third Reich. These problematic practices did not prevent the Neckermann firm, alongside other local companies, such as Otto and Quelle, from becoming one of the most important German mail order companies in the post-war decades. The mail order business became an alternative to the classic, middle-class department store. While the department store, as a theatre of carefully staged goods and self-promotion, was aimed at female consumers, the mail-order business with its catalogues offered other groups, such as men, an entry point into the world of mass consumption.

The slogan 'Neckermann makes it possible' became a byword for the post-war German economic miracle. The Neckermann mail order business delivered everything from clothes, linen, and shoes, to TVs, radios, and refrigerators, as well as holiday travel packages, insurance policies, and prefabricated housing. In the mid-1950s the company already employed several thousand people, mailing millions of catalogues to households in Germany and throughout Europe. As an article in the German periodical *Der Spiegel* explained in 1955, 'Through films and illustrated magazines, even the last village knows what is modern. ... The long way to the city is difficult in the bad season, and so the consumers far away from the big cities reach for the catalogue, which you can study in peace on the sofa in the evening. Even if an order is then placed, there is no risk, because the mail order business takes back goods that the customer does not like without any problems.'[18]

Every day around 30,000 orders reached the headquarters of Neckermann in the German city of Frankfurt and had to be administered, packed, and shipped. For this process of mass distribution, the company relied strongly on automation: 'Large wire baskets with many compartments turn their rounds here at a speed that can be regulated at will. ... Helpers accompany one basket at a time on its journey and, during the tour, put the goods marked on the order slips into the compartments. The packages roll on conveyor belts to the packing station. Then they slide down a slide into the cellar: into Neckermann's own post office.'[19] Much of Neckermann's advantage over conventional retail and a large part of its profit derived from rationalization of the process of promoting, packaging, and shipping consumer goods.

These distribution modes for mass consumption goods, such as mail order, had to be given new spatial forms. When Egon Eiermann had to design a new distribution centre for Neckermann in Frankfurt, he did not model his project on the typology of the early twentieth-century department store but rather designed a 400,000-square-metre building that was as rational and as flexible as the mail order processes themselves. With an extremely limited construction time of 180 days, Eiermann decided not only to base the entire 257-metre-long building on a rigid grid of six by six metres but also to divide it into 21 independent construction stages separated by expansion joints. This allowed different construction companies to participate in the construction.

Eiermann kept the interior of the building completely open to ease the 'flow' of consumption goods. Four towers, each with stairs, elevators, and service rooms, are arranged in front of the building. The front façade is further dominated by emergency balconies and cascading stairways. The main entrance with its striking red roof is located in a free-standing central tower, which is connected by glass bridges to the main building housing Neckermann's shipping division on its ground floor and first three upper floors. In the basement are changing rooms for the staff. On the top two floors, offices, archives, rooms for the executive committee, and the company canteen are arranged between two accessible patios.

Neckermann was no exception. In the decades following World War II numerous companies selling mass-consumption products, whether in the mail-order business or in conventional retail, commissioned architects to design distribution centres. The Swiss architect Heinz Isler designed a distribution centre for the Swiss Coop supermarkets in Olten (Switzerland, 1960); the Japanese Kenzo Tange conceived a technical centre and distribution centre in Yokohama for the Italian typewriter manufacturer

Olivetti (Japan, 1970); and the British architect Norman Foster realized a distribution centre for the French car producer Renault in Swindon (UK, 1982). All these distribution centres were typically rationally organized and well connected to road infrastructures so that the goods could be efficiently and rapidly distributed by truck to consumers in the surrounding geographies. In the decades following World War II the distribution centre would become one of the most tangible hallmarks of how mass goods were circulated in territories.

→ Figs. 2.4–6

The Planetary Shopping Mall

The goods originating from distribution centres were sometimes shipped directly by truck to the houses of individual citizens, but more often they ended up in another hallmark of mass consumption and automobility — the shopping mall.[20] This new building typology emerged in the mid-1950s in the United States and rapidly spread to other parts of the world during the post-war period. The Viennese émigré architect Victor Gruen, who had settled in the US in 1938, played a key role in the design and global proliferation of the shopping mall.[21] In developing this building typology, Gruen balanced high-culture modernist discourses on the necessity of new public spaces in expanding post-war cities with the reality of the popular culture of mass consumption and automobility.[22]

The creation of new central public spaces for collective practices often conflicted with the fundamentally individual character of consumption in the single-family home and driving in a private car, as highlighted in Gruen's publications. In *The Heart of Our Cities: The Urban Crisis, Diagnosis and Cure* (1964), Gruen asserts: 'The automobile population has a higher birth rate than the human one,' and continues, 'It appears that the internal combustion engines, in their mass assault, have led to the external combustion of the city.'[23] He even labelled the automobile 'the means by which the last vestige of community coherence was destroyed.'[24] Gruen observed the increasing sprawl of territory in the US as the land filled with an extensive and continuously growing labyrinth of suburban roads and parking areas in which various urban functions were dispersed. In his view this created a danger of 'enforced mobility' a condition in which people are obliged to spend part of their daily life driving.

Gruen also understood, however, that any account of public life in the US in the 1950s and 1960s would have to involve acknowledgement of mass consumption culture with its intense circulation of consumer goods and strong reliance on private motorization. In Gruen's view, the establishment of the shopping centre as the core of public life depended on planning of car traffic, which he analysed through schematic and detailed tabulations.
→ Fig. 2.7

For Victor Gruen and others, designing a building type that could create points of encounter within the motorized flows of goods and people became the key challenge in shopping mall design. Gruen's designs may be understood as attempts to generate moments of relative standstill within the circulation of people. To achieve this, Gruen designed introspective, closed-box buildings in which all the technology and infrastructure needed for the flows of people and goods is kept outside, far away from the interior, where collective practices involving citizens are to unfold. In Gruen's early shopping mall projects the exterior is considered an infrastructural realm that deserves mainly technical attention from the architect or urban designer. The external mute and generic character of loading docks, access roads, and parking lots contrasts with the well-studied and -designed sensorial experience of spatially impressive and colourful interior spaces that function as a setting for social gathering.

An example of a pioneering early design proposal for a shopping centre with clear separation between infrastructural exterior and commercial and public interior is Southdale Centre, near Minneapolis, which opened in 1956. Southdale was one of the first closed malls in which urban scenery and artificial climate were melded into a commercial strategy. The consumers of Southdale were led, through a small number of porticoes, from the parking lot to the main interior pedestrian area with its three-storey central court and air conditioning systems that ensured an 'atmosphere of eternal spring'.[25] In the post-war US Victor Gruen's Southdale Centre introduced new and optimistic urban spaces for commercial and social gathering throughout the year, '[keeping] out both cold war worries and actual cold.'[26] Architectural critics and historians lauded this experiment. The Swiss critic Sigfried Giedion, in his well known book *Architecture You and Me* (1958), listed Southdale Centre among the most important architectural achievements of its time, claiming that 'The out-of-town shopping centre, developed for purely commercial reasons, here begins to take on some attributes of a centre of social activity.'[27]

→ Figs. 2.8–9

Southdale was the start of a long and continuous development. From the mid-1950s forwards, a mycelial pattern of about 1200 enclosed suburban shopping malls emerged across the United States. The spread of these commercial isolated domes was propelled by specific political and legal measures. Their development was encouraged by the 'accelerated depreciation laws' of 1954, which allowed real estate developers to rapidly write off construction of new business buildings and even claim losses against unrelated income. As a result, shopping centres and other new commercial constructions on greenfield sites in the urban fringe became a lucrative tax shelter for investors.[28] These tax laws were accompanied by political measures such as the National Interstate and Defense Highway Act of 1956, a massive road-building programme that facilitated access to inexpensive land and led to large-scale subdivisions, which typically included commercial mall development or were located near new suburban malls. A third stimulus came from legislation passed in 1960 which allowed investors to band together in REITs (Real Estate Investment Trusts) to avoid corporate income tax. Together, these laws and measures helped shape the US' prototypical exurban landscape composed of gas stations, motels, drive-in fast-food restaurants, and enclosed shopping malls.[29]

Ever since its first appearance, the enclosed shopping mall has provoked strong reactions in architectural culture and discourse. On the one hand, it was immediately hailed as a new space of urban gathering, a 'notable attempt in the United States to give the pedestrian a meeting place,' as Spanish architect Josep Lluís Sert put it at an urban design seminar at Harvard's Graduate School of Design in the 1950s.[30] On the other hand, scholars such as Margaret Crawford have underlined that despite its social ambitions, the enclosed shopping mall often remained a straightforward space of controlled and disciplined mass consumption.[31] Many architectural critics and theorists have commented on the shopping mall's Janus-faced character as a new figure of urban sociability but simultaneously an interiorization of urban life disconnected from the wider urban territory. The French urban anthropologist Marc Augé described the shopping mall, together with airports and international train stations, as a 'non-place' that is a clear expression of the condition of supermodernity in the latter half of the twentieth century.[32]

The enclosed shopping mall not only transformed the American urban landscape in the second half of the twentieth century but also soon spread around the world to accommodate the ever-increasing flows of goods in geographies beyond the United States. Gruen's enclosed mall turned into a global typology of mass consumerism, whose architectural design adapted as it was 'resettled' in diverse spatial, economic, social, and political contexts. As early as 1900, the American businessman Bradford Peck published the utopian book *The World a Department Store: A Twentieth Century Utopia*.[33] A few decades later, the imagined globalization of American consumerism was gradually realized through the proliferation of Gruen's new architectural type. 'The world of the shopping mall ... has become the world,' as Margaret Crawford critically claimed.[34]

This globalization of the enclosed shopping mall, however, did not come without challenges. Ever-diminishing attention to the social and public role that the enclosed shopping mall could play was certainly one of them. Gruen was critical of designers who neglected the mall's ambition as a 'new planning concept that could expand beyond the goal of creating merely machines for selling and could satisfy the demand for urban crystallization points and thus offer the suburban population significant life experiences,'[35] saying: 'I refuse to pay alimony for those bastard developments.'[36] In 1972, in a clear attempt at redemption for this out-of-control spread of commercial design, Gruen wrote a new manifesto, titled 'The Charter of Vienna', mixing his design principles for shopping centres with an ecological interpretation of the renowned Athens Charter that the Congrès Internationaux d'Architecture Moderne (CIAM) had published 40 years earlier.[37]

Despite the criticism in architectural circles, in the second half of the twentieth century shopping malls became a globalized phenomenon that hybridized with all types of urban function to create new centralities. A good contemporary example is the Abraj Al Bait shopping centre (2004–2012) with its iconic clock tower in the city of Mecca in Saudi Arabia.[38] Directly opposite the King Abdul Aziz Gate of the Holy Mosque, this shopping centre contains a hotel, a museum, a prayer room, and an Islamic research centre. Almost an extension of the religious space of the Grand Mosque, this enclosed mall is one of the key central places in the holy city. Worldwide, large shopping malls became central places of everyday life — isolated entities in the suburban sprawl but also integral parts of dense cities.

Illustrative of this latter approach is Canal City Hakata, designed in the late 1980s for Fukuoka, a city which was struggling with a massive influx of people, a dying shopping district, and no sense of community. John Jerde, an American architect based in Los Angeles, designed this, the largest privately developed project in Japan's history, as a composition of several commercial buildings along a new canal. At its core Jerde situated a half 'negative sphere', intended to function as a theatrical and ceremonial gathering space. Jerde's references to theatre sets, entertainment environments, and film set designs are combined into a continuous 'climax by taking the entire discarded repertoire of architecture and returning it as a farce'.[39] Whereas Gruen aimed at a 'transfer' by which 'destination buyers' were transformed into 'impulse shoppers',[40] the 'Jerde transfer' occurs when consumers are intoxicated by excessive spatial stimulation without being aware of where they are, where to go, or how they got there.[41] If in his projects Gruen sought refuge from suburban chaos, Jerde instead aimed to strengthen it in order to disorient 'homo consumens' in his capacity as hero-actor-spectator.[42,43] Gruen's enclosed minimalist, box-like buildings are turned into an open-air, eclectic Hollywood experience. Experiential amplification, visual bombardment, and entertainment — terms used by the critic Norman M. Klein to describe Jerde's shopping mall — are key words for this 'electronic Baroque'.[44]

Spaces for Display

Architecture and urbanism have not only provided for the distribution and consumption of mass goods but also engaged with their display, promotion, and advertisement. International trade fairs became important actors in promoting the circulation of consumer goods. Periodicals such as the American *Foreign Commerce Weekly* illustrated the enormous number of trade fairs organized around the world. In 1960 numerous international trade fairs were held across the globe, from Kabul in Afghanistan to Lima in Peru and Zagreb in Yugoslavia.[45] Not only business leaders but also politicians viewed international trade fairs as ideal forums for the promotion of nationally produced consumer products.

In France, for instance, the politicians of the French Senate maintained in an official report that 'the representation of our country at international fairs is a means that guides our export activity and makes our products known. This publicity and presence are essential for the French flag to fly high where there is international competition.'[46] In a single year, 1960, French commercial interests were represented at international fairs in a wide variety of cities and countries, including Johannesburg, Milan, Casablanca, New York, Barcelona, Poznan, Kabul, Thessaloniki, Leipzig, Munich, Dallas, Philadelphia, and Gothenburg.[47] The French Senate concluded that these international trade fairs were 'certainly an effective aid to the development of our exports.'[48]

A good example is the fair in Casablanca, Morocco, organized by the local chamber of commerce on a yearly basis since 1937. *Foreign Commerce Weekly* reported in 1961 that at the International Fair of Casablanca good business could be done by American producers of mass consumer products since 'a market reportedly exists for household equipment such as water heaters, food-processing machinery, packaging equipment, washing machines, and tailoring machines.'[49] Besides American companies, European businesses, such as the Swedish car and vehicle maker Volvo and the French car manufacturer Renault, maintained a conspicuous presence at the fair in Casablanca to promote their products. Nor was it only western nations that presented their products: countries such as China also received ample attention, as the Moroccan politician and independence fighter Mehdi Ben Barka recalled: 'Observers are unanimously struck by the immense success of the Chinese pavilion at the Casablanca International Fair. This is due to the fact that China presents itself as the country with the most similarities to ours, in its past, by the immense delay it has had to catch up, and by the mistakes also made after liberation.'[50]

In 1952 the Moroccan authorities decided that the International Fair of Casablanca needed new premises, and the event was moved from the harbour to a 130,000-square-metre site bordering the medina and the city's infamous gigantic open-air swimming pool. Planning of the fair's grounds was led by the Service de l'Urbanisme, the main planning administration in the French protectorate, under the leadership of the French urban designer Michel Ecochard.[51] The main exhibition hall for the Casablanca trade fair, the so-called 'Grand Palais', was the result of a competition and designed by the French architects Robert Maddalena and Raymond Lucaud, who created a project for a vaulted exhibition hall punctured by numerous circular skylights, offering maximal flexibility for showcasing a variety of consumer products. Two hundred metres long and 90 metres wide, this project not only offered a spectacular 18,000 square metres of interior exhibition space but was also, at the time of its construction in 1953, the longest concrete vault in the world. At the entrance to the fairground, in 1960 the French-Moroccan architect Jean-François Zevaco designed the so-called Entrance Pavilion of the City in the form of a reversed concrete pyramid. Like many other buildings on the fairground, this pavilion symbolized the modernity not just of architecture but also, and especially, of the consumer products it showcased.

→ Fig. 2.10

Another example was the International Fairground in Tripoli in northern Lebanon, whose construction was initiated in 1962 by the Lebanese president, Fuad Chehab.[52] The 1960s were Lebanon's glory days, and it was hoped that this project would serve as a bridge between the country's different communities and as the hallmark of a modern state seeking progress and peace. The Lebanese government invited the Brazilian architect Oscar Niemeyer to design a permanent international fair complex for Tripoli, specifically because he had recently completed a governmental building complex in Brazil's new capital of Brasília, which vividly expressed the cultural pride of a developing nation.

Niemeyer's ambitious plan for Tripoli proposed a new city quarter including zones for commerce, sports, entertainment, and housing with the fair at its centre. His original design envisaged the individual pavilions under a single flat, curved canopy, 750 by 70 metres. As part of the fair, Niemeyer also conceived two types of housing — one, a tall building of several storeys; the other, a single-family villa. A small train was to transport people through the site. There were also to have been an experimental theatre, an open-air theatre, and a space museum. Construction started in 1962, but by the time the fairground was finally ready to open in 1975, over a dozen years after its inception (phased opening had never been part of the plan), the Lebanese civil war had broken out; the site was abandoned and remained frozen in time.

→ Fig. 2.11

That the display of goods also became part and parcel of modernization and nation-building projects during the post-war period is made clear by the International Trade Fair in Accra, Ghana. This project was commissioned in 1962 under the leadership of President Kwame Nkrumah, who saw the fair as a platform to bolster international trade and economic development and showcase Ghana's industrial and agricultural potential to the world.[53] The design incorporated state-of-the-art facilities, including exhibition halls, pavilions, and conference centres, in a bid to attract international exhibitors and visitors. The fair was strategically located in Accra, the Ghanian capital, to maximize accessibility and impact.

The fair's design and construction were led by two young architects from socialist Poland, Jacek Chyrosz and Stanisław Rymaszewski, in collaboration with Victor Adegbite, the Ghanian chief architect. All three worked for Ghana National Construction Corporation (GNCC), which was responsible for the design, construction, and maintenance of governmental buildings and infrastructure in Nkrumah's Ghana and managed the design and construction of the International Trade Fair between 1962 and 1967. Chyrosz and Rymaszewski were employed by GNCC through a contract with Polservice, Poland's central agency for foreign trade, which facilitated export of labour from socialist Poland. At GNCC they worked alongside Ghanaian architects and various foreign professionals, many of whom were from socialist countries.

Relying on various networks of architectural knowledge, the design of the buildings at the fair followed the principles of modern tropical architecture as defined by the British architects Jane Drew and Maxwell Fry. In their book *Tropical Architecture in the Humid Zone* (1956) and other publications Drew and Fry identified climate, local materials and technologies, and people's needs and aspirations as the 'main considerations influencing architectural design in the tropics'.[54] The Polish and Ghanaian architects employed these principles to create a modern architecture suited to displays of goods, numerous restaurants and snack bars, a cinema, an exhibition gallery, and Ghana's first drive-in banking window. The various pavilions explored the relationship between space and goods, balancing architectural expression between recognizable stereotypes and enlivening surprises. At the Accra International Trade Fair modern tropical architecture became an accepted idiom to articulate a new

Ghanian consumer culture embraced by avant-garde architects as well as the political and commercial establishment. The fair's inauguration in 1967 was a significant milestone in Ghana's post-independence history, symbolizing the nation's aspirations for economic growth and international cooperation.

→ Fig. 2.12

Dead Malls: the Rise and Fall of Flows of Goods

In 1989, the year of the fall of the Berlin Wall, the World Wide Web was invented by the English computer scientist Berners-Lee.[55] The emergence of the web rapidly resulted in the superimposition of a new digital layer on flows of goods and people. Online versions of real-life stores and fully digital shops proliferated in the years and decades following the public launch of the internet, resulting in an augmented reality of web-based mass distribution and consumption. The broad rise of e-commerce, or internet-based shopping, radically transformed shopping habits in many parts of the world, offering faster, cheaper, and more convenient ways of selling and buying. Echoing the Sears advertisements of the mid-twentieth century, e-commerce fuelled the idea that goods and goods could travel across territories more quickly and effortlessly than ever. In many parts of the world, platform commerce became the dominant mode of mass advertisement, distribution, and consumption.

This new way of displaying, distributing, and purchasing goods also affected built spaces of mass distribution and consumption. Old distribution centres were repurposed, and new ones were built to accommodate the dream of effortless and free circulation of goods. Platform commerce also called into question existing building typologies for mass consumption, especially the enclosed shopping mall. In the United States the overbuilding of malls had by the 1980s already resulted in an oversaturated market where supply far exceeded demand. The rapid rise of e-commerce drastically altered shopping habits, making it more convenient for consumers to purchase goods online rather than by visiting physical stores. This shift led to reduced foot traffic in malls, causing many retailers to close their bricks-and-mortar locations. As a result, in the late twentieth century, so-called 'dead malls', part of a new territory of 'greyfields', became a notable phenomenon in the United States.

Similar patterns emerged elsewhere, particularly in countries that had adopted the American-style mall concept. In Europe and parts of Asia, changing consumer preferences and economic fluctuations led to the decline of many large shopping centres.[56] As a result, dead malls became a global issue, with abandoned or repurposed shopping centres reflecting broader shifts in the circulation of goods. In response, architects, urban planners, and local communities started to explore innovative ways to repurpose these spaces, transforming them into mixed-use developments, community centres, or even residential areas in order to breathe new life into these once-bustling hubs of mass distribution and consumption.

1   George Katona, *The Mass Consumption Society* (New York: McGraw-Hill, 1964).
2   Lizabeth Cohen, 'A consumers' republic: The politics of mass consumption in post-war America', *Journal of Consumer Research*, No. 31 (2004), pp. 236–239.
3   Walt Whitman Rostow, *The Process of Economic Growth*, 2nd ed. (Oxford: Clarendon Press, 1960).
4   Victoria de Grazia, *Irresistible Empire. America's Advance through Twentieth-Century Europe* (Cambridge Mass.: The Belknap Press of Harvard University Press, 2005).
5   Jean Fourastié, *Les Trente Glorieuses: ou la révolution invisible de 1946 à 1975* (Paris: Fayard, 1979).
6   Yutaka Kōsai and Yoshitarō Ogino. *The Contemporary Japanese Economy* (London: Macmillan, 1984).
7   Matthew Hilton, *Consumerism in Twentieth-Century Britain: The Search for a Historical Movement* (Cambridge: Cambridge University Press, 2003).
8   David W. Jones, *Mass Motorization and Mass Transit: An American History and Policy Analysis* (Bloomington, IN: Indiana University Press, 2008).
9   'The Interstate Highway System'. Online. Available https: https://www.history.com/topics/interstate-highway-system (accessed 10 August 2018).
10 See Richard Vahrenkamp, 'Driving globalization: The rise of logistics in Europe 1950–2000', *European Transport \ Trasporti Europei*, No. 45 (2010), p. 3.
11 Sigfried Giedion, *Mechanization Takes Command* (Oxford: Oxford University Press, 1948), p. 43.
12 Victoria de Grazia argues that Henry Ford should be considered one of the founders of united Europe since he was the first to consider the whole of Europe as a single unique selling area. See Victoria de Grazia, op. cit. (note 4), p. 90.
13 Ibid.
14 In the Leicester Traffic Plan of 1964 urban planner Konrad Smigielski depicted the car as a family pet, housed in its own special kennel-garage. W. Konrad Smigielski, *Leicester Traffic Plan: A Report on Traffic in Urban Policy* (Leicester, 1964), p. 23. Quoted in Simon Gunn, 'People and the car: the expansion of automobility in urban Britain, c. 1955–1970,' *Social History*, 38:2, (2013), pp. 231–232.
15 Kingsley Dennis and John Urry, *After the Car* (Cambridge, 2009), p. 39. In Simon Gunn, op. cit. (note 14), p. 221.
16 James C. Worthy, *Shaping an American Institution. Robert E. Wood and Sears, Roebuck* (Champaign-Urbana: University of Illinois Press, 1984).

17 In 1935 Neckermann took over the Mercur emporium and a textile department store in Würzburg from Siegmund Ruschkewitz. Other similarly 'Aryanised' businesses were later added to the list: the Vetter department store in Würzburg and, most importantly, the Karl Joel clothing business in Nuremberg and Berlin. Due to the Nuremberg racial laws, the Jewish owners had been forced to 'sell' their companies at well below their real value.
18 'Kataloge gegen Kartelle', *Der Spiegel*, 26.10.1955.
19 Ibid.
20 For an introduction to this building typology see Tom Avermaete and Janina Gosseye (eds.), *Acculturating the Shopping Centre* (London: Routledge, 2018); Janina Gosseye, Tom Avermaete (eds.), *Shopping Towns Europe: Commercial Collectivity and the Architecture of the Shopping Centre, 1945–1975* (London: Bloomsbury, 2020).
21 M. Jeffrey Hardwick, *Mall Maker. Victor Gruen, Architect of an American Dream* (Philadelphia: University of Pennsylvania Press, 2004).
22 Jacqueline Tyrwhitt, Josep Lluís Sert, Ernesto N. Rogers (eds.), *The Heart of the City — Towards the Humanisation of Urban Life* (London: Lund Humphries Ltd, 1952; New York: Pellegrini and Cudahy, 1952). See also Leonardo Zuccaro Marchi, *The Heart of the City: Legacy and Complexity of a Modern Design Idea* (London: Routledge, 2018).
23 Victor Gruen, *The Heart of Our Cities — The Urban Crisis Diagnosis and Cure* (New York: Simon and Schuster, 1964), p. 84.
24 Victor Gruen, Larry Smith. *Shopping Town USA. The Planning of Shopping Centers* (New York: Reinhold Publishing Corporation, 1960), p. 19.
25 Malcolm Gladwell, 'The Terrazzo Jungle', *The New Yorker* (15 March 2004). Online. Available http: https://www.newyorker.com/magazine/2004/03/15/the-terrazzo-jungle (accessed 3 February 2015).
26 Timothy Mennel, 'Victor Gruen and the Construction of Cold War Utopias', *Journal of Planning History* 3 (2004), p. 129. Online. Available doi: 10.1177/1538513204264755 (accessed 4 June 2014).
27 Sigfried Giedion, *Architecture You and Me* (Cambridge: Harvard University Press, 1958), p. 212.
28 Thomas W. Hanchett, 'U.S. Tax Policy and the Shopping-Centre Boom of the 1950s and 1960s', *The American Historical Review*, Vol. 101, No. 4, 1996, pp. 1082–1110. JSTOR. Online. Available https: https://doi.org/10.2307/2169635 (accessed 9 July 2024).

29 Ibid.
30 Josep Lluís Sert, 'Urban Design Seminar: The Human Scale', GSD Harvard, Cambridge, 1957, Twelfth Meeting, 1–3, and Thirteenth Meeting, 1–2 (HU sc Loeb), quoted in Eric Mumford, *Defining Urban Design — CIAM Architects and the Formation of a Discipline, 1937–1969* (New Haven and London: Yale University Press, 2009), p. 135.
31 Margaret Crawford, 'The World in a Shopping Mall', in: M. Sorkin (ed.), *Variations on a Theme Park. The American City and the End of Public Space* (New York: Hill and Wang, 1992), p. 6.
32 David Smiley, *Pedestrian Modern. Shopping and American Architecture, 1925–1956* (Minneapolis: University of Minnesota Press, 2013), p. 5.
33 Bradford C. Peck, *The World a Department Store: a Twentieth Century Utopia* (Lewiston, Maine: Bradford Peck, 1900).
34 Crawford, op. cit. (note 31), p. 30.
35 Victor Gruen, *Centers for the Urban Environment. Survival of the Cities* (New York: V.N.R. Company, 1973), p. IX.
36 M. Jeffrey Hardwick, *Mall Maker. Victor Gruen, Architect of an American Dream* (Philadelphia: University of Pennsylvania Press, 2004), p. 216.
37 Victor Gruen, 'The Charter of Vienna', Victor Gruen Papers: Box 48, Folder 5, Library of Congress, Washington. See also Leonardo Zuccaro Marchi, 'Victor Gruen: the Environmental Heart', *The Journal of Public Space*, Vol. 2, No. 2 (2017), pp. 75–84. Online. Available https://doi.org/10.5204/jps.v2i2.94 (accessed 23 July 2018).
38 Online. Available http: http://www.dar.com/work/project/makkah-clock-tower (accessed 23 July 2018).
39 Herman Daniel, 'Jerde Transfer', in: Koolhaas Rem et al. (eds.), *Harvard Design School — Guide to Shopping*, (Los Angeles: Taschen, 2001), p. 403.
40 Crawford, op. cit. (note 31), p. 14.
41 Herman Daniel, op. cit. (note 39), p. 403.
42 See Zygmunt Bauman, *Homo consumens. Lo sciame inquieto dei consumatori e la miseria degli esclusi* (Gardolo (TN): Edizioni Erickson, 2007).
43 Norman M. Klein, 'The Electronic Baroque: Jerde Cities', in: Ray Bradbury, Margaret Crawford, Frances Anderton (eds.), *You are Here* (London: Phaidon Press Limited, 1999), p. 114.
44 Ibid., p. 112.
45 For an overview of all trade fairs in 1960, see, for instance *Foreign Commerce Weekly*, No. 64/1 (Washington: US Department of Commerce, 1960).
46 Senat, *Rapport Général*, 1 Decembre 1959, p. 9. Online. Available https://www.senat.fr/rap/1959-1960/i1959_1960_0066_03_11.pdf (accessed 26 August 2024; translation by author).
47 Ibid.
48 Ibid., p. 11.
49 *Foreign Commerce Weekly*, Washington: US Department of Commerce, Vol. 65, No. 2, 1961, p. 41.
50 Mehdi Ben Barka, 'Quatre entretiens avec Raymond Jean (Juin 1959)', *Écrits politiques 1957–1965* (Paris: Syllepse, 1999), p. 128. Translation by author.
51 For an introduction to the Service de l'Urbanisme and to Michel Ecochard, see, amongst others, Tom Avermaete, Maristella Casciato, *Casablanca-Chandigarh: A Report on Modernization* (Zurich: Park Books, 2015).
52 See the chapter 'A Lebanese Heterotopia?' in: Meier, Daniel and Rosita Di Peri, *Mediterranean in Dis/order: Space, Power, and Identity* (University of Michigan Press, 2023), https://doi.org/10.1353/book.115923, accessed on 14 January 2024.
53 Łukasz Stanek, 'Architects from Socialist Countries in Ghana (1957–1967): Modern Architecture and Mondialisation', *Journal of the Society of Architectural Historians*, 1 December 2015; 74 (4): pp. 416–442. Online. Available https://doi.org/10.1525/jsah.2015.74.4.416 (accessed 7 January 2024).
54 Maxwell Fry and Jane Drew, *Tropical Architecture in the Humid Zone* (New York: Reinhold, 1956), p. 23 and Maxwell Fry and Jane Drew, *Tropical Architecture in the Dry and Humid Zones* (New York: Reinhold, 1964).
55 Tim Berners-Lee, Robert Cailliau, Bernd Pollermann 'World-Wide Web: The Information Universe', *Internet Research*, Vol. 2, No. 1, 1992, pp. 52–58. Online. Available https://doi.org/10.1108/eb047254 (accessed 26 August 2024).
56 See Gabriele Cavoto, *Demalling. A response to the demise of retail buildings* (Milano: Maggioli, 2014).

World's Largest Conventio

McCormick Place at Night

3 Mobility: Automobiles, Trains, Airplanes, and New Building Types

Michelangelo Sabatino

Fig. 3.1
'World's largest convention center', postcard showing McCormick Place, Chicago (Shaw, Metz & Dolio with Edward Durrell Stone, 1958–1960).

The concept of globalization reflects the sense of an immense enlargement of world communication, as well as of the horizon of a world market, both of which seem far more tangible and immediate than in earlier stages of modernity.
— Frederic Jameson, *Globalization and Architecture*[1]

In order to understand why major cities with different histories and cultures have undergone parallel economic and social changes, we need to examine transformations in the world economy. Yet the term *global city* may be reductive and misleading if it suggests that cities are mere outcomes of a global economic machine.
— Saskia Sassen, *The Global City: New York, London, Tokyo*[2]

The exponential increase in mobility since World War II, with individuals facing ever fewer physical challenges in moving between cities, regions, and nations, dramatically increased interconnectedness in the late nineteenth through to the first half of the twentieth century.[3] As a consequence of increased professional and leisure-related mobility, a set of new 'hybrid' building types emerged. Although some buildings drew from existing types, such as hotels, railway stations, and exhibition halls, from World War II onwards they gradually veered in scale and focus toward being aimed at a markedly more global audience.[4] Most importantly, these new buildings typically shifted from having self-contained programmes to being part of an integrated and complex transport system consisting of highways, roads, and metro systems.[5] Examples of these new building types range from the motel and the airport to the international chain hotel and the convention centre. Ultimately, they have facilitated global transfer of knowledge, reshaped the cities (and countryside) in which we live, and given rise to a different culture of architectural practice and image of the architect.[6]

→ Fig. 3.1

Fig. 3.2
'The Strip', Las Vegas, Nevada, photograph by G. E. Kidder Smith, 1971.

3 Mobility

Fig. 3.3
Still from the film *Stazione Termini* (released in the US as *Indiscretion of an American Wife*), directed by Vittorio De Sica, Columbia Pictures, 1953.

Fig. 3.4
Aerial view of American Airlines terminal 3 at O'Hare International Airport, Chicago (Ralph H. Burke Associates, 1962), c. 1970.

Fig. 3.5
Postcard, 'Chicago-O'Hare International Airport (Richard J. Daley, mayor)', c. 1960.

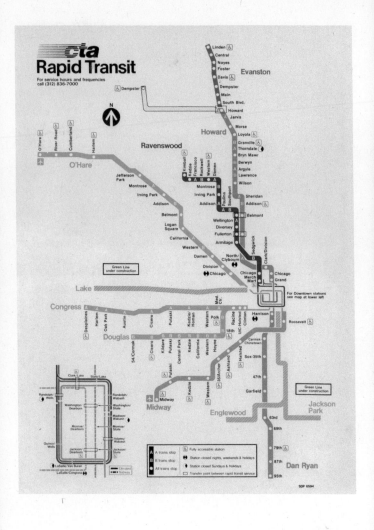

Fig. 3.6
Rapid transit map, Chicago Transit Authority (with colour-aided legibility introduced for the first time), 1991.

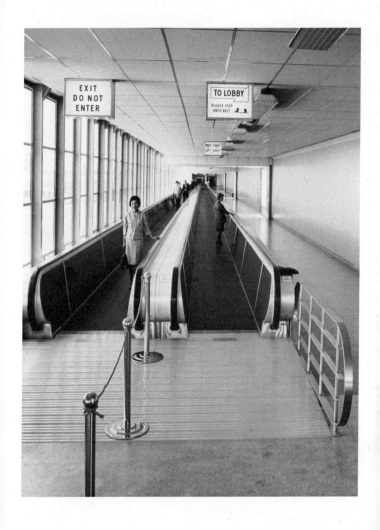

Fig. 3.7
United Airlines twin speedwalk passenger conveyors ('moving sidewalks'), San Francisco International Airport, 18 June 1964.

3 Mobility

Fig. 3.8
Postcard, '50th on the Lake Motel' (Frank J. Lapasso, 1958), Chicago.
Fig. 3.9
Book, Conrad N. Hilton, *Be my guest* (Englewood Cliffs, N.J: Prentice-Hall Press, 1957).
Fig. 3.10
Advertisement for the Nile Hilton, Cairo, 1959.

Automobiles, Trains, Airplanes, and New Building Types

Fig. 3.11
Grand Central Station and the Pan Am (now: MetLife) Building, New York (Richard Roth, Walter Gropius, and Pietro Belluschi, 1959–1962), 1988.

Fig. 3.12
'The evolution of Pan Am's Flying Clippers', illustration in brochure, Pan American World Airways, Inc., 1946.

3 Mobility

Fig. 3.13
DC-8, United Airlines (designer: Raymond Loewy), c. 1959.
Fig. 3.14
'KLM chief flight attendant serves the meal during the flight in a KLM passenger plane', c. 1950.

Fig. 3.15
Duty-free shopping, Gatwick Airport, West Sussex, England, 1987.

Mobility and Patterns of Settlement

In parts of the world the availability of the automobile to large sections of the population dramatically reshaped the landscape and patterns of settlement in the first half of the twentieth century but especially after World War II — and especially in the US, where it led to the emergence of so-called 'automobile suburbs'.[7] Fuelled by the increasing availability of the automobile and roads, suburban growth in the US after 1945 followed a different pattern to that of the turn of the century.[8] No longer constrained by the need to maintain close, i.e. walkable or cyclable, proximity to a railway station, streetcar stop, or the centre of a town or city, the new suburbs were free to sprawl wherever there was a road or highway.[9] This development was not tied to or dependent upon a densely built-up urban centre. Its daily needs were catered for by relatively dispersed amenities, such as shopping malls and 'centres', strip malls in various locations nearby, and jobs usually in locations a greater distance away. One result of this reshaping of the American suburb was a local homogenization:

> Any residue of the relatively heterogeneous society of the streetcar suburb, with its tradespeople and local service workers, was eliminated by the capability of the automobile to support a spatially extensive highly differentiated mosaic of socially uniform suburban localities.'[10]

Another was the hollowing out of the densely built-up city centre. America's downtowns were to a large extent abandoned to those who could not afford to live outside them — the economically disadvantaged. In these and other ways automobile mobility brought not just the reshaping of the American suburb but also a reshaping of the substance and image of the American way of life. It affected not just where Americans lived but how they lived — where they shopped, of what they dreamed and to what they aspired, how they perceived differences in social and economic class, and how they met one another.

→ Fig. 3.2

Leisure and Mobility

Whereas the Grand Tour, a characteristic feature of the seventeenth and eighteenth centuries, influenced architectural design and pedagogy among an elite circle of architects and artists serving the upper class, post-World-War-II mass motorization — the spread of both cars and trucks — was the engine of a new global turn governing the distribution and consumption of goods, fostering the rise of new commercial architecture, such as the shopping mall or shopping centre.[11] Additionally, during the post-war years other types of buildings came into existence in response to a new global transportation network which was transforming both the regional landscape and the social habits of an ever more consumer-oriented society. In particular, the upsurge in international mass tourism and intensified patterns of travel required new buildings that could accommodate and symbolize the connections between different modes of automotive, pedestrian, and air travel but also serve as new places of collective gathering. New places of arrival-accommodation-departure — namely train stations, airports, hotels, and motels — opened up new challenges arising from the overlapping of interwoven, multi-layered functions and complex uses.[12]

The social turn to mass tourism, involving the unprecedented movement of millions of new vacationers from the 1950s forwards, favoured the spread and transformation of these typologies.[13] If the Grand Tour had been an elitist and educational social privilege, vacation travel, in contrast, now became common practice — a 'commonplace ... a common consumer good' enjoyed by the entire middle class.[14] For the first time in history, millions of people spent vacations either within their regional borders or abroad in other countries; tourism became part of an unprecedented pattern of global mass consumption. One side effect was the considerable challenges it generated for heritage.[15]

The primary medium of influence luring middle-class tourists to vacation was the travel catalogue or brochure. Similarly to popular magazines and journals, this literature provided information through text and especially photography, including portrayals of exotic places.[16] Vacations were promoted as a sensual pleasure and a legitimate universal right. Travel brochures were an open window on unexplored parts of the world, emphasizing romantic images of the far away and offering an escape from the normal life and work regime of quotidian existence. As a result, the 25 million travellers per year in the 1950s grew by more than 10 per cent annually to reach 160 million in 1970.[17] If in 1954 one quarter of Germans spent at least one week vacationing that involved travel — mostly in their home country — by 1975 fifty-six per cent of Germans were going on holiday, more than half of them choosing to vacation in a foreign country.[18]

In view of these numbers, theorists and historians have variously called tourism 'one of the great nihilistic movements', whose 'gigantic bacteria' are tourists (Nebel),[19] an essential manifestation of modern culture (Enzensberger),[20] and even a 'metaphor for contemporary life in Western societies'[21] (Bauman). As both 'alienated leisure' (MacCannell)[22] and 'a romantic concept of freedom',[23] tourism became another mass consumer good with the power to transform, through the 'tourist gaze' (Urry),[24] socio-spatial realms and relations. It also influenced the perception of the world itself, resulting in a division between 'those places where tourists are carefully ushered into and through and those places they are prevented from seeing.'[25]

In this new worldview in the post-war years Europe played the undisputed role of epicentre since almost three-quarters of the world's tourists, most of whom were Europeans themselves, visited destinations on the old continent.[26] In Europe tourism, coupled with other forms of mobility, such as commuting, migration, and mobile labour, propelled radical improvements in networks of railway lines, aeroplane routes, and highways. Tourism encouraged a shift in preference from train trips as a practice of 'collectivism' in the 1950s to individual mobility and air travel, made possible by the democratization and increased affordability of air travel from the 1960s forwards.[27] If in 1954 seventy-three per cent of German tourists took trains and buses, by 1975 sixty per cent were using cars and 12 per cent already preferred travelling by plane.[28] As air travel in Europe and abroad grew drastically, travel agencies thrived, leading to the rise of the charter flight. All Europe and previously unexplored non-western destinations became suddenly much more accessible to millions of middle-class people.

Railway Stations

'Railway termini and hotels are to the nineteenth century what monasteries and cathedrals were to the thirteenth century. They are truly the only real representative buildings we possess. Our metropolitan termini have been leaders of the art spirit of our time.'
— *Building News*, 1875[29]

'A station is a place where tired, excited, bored, impatient, nervous, hungry and dirty people gather per force.'
— G.E. Kidder Smith, *Italy Builds*, 1955[30]

The normalization and democratization of tourism and the growth of other forms of travel on a global scale had an enormous impact on architecture with arrival-departure functions, fuelling experimentation with new typological solutions for train stations, airports, and hotels. Originally straightforward buildings hosting separate functions, train stations became more integrated, complex systems accommodating spatial connections and functional hybridizations.

The emergence of stations and hotels serving rail connections in the middle of the twentieth century was not a new thing. In the nineteenth century too, cities had been transformed to make way for grand urban termini for travellers. In the Victorian era the British were undoubtedly at the forefront of railway technology and architecture. The leading example is St Pancras Station in London (1868), which was conceived and designed as a system consisting of two main parts, the train shed and the hotel, responding respectively to the need to gather travellers during arrival/departure and to accommodate them in a style and with a luxury appropriate to the journey they were about to make or had just completed.[31]

Designed by the engineer William Henry Barlow, the St Pancras train shed possessed at the time of its construction the most massive station roof in the world without internal supports, with a 240-foot span covering 25 bays. Constructed in cast iron and glass, this dramatic roof was made by the Butterley Iron Company at a cost of £117,000, which was about 30 per cent of the total cost of the building. Interestingly, the platforms were placed higher than street level since the line had to bridge Regent's Canal; this meant that the station could accommodate additional functions beneath it, such as storage for goods. As a result, the station's grid of iron columns was determined by the dimensions of the Burton beer barrel, 'one of the Midland Railway's most lucrative goods'.[32]

The station's hotel, named 'the Midland Grand' (1876), was designed by the Gothic Revival architect George Gilbert Scott, who won the competition with a design for a larger building than allowed by the competition brief. Seen together with the train station, the hotel possessed a physical presence which dominated its then historical context.

Over the years both station and hotel failed to prosper — largely because the Midlands Railway, of which St Pancras was the London terminus, was forced into a merger with the London, Midland and Scottish Railway, which adopted Euston Station as its principal London terminus. The Midland Grand Hotel closed as a hotel in 1935 and was used as offices for railway workers. During World War II the station mainly served military troops and children being evacuated from London, rather than travellers going on vacation. Attempts to demolish the station were made until November 1967, when its buildings were placed under a Grade 1 conservation order as 'Britain's most impressive station'.[33]

A decade earlier, the London Bridge Railway Terminus Hotel had been built to serve another railway station, the terminus of the London Brighton South Coast Railway. At the start of the second half of the nineteenth century London had few large hotels and fewer still offering facilities of the variety or standard to be found abroad, in Europe or the US.[34] The London Bridge Terminus Hotel was the second largest hotel in London after the Grosvenor;[35] its amenities included coffee rooms (including for ladies — a significant advance), a billiards room, a library, reading rooms, and corridors 'wider, and certainly more airy, than those of any other London hotel'.[36] Thus it helped fuel a trend in luxury hotels at railway stations whose commencement dated to the 1850s; interestingly, these new establishments set new standards not just for hotels at railway stations but for hotels in London in general.[37]

However, similarly to the Midland Grand Hotel, the London Bridge Railway Terminus Hotel proved less successful in operation than expected; in 1892 its owners likewise turned it into offices. Terminus hotels in other cities in Great Britain, meanwhile, thrived. By 1914 'there were railway hotels in every one of the leading cities of Great Britain except Plymouth, Portsmouth, Bristol, Cardiff, and Dundee.'[38] Often these establishments provided facilities that met new needs: if the London railway hotels for the first time offered 'ladies' coffee rooms' which women could frequent without risking social opprobrium, provincial railway hotels had rooms that could be used for meetings of all kinds, thus serving as a precursor of today's business hotels and conference centres.[39]

Railway stations and hotels of the second half of the nineteenth century were grand advertisements for a new form of travel for the 'leisure class', as Thorstein Veblen called it in his landmark study.[40] They were bold and often very expensive feats of engineering and finance that underlay the rapid creation of competing networks of railway lines. They were usually situated at the edges of or in less fashionable downtown parts of cities. The second half of the twentieth century, in contrast, saw the railway station assume a new role as an integral, well-established entity of urban development with a new centrality in the urban territory. The railway was no longer something radically new but part of a seamless system of different forms of transport that made possible rapid connections in a much more homogenized and global space — between city and countryside, between different parts of a city, between cities in one country, and between different countries.

New technologies enabled the development of high-speed railway lines which dramatically shortened distances. Japan's bullet trains in the 1960s set the pace for later high-speed projects in other countries: in France the TGV (Train à Grande Vitesse), in Germany the ICE (Intercity Express), and in Italy the Pendolino ('pendulum', designating a high-speed tilting train). Using new technologies and dedicated tracks, these faster trains — which today reach speeds of up to 320 kilometres (199 miles) per hour — introduced millions of different types of travellers to a modern experience of space-time compression.[41]

In parallel with these new technologies, new approaches in urban design were developed to accommodate the functional complexity of the stations. Shinjuku Terminal (1960) in Tokyo is an important example of the railway station as a new entity of urban development. Its site is one of the most crowded commercial and amusement centres in the Japanese capital. In 1960 the Japanese architects Fumihiko Maki and Masato Osawa proposed a new project for reordering the existing chaotic traffic around the terminal, including flows of trains, subway trains, buses, automobiles, and pedestrians. The new, more organized pattern was based on a flexible, dynamic, and expandable 'master form'. The purpose of the project was to foster different types of human association — 'gathering' in amusement squares and 'contemplating vistas' from roof gardens — as an 'attempt to express the energy and sweat of millions of people in Tokyo in the breath of life and poetry of leaving.'[42] More importantly, this project was not intended to be merely a scheme for the Shinjuku Station area but a demonstration of theoretical assumptions behind the theory of the 'group form', which Fumihiko Maki had elaborated during two years of travel research in Asia, the Middle East, and Europe. With its complexity and multi-layered functions the Japanese station realized Maki's notion of an urban order based on a combination of elements.[43]

A similar complexity — this time more an interweaving of history and technology — is to be found in another groundbreaking design for a station: Termini Station in Rome, Italy. Situated directly opposite the Baths of Diocletian ('the Terme'), in the very centre of Rome, Termini Station is an interesting architectural-cultural 'battleground of history'.[44] The result of different overlapping projects, ideas, and interpretations of the railway station from the end of the nineteenth century to the period following the end of World War II, it reflects sociopolitical-economic ideals during the transition from the Papal State to the Kingdom of Italy and from a fascist dictatorship to the rise of a democratic republic.

→ Fig. 3.3

The first project for the station was developed through a competition announced in 1867 in response to the modernizing ambitions of Pope Pius IX for the Papal State (751–1870), of which Rome was still a part. However, in 1874, when the station designed by the Italian architect Salvatore Bianchi was inaugurated, this 'papal project' was acclaimed as the central station of the capital of the newborn Kingdom of Italy.

A modern gateway through the ancient defensive wall, Termini Station was designed with two main parallel wings linked by a roof of iron and glass. With a typological setting similar to that of the Gare de l'Est in Paris, it has been described as 'an attempt to merge iron architecture with the orders of Vignola', a marriage of classical references and nineteenth-century iron construction.[45]

Its structure was nevertheless considered inadequate by the new political powers only a few years later. As early as 1937, the new fascist government decided to construct a new station of grandiose dimensions to better mirror the magnificence of Rome as the imperial capital of fascism. The Italian architect and engineer Angiolo Angelo Mazzoni, designer of other elegant stations throughout Italy under the fascist regime,[46] was commissioned to develop a number of different solutions, of which the final version was only partially realized due to the pressures of World War II. The two principal lateral wings containing most of the services were built; the monumental façade with a classical colonnade, on the other hand, remained unrealized, its design to be decided by a free competition after the war's end. In 1947 this competition was won by two teams of Italian architects — one composed of Leo Calini and Eugenio Montuori, the other of Massimo Castellazzi, Vasco Fadigati, Achille Pintonello, and Annibale Vitellozzi — who then collaborated on merging the most significant features of the two proposals into a final project.

The two teams' new station façade is characterized by transparency and lightness. The era's international travellers flowed from Piazza Cinquecento — a public square containing the Servian Wall, a fourth-century century Roman defensive barrier — into an impressive internal hall accommodating a variety of functions. The transparency and lightness of the station embodied the new ideals which were forcefully reshaping Italian society into a democracy, following the demise of Mussolini's dictatorship. The iconic floating cantilever roof in reinforced concrete, dubbed 'the dinosaur', was curved in order to leave the Servian Wall visible from the central hall, so as to 'urbanistically solve and valorize the presence of the ruins'.[47] The authors set out to connect past and present, static historical presences and rapid modern flows of travellers and transport. They described their project as a response to the need to cast aside the rhetoric of the 'excessively monumental character' of the previous proposal, which had been imbued with fascist ideology, 'for the benefit of a more human and more sincere feeling'.[48] The project garnered much praise; some critics even hailed it as 'the finest station entry in Europe'.[49]

Both Tokyo's Shinjuku Station and Rome's Termini Station are examples of railway termini that are firmly embedded not only in their urban contexts but also in transport systems linking not just different cities but different regions and countries as well.

Unlike the railway termini of the second half of the nineteenth century, they do not have to advertise the idea of travel by rail as a fundamentally new form of transport; they are parts of systems which, at the time of their construction, were becoming ever more global.

Airports

'Pre-war aviation was a sport; during the war it was a military weapon; after the war it will be one of the transport industries.'
— M. d'Aubigny, member of French parliament, 1918[50]

'The nation that controls the air will control the earth.'
— Sir Alan Cobham, English aviator, 1920s[51]

'One sunny afternoon Auguste Perret, with whom I was working, burst into the atelier, brandishing a freshly printed *Intransigeant*: "Blériot has crossed the Channel! Wars are finished: no more wars are possible! There are no longer any frontiers!"'
— Le Corbusier, Swiss-French architect, 1935[52]

On the eve of the twentieth century airports were mainly composed of simple buildings such as sheds, hangars, and barracks containing only a few necessary functions and facilities for landing, storage, and departures of the earliest types of airplanes. These first elementary airports or 'air stations' relied for their identity on other well-established infrastructures and architectures, such as hippodromes, farmhouses, and railways. The word 'terminal', for instance, was derived from the word for a certain type of railway station.[53]

Interestingly, in parallel to these first modest examples of air stations, which still lacked a clear identity and image of their own, a number of modernist architects were proposing visionary and utopian projects that would reflect the potential of this new form of transport. The 'Stazione per treni e aerei' ('Station for trains and planes', 1914) by the Italian Futurist architect Antonio Sant'Elia had multilevel connections between stations for trains and aircraft. The French architect Eugène Hénard's 'Rue

Future' ('Street of the Future', 1919) showed airport-platforms at the top of houses whose various levels accommodated both residential apartments and different forms of transport. And the masterplan for the 'Ville contemporaine de trois millions d'habitants' (1922) by the French-Swiss architect Le Corbusier included a central air station. In these projects modernist architects offered a glimpse of the complexity of interwoven functions and urban implications which would be fully explored in airport design a few decades later.

In the post-war period aviation ceased to be either mere sport or a military weapon and grew to become a transport and 'commercial' mass-travel industry.[54] The first civil air route with an established flight plan was created as early as 1919; it flew from Berlin to Weimar.[55] It was only in the post-war period, however, that commercial air travel took off as a standard form of transportation. Its expansion drove a boom in construction of new commercial terminals and facilities in the form of various experimental typologies. Far from being simple sheds in the rural landscape on the edge of the city, these new airport projects embodied a clear typological complexity of connections and functions. As air transportation developed, airport proposals became more complex and sophisticated. The new typological features had to handle the steady increase in post-war travel; they involved, for instance, proposals for differentiation of flows, parking, access, flexibility, security, new facilities, logistics, and much else.

One of the new types of airports was based on the 'transporter configuration'. Up to this point, given that planes did not park adjacent to airport terminals but stood on aprons, passengers had been forced to walk out of the terminal in order to board; this left them exposed to all types of weather and having to walk increasingly long distances as the number and size of airplanes increased. To supply this missing connection, shuttle buses (introduced at Amsterdam Schiphol in the 1950s) and 'mobile lounges' began to be introduced to bridge the gap between the terminal and the planes. This service became even more necessary with the introduction of airplanes powered by jet engines, which needed both more space and an enclosed interchange to protect passengers from high levels of noise and air displacement.

In the 1950s 'pier finger' airports and star-shaped terminals were developed in Europe and the USA. These gathered passengers in a central area and then transferred them directly to the aircraft through linear, finger-like extensions, allowing the airport to receive a greater number of aircraft. Examples of 'pier fingers airports' include Chicago's O'Hare International Airport (Ralph H. Burke Associates) and Amsterdam's Schiphol.[56] Chicago's O'Hare boasted of playing a particularly large role given its midwestern location between the east and west coasts of America.[57] After the original Terminal 1 at O'Hare International was demolished and redesigned by Helmut Jahn, its reopening in 1987 generated a considerable fanfare. This also coincided with the Chicago Transit Authority gradually expanding public access (Blue Line) to O'Hare. Splitting departure and arrival into two separate floors enabled functional differentiation of flows. When the large number of piers resulted in passengers walking long distances, airports introduced 'moving sidewalks' (*tapis roulants*) to speed up pedestrian connections. Another technological and typological invention was the jetway, an all-weather dry connection between the pier and the aircraft. 'Not quite in the airport, not quite in the airplane,' the jetway or 'finger' became a flexible bridge, a threshold element that fascinated the architect's imagination.[58] It also, interestingly, became an element of a residential building at Het Breed, the housing complex in Amsterdam built in 1962 to 1968 to a design by the architect Frans van Gool, who here used airbridges to connect the individual residential blocks (at about the same time as his project for a terminal at Schiphol Airport).[59] OMA's project for Zeebrugge Sea Terminal (1988) remains an outstanding design proposal; here the movable fingers highlight the terminal's symbolical and functional role as a 'Working Babel' of different European tribes embarking on a united future.[60]

→ Figs. 3.4–7

Another type of airport was the 'satellite' — an insular, freestanding building situated apart from other airport structures. This isolation enables airplanes to use the entire circumference of the structure for parking and connections. The earliest design for London Gatwick Airport (Hoar, Marlow & Lovett, 1936) pioneered — and even attempted to patent — this airport terminal type.[61] Nicknamed 'the Beehive', the terminal had an underground pedestrian tunnel connecting it with the railway station 120 metres away, allowing passengers arriving by train from London to enjoy protection from the weather from the moment they arrived at Victoria Station in the centre of the city until the time their aircraft reached its destination; telescoping passageways connected directly with the planes.[62] If airplanes were becoming 'as much a part of daily life as the motor car', as the American critic Lewis Mumford claimed in 1945, many airport designs strove to merge air, bus, and car traffic through the use of ever more complicated solutions.[63]

The intermodal connection between aircraft, terminal, and city was necessary to avoid airports appearing totally alienated from the urban-social landscape — a detachment which would have been even more intrusive given the grand scale of the new airport types. The planning of 'airports of the future' thus needed to involve total planning of a territory, 'from regional plan covering the entire territory influenced by the community, down to the smallest detail at the airport itself.'[64]

Car parking: welcome to the airport

As airports became larger and further from city centres, links between terminal buildings and parking facilities became crucial in order to keep walking distances in check. Architects experimented with radical designs. One such was the design for Dallas/Fort Worth (architect: Gyo Obata) based on the concept of 'park-and-fly' (1973). This new airport, the world's largest and most expensive at the time of its construction, consisted of a central infrastructural spine of parking spaces and roads, to which were attached semi-circular terminals, each more than a mile in circumference. 'Our idea is to have a parking space,' wrote the architect, 'and out of the parking space, you can go directly to the gate. No crowds, no confusion, no pain.'[65] Plans for megastructures integrating parking and terminals were experimented with in several other projects of this time. For Paris the French architect Paul Andreu envisaged an airport as a continuous infrastructural network or 'omnibuilding',[66] in which the structure rises out of the road system itself rather than depending on references relating to aviation.[67] 'A good airport,' said Andreu, 'is beyond a building; it is a landscape.'[68] The first, octopus-like, terminal at Charles de Gaulle (1974) is a nine-storey circular building with an empty core which vertically condenses both essential airport functions and traffic. Parking is on the upper floors and roof, while the other functions — technical operations, shops, and restaurants, check-in counters, and so on — overlap on the other rings below. Underground walkways link the main building to seven satellites with boarding gates. The second terminal (1972–1994) 'starts while you are still in the car',[69] emphasizing to an even greater extent the interconnection between car and air traffic. Similarly to Dallas, it consists of a linear spine containing a service highway and connecting seven sub-terminals, creating a direct link between parking one's car and boarding an aircraft.

'It's a Mall ... It's an Airport ... It's Both'[70]

The new generation of airports were of immense dimensions and extremely complex in their connections; they also accumulated and housed an increasing variety of facilities, programmes, and amenities. In addition to the new security services and locked areas which were introduced to tackle the growing issue of terrorism from the 1970s forwards, airports now contained hotels, congress rooms, cinemas, exhibition rooms, spaces for athletic activities, chapels, restaurants, and shops. The early modest hangar-airport had become a condensed urban landscape that increasingly resembled a shopping centre. The first airports had to find a new identity of 'airportness' since 'there was no past,' as Paul Andreu remarked; 'now many seemingly different building types converge around shopping experience.'[71]

Airports were transformed into perfect consumerist domes where travellers were forced to walk slowly through a labyrinth of shopping zones — without being left an escape path — while waiting hours before they could take a seat in their plane. This commercial imprisonment, or 'controlled laboratory experiment,'[72] became vital for the economic survival and self-financing of airports as they faced diminished government funding.[73] Eventually, the legacy — or bastardization, as Victor Gruen would have seen it — of the shopping mall engulfed airports, as well as all the other types of travel stations throughout the world. 'All vestiges of utopia have been lost' is the verdict of the American critic Alastair Gordon, lamenting the lost possibilities for visionary creation in airport design.[74] Visions such as Le Corbusier's — of a 'naked airport' in which the airport building and infrastructure would disappear from sight in order to clear the stage for the extraordinary spectacle of airplanes taking off and landing — increasingly gave way to uniform commercial megastructures that are plugged into the economies of entire regions.

Hotels-Motels

Post-war mass tourism became an engine for the proliferation, mutation, and redefinition of the hotel (and its hybrid offspring, the motor hotel or 'motel') on a global scale.[75] The Global Turn was characterized by the rise of hotel lobbies and lounges that increasingly became theatres for 'global nomads'.[76] Travel's sudden transition from exclusive, elitist tour to affordable, common, and consumerist good was anything but without consequences. With respect to accommodation, it provided the premise and propellant for a radical transformation of the status of the hotel. The proliferation of 'grand hotels' for the upper and middle classes had in the previous century transformed the landscape of idealized tourist locations — in, for example, the Swiss Alps and on the French Riviera in Europe; now the growing need to provide places to sleep for a steadily increasing number of travellers changed the tourism and accommodation business worldwide.
→ Fig. 3.8

In the post-war era new transatlantic hotel chains offered efficient, normalized accommodation that embodied a 'modernist, universal standard'.[77] Such hotels attempted, to various degrees of success, a dialectical balancing act between standardization of the design of identical elements and interior spaces on the one hand and reflection of local environmental-cultural-political presences on the other.

'Be my guest'[78]

One of the most prominent international accommodation businesses was the Hilton Hotels Corporation, founded by the American businessman Conrad Hilton in 1919. Although the American hotel has a storied tradition, Hilton's name became so well known to people everywhere that it became 'synonymous worldwide with the word "hotel"'.[79]
→ Figs. 3.9–10

The epitomized 'hotel' — the Hilton — was anything but just a business. It embodied and carried out multifaceted roles that involved an interweaving of architectural, political, economic, and cultural aspects in the politicized post-war era. The chain's economic activities were imbued with symbolical-cultural nuances and influences that were represented in the modernist architecture of its hotels.

The Hilton was, foremost, a transplantation of the suburban American way of life to foreign settings. By planning and constructing massive luxury hotels on foreign soil — 17 between 1949 and 1966[80] — Hilton advertised and extolled a way of life — the American way of life — which was distinct from that of the local communities into which the hotels were inserted.

On the one hand, the Hilton offered to its American/western guests an opportunity to continue safely and comfortably practising their American/western habits and enjoying the technological pleasures of the west in places and countries that were exotic or had different customs. The Hilton offered a globalized version of hotel culture. Specifically, it reproduced the familiar ambience of the American suburb within an alien external setting abroad, cocooning its guests with the technology (for instance, air-conditioning, radio, television, and iced water), food, and cultural events to which they were accustomed at home.[81] This standardization of architecture and services, however, awakened in the traveller an adrenalin-rich sense of escape and adventure that came from being in a transitional area, beyond a person's customary comfort zone.

On the other hand, each Hilton hotel was a peaceful colonization carried out by capitalist American-style democracy in a non-western peripheral-political context. As early as 1916, the American president Woodrow Wilson had praised the fight of the USA — the 'Irresistible Empire' — 'for the peaceful [commercial] conquest of the world';[82] in the Cold War era this ideal, imbued with democratic, symbolical, and patriotic inflections, was perfectly fulfilled by the Hilton hotels.

'Each of our hotels is a "little America",' boasted Conrad Hilton at the opening ceremony for the Istanbul Hilton in 1955, 'not as a symbol of bristling power, but as a friendly centre where men of many nations and of goodwill may speak the language of peace.'[83] Hilton was a vigorous advocate of a dream of worldwide peace and freedom exported and popularized by the USA as a counterforce to the 'essence of Communism, [which] is the death of the individual and the burial of his remains in a collective mass', as he put it in his book *Be my guest*.[84] The global spread of Hilton hotels carried heavy political and ideological connotations, particularly in countries such as Turkey and Egypt.

The opening of a Hilton hotel was often influenced by governmental actors and plans, often involving a partnership between the hotel corporation and the host country. According to the architectural historian Annabel Jane Wharton, Hilton hotels abroad were not usually owned by the Hilton Corporation. The investment capital was provided either by local institutions and investors or indirectly by the American government, sometimes even through the Marshall Plan and the Economic Cooperation Administration.[85] The Hilton Corporation ran the finished hotel, receiving a third of the profits.[86] Building a cultural-commercial American symbol was popular with local legislatures in foreign countries. In Turkey, for instance, the minister of internal affairs personally escorted the Hilton committee during the site visit in Istanbul and in 1951 signed the final agreement for construction of the hotel.[87] In 1955 the opening of the Hilton Istanbul Bosphorus, the city's first international five-star hotel, heralded 'a revolution in the [entire country's] hospitality industry'.[88] The project was designed by the American firm Skidmore, Owings & Merrill (SOM) in collaboration with the local Turkish architect Sedad Hakkı Eldem. The result of this design cooperation was a synergy between modernism and vernacular architecture, a fusion of the comfort of American consumerist culture (in the guest rooms, for instance) with local Turkish character (in the public spaces, furniture, and uniforms worn by the personnel).[89]

The Hilton's modern architecture also played a crucial role as ideological advertisement and influence on its local surroundings. It had a political impact on the host countries, promoting American hegemony and 'serving humanity worldwide',[90] always under the guise of pursuit of the economic interests of a private business. In addition to the Hilton's modern technology and standardized interiors — from lobbies to the layouts of the bathrooms — Wharton particularly emphasizes the prominence of plate glass as the ultimate modern material. Plate glass transformed the Hilton into a 'machine for viewing' and 'the anxiety of being observed into a pleasure'.[91] 'A balm, a salve, a glass of Alka-Seltzer,' the Hilton was extolled by *Vogue* in 1965 as a 'tall glass oasis' offering safety and distance from the indigenous, unfamiliar world outside.'[92] From the (pre)modern avant-garde of the curtain wall to the creation of 'little Americas', from political oasis to voyeuristic 'fish-bowl' — as underlined by John Lennon and Yoko Ono's Bed-In for Peace at the Amsterdam Hilton in

1969[93] — the Hilton fed on the modern global transfer of architecture and technology. Positioned opposite and adjacent to, detached from, yet absorbing local vernacular presences, the Hilton, to rephrase and re-interpret Ian McCallum,[94] itself became a modern 'vernacular' — a syntax of common everyday practice and a standard mode for the traveller in whatever part of the world. While Hilton was amongst America's most visible 'brands' associated with modern buildings, one could argue the Pan American World Airways (Pan Am) brought considerable visibility to American innovation to the airline industry. The Pan Am headquarters opened in New York City in 1963 and was designed in collaboration with Richard Roth, Walter Gropius, and Pietro Belluschi.[95]

→ Figs. 3.11–12

Escaping Global Uniformity

The process that witnessed, from the post-war years onward, a shift (global turn) in the experience of travelling from elitist privilege to collective practice and standard consumer good influenced the architectural typology of transport buildings and their underlying business model. More and more, business and tourist travel was bolstered with an overall branding strategy that impacted the design of airlines and employee outfits to the experience of duty free shopping. If train stations and hotels in the twentieth century acquired a new status through their use of new typological and technological solutions in response to new socio-political exigencies, airports were a brand-new type of infrastructure with no past to which they could refer. This lack of a past encouraged modernist architects in the early part of the century to speculate in a visionary manner on the city of the future, opening up possibilities for adventurous typological quests later in the twentieth century. As time wore on, however, exploration gave way to standardization: the variety of typological solutions was absorbed in standard commercial strategies and layouts. Consumerism became the dominant hybridization force as shopping facilities took up increasing amounts of space in all the types of transport building analysed here. The shift towards commercialism in hotels, stations, and airports ensured a familiar, safe, and uniform travel experience for the new global network of bourgeois travellers. In Hilton hotels the exportation of modern American consumerism abroad was coloured with political statements against communism in the ideological context of the Cold War. A kind of 'little America' abroad, the Hilton played an ambassadorial/colonizing role. Nevertheless, certain of the new transport and travel structures — Rome's Termini Station and the Istanbul Hilton, for instance — showed remarkable equipoise between modern architecture and historical-local context, incorporating in their designs, respectively, the Servian Wall and local Turkish elements. In this they demonstrate how commercialization and global uniformity can be overcome by more nuanced and contextual approaches to design and construction.

→ Figs. 3.13–15

3 Mobility

1   Frederic Jameson, 'Globalization and Architecture', in: Sang Lee and Ruth Baumeister (eds.), *The Domestic and the Foreign in Architecture* (Rotterdam: 010 Publishers, 2007), p. 94.
2   Saskia Sassen, *The Global City: New York, London, Tokyo* (Princeton, NJ: Princeton University Press, 2001; 2nd edition), p. 4.
3   Emily S. Rosenberg (ed.), *A World Connecting 1870–1945* (Cambridge, MA: The Belknap Press of Harvard University Press, 2012).
4   Nikolaus Pevsner, *A History of Building Types* (Princeton, NJ: Princeton University Press, 1976). In particular, see the chapters on hotels (pp. 169–192); railway stations (pp. 225–234); and market halls, conservatories, and exhibition buildings (pp. 235–256).
5   See Jilly Traganou and Miodrag Mitrasinovic (eds.), *Travel, Space, Architecture* (Burlington, VT: Ashgate, 2009), pp. 2–3.
6   Andrew Saint, *The Image of the Architect* (New Haven: Yale University Press, 1983), Chapter 7, 'The Architect as Entrepreneur,' pp. 138–160. See also Dana Cuff, *Architecture: The Story of Practice* (Cambridge, MA: The MIT Press, 1991) and Spiro Kostof (ed.), *The Architect. Chapters of the History of the Profession* (New York: Oxford University Press, 1977).
7   See, for instance, Carolyn T. Walker, 'Automobile Suburbs', *The Encyclopedia of Greater Philadelphia*. Online. Available https https://philadelphiaencyclopedia.org/essays/automobile-suburbs/#:~:text=Later%20designated%20on%20the%20National,part%20of%20Philadelphia's%20western%20boundary (accessed 16 August 2024); Peter O. Muller, 'The Evolution of American Suburbs: A Geographical Interpretation', *Urbanism Past & Present*, No. 4 (summer 1977), pp. 1–10; James J. Flink, 'Three Stages of American Automobile Consciousness', *American Quarterly*, Vol. 24, No. 4, pp. 451–473.
8   Road construction throughout the US took off with the federal programme for construction of an Interstate Highway System, launched by the Federal-Aid Highway Act of 1956.
9   Robert Bruegmann, *Sprawl: A Compact History* (Chicago: University of Chicago Press, 2005).
10   Muller, op. cit. (note 7), p. 7. See also Walker, op. cit. (note 7): 'By the 1970s, the social mixing of residents that had been common in earlier streetcar suburbs had become distinctly uncommon in suburbs. Inner suburbs had become home to many working-class and immigrant households. In contrast, the greatest number of middle-class suburbs were arrayed at the outer edges of the metropolitan area, where land prices were affordable. The suburban towns with the highest household incomes in the region clustered in Pennsylvania at mid-distance between downtown Philadelphia and the region's edge, where land prices had risen historically in older suburbs served by commuter railroads.'
11   See, for example, Geoffrey H. Baker and Bruno Funaro, *Shopping Centers. Design and Operation* (New York: Reinhold, 1951); Richard W. Longstreth, *City Center to Regional Mall: Architecture, the Automobile, and Retailing in Los Angeles, 1920–1950* (Cambridge: The MIT Press, 1997).
12   On motels, see, for instance: John A. Jakle, Keith A. Sculle, Jefferson S. Rogers, *The Motel in America* (JHU Press, 1996); Bruce Bégout, *Common Place: The American Motel* (Seismicity Editions, 2010); Andrew Wood, 'The Rise and Fall of the Great American Motel', *The Smithsonian Magazine*, 30 June 2017.
13   See Erkan Sezgin and Medet Yola, 'Golden Age of Mass Tourism: Its History and Development'. Online. Available doi: 10.5772/37283 (accessed 17 August 2024), p. 73.
14   Christopher M. Kopper, 'The breakthrough of the package tour in Germany after 1945', *Journal of Tourism History*, 1:1 (2009), p. 82. Online. Available https: https://doi.org/10.1080/17551820902742798 (accessed 22 August 2024).
15   Nezar AlSayyad (ed.), *Consuming Tradition, Manufacturing Heritage: Global Norms and Urban Forms in the Age of Tourism* (London and New York: Routledge, 2001).
16   Joan Ockman and Salomon Fausto (eds.), *Architourism: Authentic, Escapist, Exotic, Spectacular* (Munich and New York: Prestel, 2005).
17   Gürhan Akdag, Zafer Öter, 'Assessment of world tourism from a geographical perspective and a comparative view of leading destinations in the market', *Procedia: Social and Behavioral Sciences*, December 2011, pp. 217–218.
18   Ivan T. Berend, *An Economic History of Twentieth-Century Europe: Economic Regimes from Laissez-Faire to Globalization* (Cambridge: Cambridge University Press, 2006), pp. 237–238.
19   'Occidental tourism is one of the great nihilistic movements, one of the great western epidemics whose malignant effects barely lag behind the epidemics of the Middle and the Far East, surpassing them instead in silent insidiousness. The swarms of these gigantic bacteria, called tourists, have coated the most distinct substances

with a uniformly glistening Thomas-Cook-slime, making it impossible to distinguish Cairo from Honolulu, Taormina from Colombo', Gerhard Nebel, *Unter Kreuzrittern und Partisanen* (Stuttgart: Klett, 1950); Hans Magnus Enzensberger, 'A Theory of Tourism', *New German Critique*, No. 68, Special Issue on Literature (spring–summer, 1996), p. 131.
20   Enzensberger, op. cit. (note 19).
21   Zygmunt Bauman, quoted in Adrian Franklin, 'The Tourist Syndrome: An Interview with Zygmunt Bauman', *Tourist Studies* 3 (2003) p. 207. Online. Available https: https://journals.sagepub.com/doi/10.1177/1468797603041632 (accessed 22 August 2024).
22   Dean MacCannell, *The Tourist: A New Theory of The Leisure Class* (New York: Shocken, 1989).
23   Enzensberger, op. cit. (note 19), p. 132.
24   John Urry, *The Tourist Gaze: Leisure and Travel in Contemporary Societies* (Newbury Park and London: Sage Publications, 1990).
25   Zygmunt Bauman, quoted in Adrian Franklin, op. cit. (note 21), p. 207.
26   Allan Williams, Gareth Shaw (eds.), *Tourism and Economic Development: European Experience* (Wiley, 1998). Quoted in Berend, op. cit. (note 18), pp. 237–238.
27   Kopper, op. cit. (note 14), p. 75.
28   Ibid.
29   *Building News*, 29 (1875), p. 133. Quoted in Carroll L. V. Meeks, *The Railroad Station: An Architectural History* (New York: Dover Publications Inc., 1995), p. 90.
30   G. E. Kidder Smith, *Italy Builds: Its Modern Architecture and Native Inheritance* (London: The Architectural Press, 1955), p. 234. Angelo Maggi, *G. E. Kidder Smith Builds: The Travel of Architectural Photography* (Novato, CA: Applied Research + Design Publishing, 2022), in particular M. Sabatino, 'G. E. Kidder Smith's Reputational Shadow,' pp. 8–17.
31   Simon Bradley, *St Pancras Station* (London: Profile, 2007); Alastair Lansley, *The Transformation of St Pancras Station* (London: Laurence King, 2008).
32   'The history of London St Pancras International Station'. Online. Available https://www.networkrail.co.uk/who-we-are/our-history/iconic-infrastructure/the-history-of-london-st-pancras-international-station/ (accessed 20 August 2024). 'St Pancras Station and former Midland Grand Hotel'. Online. Available https://historicengland.org.uk/listing/the-list/list-entry/1342037 (accessed 15 August 2024).

33   'St Pancras Station and former Midland Grand Hotel'. Online. Available https://historicengland.org.uk/listing/the-list/list-entry/1342037 (accessed 20 August 2024).
34   *The Mercury*, July 3, 1862. Online. Available https://trove.nla.gov.au/newspaper/article/8808302 (accessed 15 August 2024).
35   Ibid.
36   Ibid.
37   Jack Simmons, 'Railways, Hotels, and Tourism in Great Britain 1839–1914', *Journal of Contemporary History*, Vol. 19, No. 2, 1984, p. 204.
38   Ibid, p. 205.
39   Ibid, p. 205.
40   Thorstein Veblen, *The Theory of the Leisure Class: An Economic Study of Institutions* (New York: Macmillan, 1908; Oxford University Press, reissue edition, 2009).
41   Online. Available https://www.jrailpass.com/shinkansen-bullet-trains (accessed 20 August 2024).
42   Fumihiko Maki, *Investigations in Collective Form* (St. Louis: Washington University, 1964), p. 59.
43   Fumihiko Maki, David Stewart, Mark Mulligan, Kenneth Frampton, *Fumihiko Maki* (London: Phaidon Press, 2009), pp. 16–17.
44   Arthur Weststeijn, Frederick Whitling, *Termini. Cornerstone of Modern Rome* (Rome: Edizioni Quasar, 2017), pp. 79–80.
45   Antonio Caiola, 'Da Villa Montalto a Piazza dei Cinquecento', p. 202. Quoted in Weststeijn, Whitling, op. cit. (note 44), p. 70.
46   *Angiolo Mazzoni (1894–1979): architetto ingegnere del Ministero delle comunicazioni* (Milano: Skira, 2003).
47   Leo Calini. 'Il progetto prescelto', *La Nuova Stazione di Roma Termini* (Rome: Collegio ingegneri ferroviari italiani, 1951), pp. 62–71. Quoted in Weststeijn, Whitling, op. cit. (note 44), p. 132.
48   Ibid.
49   G.E. Kidder Smith, op. cit. (note 30), p. 232.
50   Jean Dargon and Philip Nutt, *The Future of Aviation* (London: Nutt, 1919). Quoted in W. Voigt, 'From the Hippodrome to the Aerodrome' in: J Zukowsky (ed.), *Building for Air Travel* (New York: Prestel, 1996), p. 31.
51   Lowell Thomas, *European Skyways: The Story of a Tour of Europe by Airplane* (Boston: Houghton Mifflin Company, 1927), p. 90. Also quoted in Alastair Gordon, *Naked Airport: A Cultural History of the World's Most Revolutionary Structure* (Chicago: University of Chicago Press, 2008), p. 74.

52 August Perret in Le Corbusier, *Aircraft. The New Vision* (London, New York, 1935), p. 7. Quoted also in Voigt, op. cit. (note 50).
53 Voigt, op. cit. (note 50), p. 33.
54 John Zukowsky (ed.), *Building for Air Travel: Architecture and Design for Commercial Aviation* (Munich and New York: Prestel and the Art Institute of Chicago, 1996).
55 Voigt, op. cit. (note 50), p. 31.
56 See Koos Bosma, 'European Airports, 1945–1995: Typology, Psychology, and Infrastructure', in John Zukowsky (ed.), op. cit. (note 54). Paul Meurs, *Schiphol: Groundbreaking Airport Design 1967–1975* (Rotterdam: nai010 uitgevers 2019).
57 Neal Samors and Christopher Lynch, *Now Arriving. Traveling To and From Chicago By Air. 90 Years of Flight* (Chicago: Chicago's Books Press, 2015). See the exhibition at the Chicago Architecture Foundation (Jan-May 2009) on O'Hare International Airport curated by Charles Waldheim.
58 Christopher Schaberg in Harriet Baskas, 'A short history of the much-maligned jet bridge. Special for USA TODAY' (16 August 2017). Online. Available https://eu.usatoday.com/story/travel/flights/2016/02/24/jet-bridge-jetway/80806044/ (accessed 19 December 2019).
59 See 'Plan van Gool' (1968). Online. Available https: https://www.arcam.nl/en/plan-van-gool/ (accessed 19 December 2019).
60 OMA, Zeebrugge Sea Terminal (1988). Online. Available https: https://oma.eu/projects/zeebrugge-sea-terminal (accessed 19 December 2019).
61 'Beehive, Gatwick Airport', Wikipedia. Online. Available https: https://en.wikipedia.org/wiki/Beehive,_Gatwick_Airport (accessed 16 August 2024).
62 See Voigt, op. cit. (note 50), p. 47. See also John King, Geoffrey Tait, *Golden Gatwick: 50 Years of Aviation* (London: Royal Aeronautical Society, 1980).
63 Lewis Mumford, 'An American Introduction to Sir Ebenezer Howard's "Garden Cities of Tomorrow"', *New Pencil Points* (March 1945), p. 73. Quoted in Gordon, op. cit. (note 51), p. 146.
64 J. Gordon Carr, 'Airports of the Future', *Architectural Record*, Vol. 94, No. 1 (July 1943) p. 67.
65 Quoted in Gordon, op. cit. (note 51), p. 243.
66 Bosma, op. cit. (note 56), p. 56.
67 Ibid.
68 Paul Andreu in Vladimir Belogolovsky, 'Paul Andreu: "I Would Only Take On a Project if the Ideas Were Mine. Otherwise, I Am Not Interested"', Archdaily.com. Online. Available https: https://www.archdaily.com/806698/paul-andreu-i-would-only-take-on-a-project-if-the-ideas-were-mine-otherwise-i-am-not-interested (accessed 19 December 2019).
69 Bosma, op. cit. (note 56), p. 60.
70 Jennifer Steinhauer, 'It's a Mall … It's an Airport … It's Both: The Latest Trend in Terminals', *The New York Times* (10 June 1998). Online. Available https: https://www.nytimes.com/1998/06/10/business/it-s-a-mall-it-s-an-airport-it-s-both-the-latest-trend-in-terminals.html (accessed 8 January 2020).
71 'PA: Because everything was so new. There was no past. The very first commercial airports started to appear in the 1920s. So by 2000, working on airports for almost 40 years, I was involved in designing this building type for half of its existence, and it really started to grow and change dramatically right at the time when I started. Airports no longer change; they just grow in size; there is no new concept. And, unfortunately, now many seemingly different building types converge around shopping experience. So many projects have become very commercial. There are airport versions of commercial malls, railway station versions, museum versions … Everything is a commercial centre.' Online. Available https: https://www.archdaily.com/806698/paul-andreu-i-would-only-take-on-a-project-if-the-ideas-were-mine-otherwise-i-am-not-interested (accessed 22 August 2024).
72 Sze Tsung Leong, 'Captive', in: Rem Koolhaas, Chuihua Judy Chung, Jeffrey Inaba, Sze Tsung Leong (eds.), *Harvard Design School: Guide to Shopping* (Los Angeles: Taschen, 2001), p. 178.
73 Ibid.
74 Gordon, op. cit. (note 51), p. 264.
75 Giampiero Aloi, *Hotel, Motel* (Milan: Hoepli, 1970); Geoffrey Baker and Bruno Funaro, *Motels* (New York: Reinhold Publishing Corporation, 1955).
76 Tom Avermaete and Anne Massey, *Hotel Lobbies and Lounges. The Architecture of Professional Hospitality* (London and New York: Routledge, 2012); Donald Albrecht, *New Hotels for Global Nomads* (London: Merrell Publishers, 2002).
77 Tom Avermaete, 'Introduction. Hotel lobbies: anonymous domesticity and public discretion', in: Tom Avermaete, Anne Massey (eds.), op. cit. (note 76), p. 1.
78 Conrad N. Hilton, *Be my guest* (USA: Prentice Hall, 1957; New York: Simon & Schuster, 1994).
79 Conrad N. Hilton Foundation, *The Hilton Legacy. Serving Humanity Worldwide* (Los Angeles, 2009), p. 6.

See also A. K. Sandoval-Strausz, *Hotel. An American History* (New Haven: Yale University Press, 2007).

80 Annabel Jane Wharton, *Building the Cold War: Hilton International Hotels and Modern Architecture* (Chicago: University of Chicago Press, 2004), p. 2.

81 Ibid.

82 President Woodrow Wilson in Detroit on 10 July 1916, quoted in Victoria De Grazia, *Irresistible Empire: America's Advance Through Twentieth-Century Europe* (Cambridge: Harvard University Press, 2005), p. 1.

83 Conrad N. Hilton Foundation, *The Hilton Legacy. Serving Humanity Worldwide* (Los Angeles: Conrad Hilton Foundation, 2009), p. 23.

84 Conrad Hilton, op. cit. (note 78), p. 269. 'An integral part of my dream was to show the countries most exposed to Communism the other side of the coin — the fruits of the free world', ibid., p. 237. 'Our Hilton house flag is one small flag of freedom which is being waved defiantly against Communism exactly as Lenin predicted. With humility we submit this international effort of ours as a contribution to world peace', ibid. p. 262.

85 Wharton, op. cit. (note 80), pp. 7–8.

86 See also Kerr Houston, 'Book Review: Annabel Jane Wharton *Building the Cold War: Hilton International Hotels and Modern Architecture*'. Online. Available doi: 10.3202/caa.reviews.2002.64; http://www.caareviews.org/reviews/460 (accessed 12 December 2019).

87 See Barbara Czyżewska, *The Story of Hilton Hotels. 'Little Americas'* (Goodfellow Publishers, Limited, 2019), p. 75.

88 '60 Years at Hilton Istanbul Bosphorus'. Online. Available https: https://www3.hilton.com/en/hotels/turkey/hilton-istanbul-bosphorus-ISTHITW/about/60-years.html (accessed 7 January 2020).

89 Mehmet Altun, 'A monument rises', *Istanbul Hilton. Ambassadors of Turkish Hospitality since 1955* (Hilton Worldwide, 2015), p. 19. See Glenn Adamson, Giorgio Riello, Sarah Teasley, *Global Design History* (London: Routledge: 2011).

90 Conrad N. Hilton Foundation, *The Hilton Legacy. Serving Humanity Worldwide* (Los Angeles, 2009), p. 6.

91 Wharton, op. cit. (note 80), p. 5.

92 See George Bradshaw, 'The View form a Tall Glass Oasis: The Subliminal Pleasures of Hilton Hotels', *Vogue* 146 (July 1965), p. 82. Online. Available https: https://archive.vogue.com/article/1965/7/the-view-from-a-tall-glass-oasis (accessed 7 January 2020).

93 Beatriz Colomina, 'The 24/7 Bed'. Online. Available https: https://work-body-leisure.hetnieuweinstituut.nl/247-bed (accessed 7 January 2020).

94 See Ian McCallum, 'Syntax: The Contribution of the Curtain Wall to a new Vernacular', *The Architectural Review* 121 (May 1957), p. 299.

95 Meredith Clausen, *The Pan Am Building and the Shattering of the Modernist Dream* (Cambridge: The MIT Press, 2005). See also Matthias C. Hühne, *Pan Am: History Design & Identity* (Berlin: Callisto Publishers, 2016).

4 Knowledge: Journals, Manuals, and Mass Media

Tom Avermaete

Fig. 4.1
Marshall McLuhan on a national television show explaining the concept of the Global Village, Canadian Broadcasting Corporation, 1965.

In 1965 the Canadian media theorist Marshall McLuhan appeared in a national television show to explain the concept of the Global Village that he had coined in 1962 in his book *The Gutenberg Galaxy*.[1] McLuhan described how new mass media increasingly remove the time and space barriers to human communication, allowing people to interconnect on a global scale. As a result, he provocatively maintained, the world will turn into a village. McLuhan was interviewed against a wall of television screens that broadcasted his slogan 'The Medium is the Message', which he coined to problematise the enormous effect that media have on the character and development of our societies and contrasted with the limited effect of the messages that are sent by these. McLuhan argued that more attention should be given to the ways by which these media alter our relations to one another and to ourselves rather than to the messages that they spread — a line of thought that he would further explore in his books *Understanding Media: The Extensions of Man* (1964) and *The Medium is the Massage: An Inventory of Effects* (1967).[2]

→ Fig. 4.1

With his television appearances and publications Marshall McLuhan pointed to a form of globalization which would play a very important role in architectural culture: the circulation of knowledge across the world. Exchanging knowledge between distant spaces and people through communication media was obviously not a new phenomenon. Nineteenth-century maps of telegraph systems illustrate the existence of a network of telephone lines that connected different continents and allowed for the instant movement of simple data across the globe. The engineer Alonzo Jackman, who was credited with creating the first transatlantic telegraph line, already envisaged that 'all the inhabitants of the earth would be brought into one intellectual neighbourhood and be at the same time perfectly freed from those contaminations which might under other circumstances be received.'[3] In the field of architecture this idea of a global 'intellectual neighbourhood' in which architectural knowledge is exchanged across cultures seems to have haunted minds for a much longer time.

→ Fig. 4.2

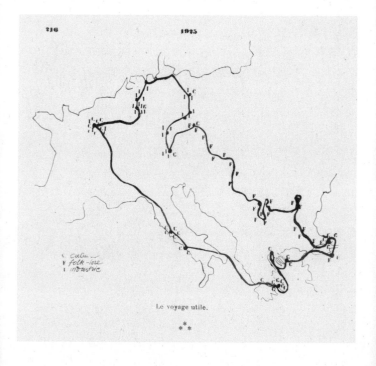

Fig. 4.2
Le Corbusier's 'Grand Tour' (here titled 'The useful trip'). The letter C stands for 'Culture' (Paris, Rome, Naples, Pompeii, Athens, etc); F, for 'Folklore' (Balkans, Romania, Bulgaria, etc); and I, for 'Industry' (Vienna, Berlin, Munich), 1910–1911.

4 Knowledge

Fig. 4.3
A collection of plaster casts and cork models at the Technische Hochschule in Munich, Germany.

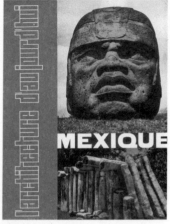

Figs. 4.4–6
L'Architecture d'Aujourd'hui, thematic issues on Brazil (1952), Mexico (1963), and Japan (1956).

4 Knowledge

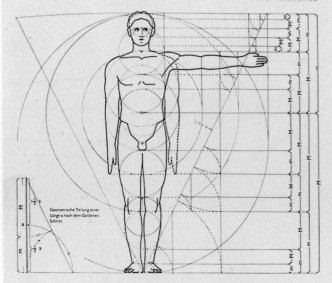

DER MENSCH
DAS MASS ALLER DINGE

Geometrische Teilung einer Länge a nach dem Goldenen Schnitt

Maßverhältnisse des Menschen,
aufgebaut in Anlehnung an die Ermittlungen von A. Zeising

Den ältesten bekannten Kanon über die Maßverhältnisse des Menschen fand man in einer Grabkammer der Pyramidenfelder bei Memphis (etwa 3000 Jahre v. Chr.). Also mindestens seit dieser Zeit haben sich Wissenschaftler und Künstler bis heute um die Entschleierung der menschlichen Maßverhältnisse bemüht. Wir kennen den Kanon des Pharaonenreiches, der Ptolomäerzeit, der Griechen und Römer, den Kanon des Polyklet, der lange Zeit als Norm galt, die Angaben von Alberti, Leonardo da Vinci, Michelangelo und der Menschen des Mittelalters, vor allem das weitbekannte Werk Dürers. Bei diesen erwähnten Arbeiten wird der Körper des Menschen berechnet nach Kopf-, Gesichts- oder Fußlängen, die dann in späterer Zeit weiter unterteilt und zueinander in Beziehung gebracht wurden, so daß sie sogar im allgemeinen Leben maßgebend wurden. Bis in unsere Zeit waren Fuß und Elle gebräuchliche Maße.

Die Angaben Dürers wurden vor allem Gemeingut. Er ging aus von der Höhe des Menschen und legte die Unterteilungen in Brüchen wie folgt fest:

½ h = der ganze Oberkörper von der Spaltung an,
¼ h = Beinlänge v. Knöchel b. Knie u. Länge v. Kinn bis Nabel,
⅙ h = Fußlänge,
⅛ h = Kopflänge vom Scheitel bis Unterkante Kinn, Abstand der Brustwarzen,
1/10 h = Gesichtshöhe u. -Breite (einschließlich Ohren), Handlänge bis zur Handwurzel,
1/12 h = Gesichtsbreite in Höhe der Unterkante Nase, Beinbreite (über dem Knöchel) usf.

Die Unterteilungen gehen bis zu 1/40 h.

Im vergangenen Jahrhundert hat vor allen anderen A. Zeising durch seine Untersuchungen der Maßverhältnisse des Menschen auf der Grundlage des Goldenen Schnittes durch genaueste Messungen und Vergleiche größere Klarheit geschaffen. Leider fand das Werk bis vor kurzem nicht die gebührende Beachtung, bis der bedeutendste Forscher auf diesem Gebiet, E. Moessel, auf seine Bedeutung hinwies und die Arbeit Zeisings durch eingehende Untersuchungen nach seiner Methode stützte.

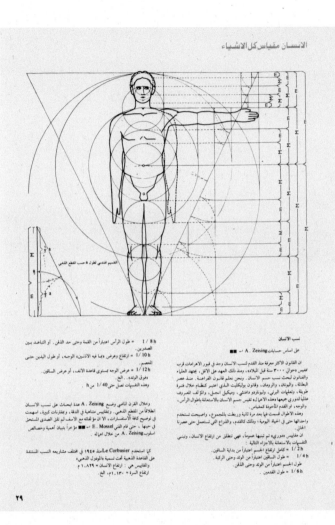

Fig. 4.7
Man as the measure of architecture. Pages from the German and Arabic editions of *Bauentwurfslehre* by Ernst Neufert, first published in Germany in 1936.

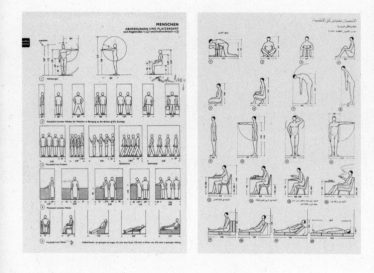

Fig. 4.8
Man as the measure of architecture. Pages from the German and Arabic editions of *Bauentwurfslehre* by Ernst Neufert, first published in Germany in 1936.

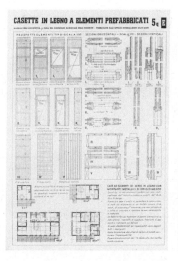 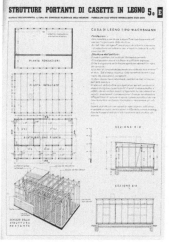

Fig. 4.9
A page from *Manuale dell'architetto* (1946) showing a modular house based on the work of the Swedish architect Eric Friberger.

Fig. 4.10
A page from *Manuale dell'architetto* (1946) showing a prefabricated wooden-frame house inspired by Konrad Wachsmann's research in his book *Holzhausbau: Technik und Gestaltung* (1931).

4 Knowledge

Fig. 4.11
Living in a mass-produced suburb. A panel from *Peanuts* by Charles M. Schulz, 1960.

Fig. 4.12
A series of packages of consumer products in a composition that resembles the urban masterplan of a modern housing estate. A still from *Deux ou Trois Choses que Je Sais d'Elle* by Jean-Luc Godard, 1967.

Of Tours and Plaster Casts

In architectural culture the circulation of knowledge was for a long time primarily facilitated by architects themselves. Historically, the well known Grand Tour is a prime example. Established in the seventeenth and eighteenth centuries, this was an itinerary for a select, elitist, upper-class group of wealthy young architects who could afford the journey to important cultural and architectural sites in Europe in search of the 'roots of Western civilization'.[4] The Grand Tour was both the culmination of their education as architects and a means to obtain patronage, commissions, and cultural cachet. More importantly, through the centuries, it became the paradigm of non-static knowledge production, as well as a marker of the architect's continuous self-education through direct physical and cross-cultural experience of buildings and cities. The Grand Tour validated and fuelled travel as a modern practice of architectural knowledge production based on encounters with unfamiliar western and non-western architectural cultures and lifting the veil of preconceptions, preconfigured ideas, and local habits. In other words, it provided the critical distance that is paramount to architectural reflection, cross-cultural understanding, and an intellectual stance.[5]

That architectural knowledge — even in its three-dimensional form — could travel more efficiently than through the sketches and photographs of architects visiting and experiencing buildings firsthand had already become clear in the nineteenth century with the generalization of the architectural plaster cast.[6] During this period many architectural schools, such as the École des Beaux Arts in Paris, the Technische Hochschule in Munich, and Cornell University in Ithaca (USA), put together collections of casts, as did museums, such as the Metropolitan Museum of Art in New York and the Victoria and Albert Museum in London, where entire courtyards were dedicated to plaster casts. These collections consisted of perfect copies of full-size architectural elements, such as doorways and balconies, as well as building details, such as reliefs and ornaments, from all over the world.[7] They promoted the idea that replicated knowledge in the form of plaster casts was as valuable as direct contact with the original; such contact was, of course, in any case usually unfeasible. The plaster cast collections played a key educational role, conferring global architectural knowledge upon students and curious citizens who were unable to travel and providing a three-dimensional quality that could not be achieved through other media, such as photography.

→ Fig. 4.3

To facilitate the global travel of architectural knowledge, it had to be replicated. In many places around the world, so-called 'plaster cast workshops' (*ateliers de moulage*) emerged in the nineteenth century, often in close proximity to important monuments, such as the Temple of Angkor Wat in Cambodia, or in relation to important museums, such as the Musée du Louvre in Paris.[8] After the plaster casts had been made, national museums and private firms, such as the Boston-based P.P. Caproni and Brother, would promote them in catalogues and distribute these artefacts of architectural knowledge across the globe.[9] Although replicas, plaster casts possessed a certain authority and authenticity thanks to the direct contact they had had with the original element or building.[10] However, rather than being mere faithful mechanical facsimiles, plaster casts were often the result of a complex artistic process characterized by 'deliberate and conscious acts of selection, assemblage, structuration, and fabrication — and even, in some cases, of falsification, refusal of information, [and] counterfeiting.'[11]

The Architectural Journal:
Part and Parcel of a Global Architectural Culture

Replicated architectural knowledge started to play an ever more important role in the second half of the twentieth century. Fast and relatively cheap modes of reproduction, such as the Xerox machine and improved forms of offset colour printing, engendered a proliferation of large and small architectural journals.[12] During the second half of the twentieth century the architectural journal with its regular publication rhythm, illustrated articles about exemplary projects, and fast delivery became a fully fledged actor in architectural culture.[13]

For some of these architectural periodicals the circulation of architectural knowledge across the globe became the principal ambition. This was, for instance, the case for the French periodical *L'Architecture d'Aujourd'hui*, founded in 1930 by the architects André Bloc and Marcel Eugène Cahen, which acted as a mouthpiece of the modern movement as defined by the Congrès Internationaux d'Architecture Moderne (CIAM).[14] The journal's main goal was clearly highlighted in its very first issue, in November 1930: to describe, advocate for, and popularize the main streams of architectural thought underpinning the idea of 'modernity'. This mission was preserved intact throughout the years. The magazine remained faithful to its ideology, stressing the foundational role of the orthodox modern movement in architecture and of its pioneers in CIAM even when the first postwar critiques began to catch on.[15]

L'Architecture d'Aujourd'hui's ambition was clearly not just to promote modern architecture; it was especially to propel cross-cultural exchange and by doing so to establish a true international modern movement. A key way to achieve this was by structurally paying great attention to architectural and urban developments beyond France. As early as 1931, articles in the journal were split into 'Architecture en France' (architecture in France) and 'Architecture à l'étranger' (architecture abroad), 'Urbanisme en France' (urban planning in France) and 'Urbanisme à l'étranger' (urban planning abroad).[16] As a result, in the period after 1945 *L'Architecture d'Aujourd'hui* played a ground-breaking role by redefining what had previously been known as 'modern Europe' to include for the first time countries such as Hungary, Poland, and the Scandinavian countries. In addition, during this period the journal published numerous thematic issues and articles on modern architecture in regions such as Brazil, Mexico, North Africa, and Japan.

→ Figs. 4.4–6

In order to grow this cross-cultural discussion of modern architecture, *L'Architecture d'Aujourd'hui* set up a dense network of international correspondents. These were architects or critics who could report on the latest architectural and urban developments in their country of origin.[17] As well as deriving from existing or long-established colonial connections, correspondents were recruited through the 'Rencontres Internationales des Architectes' (RIA), which in 1948 was reorganized as the 'Union International des Architectes' (UIA) and counted 27 participating countries at its foundation, as well as through CIAM's networks.[18] Additionally, the editorial board organized several trips abroad (to Russia, the US, Brazil, Africa, etc.), establishing new cultural encounters and professional contacts.

The results were spectacular. *L'Architecture d'Aujourd'hui* not only substantially broadened the scope of the modern movement in architecture but also propelled cross-cultural exchange on what this broadening entailed. Gradually the journal moved away from the radical character of orthodox modernism and promoted the possibility of a 'third way' between modernism and traditionalism, aiming to discover a national character and identity in each instance of modern architecture.[19] As a result, the modern movement in architecture revealed itself as a truly cross-cultural phenomenon involving architectural knowledge from all over the world. That this renewed image of the modern movement in architecture was not merely wishful thinking on the part of French architects alone emerged from subscriptions to *L'Architecture d'Aujourd'hui*. In the second half of the twentieth century the journal's subscribers literally came from all parts of the world, including Asia, Africa, and South America. In Latin America in the 1940s *L'Architecture d'Aujourd'hui* had more than 1600 subscribers, far surpassing any other architectural periodical in Brazil or Mexico.[20] For all its subscribers *L'Architecture d'Aujourd'hui* functioned not only as a source of knowledge on what was happening in other parts of the world but also as a mirror by which to understand their own position within the wider global developments of the modern movement.

L'Architecture d'Aujourd'hui was not unique. Other architectural periodicals, such as the Dutch journal *Forum* with its reports on architects' travels and the British *Architectural Review* with its series 'How Other Peoples Dwell and Build' by Erwin Antonin Gutkind, testify to a much broader interest in initiating a more global debate and articulating a more cross-cultural modern architectural knowledge — albeit informed by old colonial and new decolonial relations.[21] Another example is the highly popular 'Cosmorama' section of the British journal *Architectural Design* (formerly known as 'World News'), which in the 1960s and 1970s brought together a kaleidoscopic compilation of views, commentary, and news reports from around the world. According to Robin Middleton, its technical editor at the time:

> Cosmorama was the reason that people were buying and reading the magazine. It was the main part of the magazine. We were all saving our energy to put into Cosmorama, picking up any sort of information on new lifestyles that

we could find. Nobody was interested in pictures of new buildings. Cosmorama kept the magazine going.[22]

Common to all these post-war architectural periodicals was that they expanded the reach of modern architectural culture: the design thinking and practice of architects and urban designers in South America, Asia, or Africa was now conceived as being in direct dialogue with that of their counterparts in Europe and North America. This idea of a modern architectural culture as a 'global phenomenon' was to have lasting effects on architectural thinking and practice and also strongly influenced the way that post-war architectural culture entered the history books.

Architecture Manuals: Circulation of a Silent Design Paradigm

If architectural periodicals were often quite explicit about their ambition to support international architectural movements and engage with global publics, more silent and indirect ways of universalizing architectural knowledge could be observed in another type of architectural publication — the manual. In the 1950s and 1960s the architectural manual remained an important vector of universal architectural knowledge. The idea of creating a reference work with rational architectural knowledge that would be universally applicable was obviously not a new phenomenon: it can be traced back to the nineteenth century, when the *Précis des leçons d'architecture* (1809) by the French architect and professor Jean-Nicolas Louis Durand started to circulate in the Francophone world, or to the series *Handbuch der Architektur* (1880) by the architect and professor Josef Durm and his colleagues, which caused a furore in the German-speaking world.[23] In the twentieth century, however, the architectural manual increasingly started to play the role of 'integrator' of global knowledge.

The most widely diffused architectural manual of the twentieth century is beyond doubt *Bauentwurfslehre* (Architect's Data) by Ernst Neufert, first published in Germany in 1936.[24] This book was exported globally during the second half of the twentieth century and translated into at least 20 languages, selling more than 500,000 copies. Initially drafted by Ernst Neufert as a teaching compendium for a 'rapid design' course at the Staatliche Bauhochschule in Weimar,[25] the manual aimed at a more routine-led, accessible, and rapid design process by categorizing and rationalizing knowledge on the construction, form, size, and use of specific spaces.[26] Using more drawings than text, Neufert's manual was based on an advanced idea of standardization: specific programmes and particular constructive challenges were addressed with standard solutions. This approach means that *Architect's Data* seems to echo, embody, and emphasize the cultural pleas for functionalism, *Existenzminimum* (the minimal dwelling), and industrial standardization which were developing at this time throughout Europe. As a result, during the second half of the twentieth century the book would serve not only as an important key technical reference but also as a 'silent design paradigm' that was then applied by numerous students and professionals worldwide — sometimes without their fully realizing. As Reinier de Graaf, a partner in OMA, recently asserted, 'Neufert's architecture is everywhere.'[27]

→ Figs. 4.7–8

Architect's Data's effectiveness in the global transfer of knowledge was helped by its adaptability to the contexts and laws in different countries. Paradoxically, this manual's objective-universal standards and rules for architectural design were repeatedly acculturated to local contexts. As mentioned by architect Luigi Lenzi in the foreword to the first Italian version of the manual in 1949, this version was anything but a mere translation; it was the result of long and arduous work to adjust *Architect's Data* to the local Italian laws, practices, and climatic conditions. The fact that the drawings had not originally been geographically contextualized by the German author made this acculturation all the more feasible. The drawn data could be quickly reinterpreted and generalized.[28] As a result, the idea of an architecture based on generalized standards could be maintained even if these standards had undergone some local adaptation. Neufert's manual proved instrumental in establishing, normalizing, and globally expanding the 'mandate of standardization' in architecture,[29] based on in-depth understanding of human scale and performance.[30]

That the circulation of architectural knowledge through architectural manuals was anything but innocent is illustrated by the Italian *Manuale dell'Architetto*, first published in 1946 by the architects Bruno Zevi, Luigi Nervi, and Mario Ridolfi, together with a team of collaborators. Officially, *Manuale* was a tool to support the rapid and adequate reconstruction of Italy, which had been torn to pieces during World War II. It was also an answer to the lack of homogeneous technical knowledge and to the confusing plethora of different technical sources in different languages. The manual was a sort of integrator of technical and design knowledge generated in various countries. Put together in a rush in only 10 months, it was a compendium of technical knowledge drawn from American and German publications on the restoration and reconstruction of buildings and neighbourhoods. This knowledge was translated and catalogued in a new taxonomy of types, models, nodes, and constructive details. All the manual's sections had a pronounced graphical focus: the texts were short, and the drawings were accompanied by numerous explanatory captions; the aim was to make the manual a comprehensible and accessible tool for all professionals. Also important is that, with a print run of 25,000 copies, *Manuale dell'Architetto* was distributed free to all Italian professionals in order to guarantee its pervasive diffusion for the purpose of reconstructing the war-torn country.[31]

→ Fig. 4.9–10

That this translation and integration of foreign architectural knowledge was not a value-free venture becomes noticeable when we take a closer look at who were the publishers of *Manuale dell'Architetto*. The manual's appearance on the scene was directly linked to the American liberation of Italy:[32] its backers were the American USIS (United States Information Service) and the Italian CNR (Consiglio nazionale delle ricerche). Its chief editor, the Italian architect Bruno Zevi, had escaped from Italy during the war to avoid its racial fascist laws and studied in the USA. As leader of the editorial team, Zevi became one of the most fervent promoters of a campaign for the technical and scientific renewal of Italy under the auspices of the United States Information Service. *Manuale* became one of the most prolific results of this technical collaboration between the American 'Irresistible Empire' and Italy,[33] a country which was in need of both total rebuilding and political reshaping.

As Bruno Zevi himself later recalled, it was 'James Linen of the Time Inc. group who land[ed] in Rome, as "specialist assistant to the director, Office of War Information." Persuaded by the fact that "selling the United States or democracy" is equivalent to selling Coca-Cola or *Life* and *Time* magazines, he found[ed] the United States Information Service [USIS].'[34] It was the United States Information Service that, together with the Italian authorities, published *Manuale dell'Architetto* but also implicitly required that the model of modernization promoted by Bruno Zevi, Mario Ridolfi, and their co-editors be based on American knowledge and know-how.[35] In other words, the knowledge on the restoration and reconstruction of the built environment that was integrated in *Manuale* was not coincidental but represented business and geopolitical interests from across the Atlantic. The Italian critic Manfredo Tafuri criticized this transatlantic guidance, labelling *Manuale* a 'bottega handbook' and a 'technological Esperanto' that was affected by the politics of the American New Deal and exported as merchandise.[36]

Popular Media: Modern Norms and Forms from Charlie Brown to Jacques Tati

In addition to professional media such as the architectural periodical and the manual, popular media also played a central role in the global dissemination of architectural concepts, ideals, and aspirations. Often in a far less explicit manner than the professional media but no less incisively, they portrayed, for instance, architectural ideals of modern family living and transmitted cultural codes about privacy and publicness, domesticity, and the role of gendered inhabitants, as well as about behaviour and care in the modern house.

During the first decades following World War II modern architecture and urbanism became omnipresent in many countries around the world. Decolonized nation states, such as India, Pakistan, Chad, and Tanzania, commissioned new modern cities. All over Europe, modern housing estates and new towns sprang up. And in the United States mass-produced suburbs, such as Levittown, New York, and Park Forest, Illinois, were erected. This greater presence of modern architecture and urbanism was accompanied by the rapid introduction of new domestic technologies and appliances and the gradual universalization of mass consumer culture. Popular media played a paramount role in teaching various societies how to relate to these new phenomena. Such media may be looked upon as essential sites of negotiation with the rapid architectural, technological, and social developments taking place in post-war societies. They either underpinned the role of consumerist-driven modern ways of living or attempted, in the spirit of criticism, to open people's eyes to the inherent contradictions in consumerist logic and modern architecture and urbanism.

Peanuts, the famous comic strip for children, is a good example of how a North American image of suburban architecture and living started to travel across the globe.[37] Created by Charles M. Schulz and first published in 1950, this popular comic strip appeared in over 2600 newspapers in 75 different countries worldwide. *Peanuts'* global readership followed daily events involving Charlie Brown and his mates, all children, who live in a generic suburb of an unidentified town composed of detached houses with small gardens, an elementary school, and a summer camp in the countryside. *Peanuts* depicts suburban American life as an ideal pastoral and homogeneous social setting for the amusing adventures of a group of children. Interestingly, adults are almost absent; however, the children-protagonists themselves often behave as adults with hilarious and often thought-provoking consequences.

→ Fig. 4.11

In more than 75 countries and for a readership of 355 million, Charlie Brown and his friends popularized an ideal and, at the same time, non-innocent vision of childhood and a suburban life which is socially homogeneous, nostalgic, antiseptic, and consumerist.[38] Like other comic cartoons, *Peanuts* introduced to a broad global public the idea that it was possible to live comfortably in a modern mass-produced suburb. In order to do so, it painted the suburban dweller as a 'modern primitive', both embracing and glorifying a modern consumer capitalist lifestyle and, at the same time, a folkloristic, simplistic preindustrial life where children are free to move and act without any restrictions.[39] With its attention to a particular way of furnishing, decorating, and gardening, as well to certain appliances and props, *Peanuts* not only created a shared visual culture of the suburban context but also offered symbolic images of American post-war modernity that could be exported globally as 'vehicles for international cold warfare'.[40] This comic's embodiment of popular house styles and lifestyle expectations became part of the peaceful commercial American conquest of the world[41] and at the same time was 'the quintessential symbol of American cultural imperialism'.[42]

Mass media did not always merely promote ideals of modern living; they often also offered an incisive critique of modern architecture and urbanism, as well as of consumer society. This was, for instance, the case in French cinema. Considered far less serious than books or periodicals, the so-called 'irrational medium' of *le cinema* was free to denounce, highlight, stress, exaggerate, and poeticise new forms of social isolation and disease (such as '*Sarcellite*') and American consumerist influence on the new suburban French landscape.[43, 44] As Jean-Luc Godard argued, cinema in 1950s and 1960s France assumed the role of a 'social oracle'.[45] It often forecasted and prepared the ground for deep cultural discussion, which would later be scientifically analysed by observers, sociologists, and urbanists.[46]

From Jacques Tati's *Mon Oncle* (1958) to Maurice Pialat's *L'Amour Existe* (1960) and Jean-Luc Godard's *Alphaville* (1965) and *Deux ou Trois Choses que Je Sais d'Elle* (1967), the focus was on denunciation of social nihilism and of the disorientation that occurs inside the new modern suburbs and in the emerging French *grands ensembles* built during the post-war period. Time and time again, the directors explored how the new urban modern landscape was influencing its inhabitants' inner psychology and vice versa, using cinema as a tool for hailing the socio-spatial contradictions of the new urban question: 'a landscape is like a face', proclaims Juliette, a protagonist in Godard's movie *Deux ou Trois Choses que Je Sais d'Elle*,[47] as she surveys the monotonous façades of massive residential buildings while reflecting upon the anonymous life that she lives.

Directors such as Godard were extremely critical of the quantitative approach to housing taken by the French welfare state in the decades after World War II but also often cast a harsh eye on the social consequences of technology and consumerism. In the final shot of *Deux ou Trois Choses que Je Sais d'Elle*, Godard places a series of packages of consumer products in a composition that resembles the urban masterplan of a modern housing estate. In doing so, he compares the social alienation of inhabitants from their dwelling environment with the distance that exists between consumers and the generic products that they buy. Although Godard's movies were qualified by the artists of the Situationist International group as 'conformist' and as the 'Club Med of modern thought', his critical view on the impersonal character of housing estates, technology, and consumer products was to circulate widely and reach far broader audiences than the words of Guy Debord or any other situationist.[48]

→ Fig. 4.12

The reach of critical movies by directors such as Godard and Tati extended beyond mass audiences in France to Francophone parts of the world and sometimes beyond. From the movie *Mon Oncle* by Jacques Tati, for instance, a parallel English version was made under the title *My Uncle*, bringing it to large international audiences and even winning an Academy Award. In Tati's movies a broad public was confronted with a critical view on approaches developed by architects and urban designers to modern dwellings and cities. It should come as no surprise that *Mon Oncle* was denounced by some French critics as a reactionary or even *poujadiste* (petit-bourgeois reactionary) view of a modernizing French society which associated social and technological progress with a rise in productivity and a rationalization of the way that buildings and cities were conceived. The film's great popularity in both France and abroad soon gave way to this criticism — even in the US, where rampant consumption and a recession had made many people question the prevailing model of modernization. As a result, movies such as those of Godard and Tati not only played an important role in articulating a critique of modern architecture and urbanism for wider audiences but also indirectly shaped perspectives that gave a more central place to the inhabitant in a more global architectural discourse. In 1958 Tati maintained, 'I am not at all against modern architecture, I only think that as well as the permit to build, there should be also the permit to inhabit.'[49] Tati's critical, inhabitant-centred view of the modern built environment spread around the world, influencing a broader wave of criticism of modern architecture and urbanism.

The Global Architectural Village

Looking at the second half of the twentieth century, it becomes clear that globalization affected architectural culture by intensifying the regimes governing the circulation of architectural knowledge. Propelled by the improvement of existing media and the emergence of new ways of communicating, architectural data circulated across political and cultural geographies in unprecedented ways. In the professional field widely read architectural periodicals contributed to a more cross-cultural idea of the modern movement in architecture by fuelling international connections among architects, while much-referenced manuals not only silently introduced an international design paradigm of standardization but also participated in geopolitical tussles concerning the different paths of modernity. Popular media also played a paramount role in the circulation of architectural knowledge during the second half of the twentieth century. Comic strips introduced a global general public to the forms and norms of modern (sub)urbanity, while movies critically pinpointed social challenges within modern housing and urbanism.

As the twentieth century came to a close, global circulation of architectural knowledge once again received a new impetus as people throughout the world gained access to a new medium. Architects and urban designers could now become inhabitants of yet another 'global architectural village', located on the World Wide Web in the form of numerous websites, digital platforms, databases, streams, and blogs. This digital global village acts as a seemingly barrierless forum for cross-cultural exchange, discussion, and appraisal of architectural knowledge. It has opened up the possibility for a more equal and socially just definition of architectural knowledge which goes beyond traditional centres of knowledge production in Europe and the Americas and takes into account expertise and critical capacity in other geographies. As in all previous regimes of circulation, this unprecedented transfer of architectural knowledge across the globe needs to be scrutinized. Marshall McLuhan's invitation to critically explore how 'the medium is the message', or, as he would later formulate it, 'the medium is the massage', resonates as strongly as ever.

Journals, Manuals, and Mass Media

1 Marshall McLuhan, *The Gutenberg Galaxy: The Making of Typographical Man* (London: Routledge & Kegan Paul, 1962).
2 Marshall McLuhan, *Understanding Media: The Extensions of Man* (New York: McGraw-Hill, 1964) and Marshall McLuhan, Quentin Fiore, *The Medium is the Massage: An Inventory of Effects* (New York: Bantam Books, 1967).
3 Lynn Spigel, *Welcome to the Dreamhouse. Popular Media and Postwar Suburbs* (Durham and London: Duke University Press, 2001), p. 34 and Carolyn Marvin, *When Old Technologies Were New: Thinking About Electric Communication in the Late Nineteenth Century* (New York: Oxford University Press, 1988), pp. 200–201.
4 Paola Bianchi and Karin Wolfe, *Turin and the British in the Age of the Grand Tour* (Cambridge: Cambridge University Press, 2017) and Matt Gross, 'Lessons From the Frugal Grand Tour', Frugal Traveler (blog), *New York Times,* 5 September 2008.
5 Roxanne Euben, *Journeys to the Other Shore: Muslim and Western Travelers in Search of Knowledge* (Princeton, NJ: Princeton University Press, 2006), p. 15.
6 Mari Lending, *Plaster Monuments: Architecture and the Power of Reproduction* (Princeton: Princeton University Press, 2017).
7 Dominique de Font-Réaulx, 'S'éprendre de passion pour ces charments production naturelles … Les moulages sur nature de végétaux d'Adolphe Victor Geoffroy-Dechaume.' Quoted in Michael Falser, 'Krishna and the Plaster Cast — Translating the Cambodian Temple of Angkor Wat in the French Colonial Period', *The Journal of Transcultural Studies*, No. 2 (2011), p. 12. Online. Available https; https://doi.org/10.11588/ts.2011.2.9083 (accessed 27 August 2024).
8 Michael Falser, 'Colonial appropriation, physical substitution and the metonymics of translation: plaster casts of Angkor Wat for the museum collections in Paris and Berlin', in: Ulrich Großmann, Petra Krutisch (eds.), *2. Congress Proceedings* (2013), pp. 528–532.
9 P.P. Caproni & Brother, *Catalogue of Plaster Reproductions from Antique, Medieval and Modern Sculpture Subjects for Art Schools* (Boston (Mass.): Caproni, 1911).
10 Georges Didi-Huberman, 'Der Abdruck als Paradigma. Eine Archäologie der Ähnlichkeit', *Ähnlichkeit und Berührung. Archäologie, Anachronismus und Modernität des Abdrucks* (Köln: Dumont Literatur und Kunst Verlag, 1999), pp. 14–69. Quoted in Falser, op. cit. (note 8), p. 10.
11 Maria Tymoczko, Edwin Gentzler (eds.), *Translation and Power* (Amherst: University of Massachusetts Press, 2002), xxi. Quoted in Falser, op. cit. (note 8), p. 8.
12 David Owen, *Copies in Seconds: How a Lone Inventor and an Unknown Company Created the Biggest Communication Breakthrough Since Gutenberg — Chester Carlson and the Birth of Xerox* (Simon & Schuster, 2004).
13 Hélène Jannière and France Vanlaethem, 'Architectural Magazine as Historical Source or Object? A Methodological Essay', *Revues d'architecture dans les années 1960 et 1970 fragments d'une histoire événementielle, intellectuelle et matérielle; actes du colloque international tenu les 6 et 7 mai 2004 au Centre Canadien d'Architecture à Montreal* = Architectural periodicals in the 1960s and 1970s sous la direction d'Alexis Sornin, Hélène Jannière et France Vanlaethem (Montréal: Institut de recherche en histoire de l'architecture, 2008), p. 41 and Beatriz Colomina, Craig Buckley, and Urtzi Grau, *Clip, Stamp, Fold: The Radical Architecture of Little Magazines, 196X to 197X* (Barcelona, Spain: Actar, 2010).
14 Online. Available http; http://www.larchitecturedaujourdhui.fr/AAS-HISTORY/?LANG=EN (accessed 9 April 2019).
15 Hélène Jannière. 'La critique architectural à la recherche de ses instruments: *L'Architecture d'Aujourd'hui* et Architecture Mouvement Continuité, 1960–1974', *Revues d'architecture dans les années 1960 et 1970,* p. 272.
16 Joëlle Deyres, 'Les correspondants à l'étranger de *L'Architecture d'Aujourd'hui* et l'information sur l'actualité internationale de l'architecture (1930–1950)', in: Monnier, Gérard, Vovelle, José (eds.), *Un art sans frontières: L'internationalization des arts en Europe (1900–1950)* (Paris: Éditions de la Sorbonne, 1995), pp. 197–206. Online. Available http: http://books.openedition.org/psorbonne/457 (accessed 28 August 2024).
17 Ibid., paragraph 12.
18 Ibid., paragraphs 15–16. Regarding CIAM and UIA, see Eric Mumford, *The CIAM Discourse on Urbanism, 1928–1960* (Cambridge: MIT Press, 2000), pp. 168, 313–314.
19 See Hélène Jannière, 'Distilled Avant-Garde Echoes: Word and Image in Architectural Periodicals of the 1920s and 1930s', *Architectural Histories*, 4(1): 21 (2016), p. 12. Online. Available http: http://dx.doi.org/10.5334/ah.211 (accessed 27 August 2024).
20 Gilles Ragot, 'Pierre Vago et les débuts de *L'Architecture d'Aujourd'hui* 1930–1940', *Revue de l'Art*, jg. 89, No. 89, 1990, pp. 77–81.

21 Marcel Vellinga, '"How Other Peoples Dwell and Build": Erwin Anton Gutkind and the Architecture of the Other', *Journal of the Society of Architectural Historians*, 2019, 78 (4), pp. 409–421.
22 Lydia Kallipoliti, 'The Soft Cosmos of 2's 'Cosmorama' in the 1960s and 1970s', *Architectural Design*, No. 208, 2010, p.40.
23 Jean-Nicolas-Louis Durand, *Précis des leçons d'architecture données à l'école polytechnique*, 2 Vol. (Paris: École Polytechnique, 1809); Josef Durm et al., *Handbuch der Architektur* (Leipzig, 1880–1943). For a bibliography, see Roland Jaeger, 'Monumentales Standardwerk: Das "Handbuch der Architektur" (1880–1943): Verlagsgeschichte und Bibliographie', *Aus dem Antiquariat* (2006), pp. 343–364.
24 Ernst Neufert, *Bauentwurfslehre* (Berlin: Bauwelt-Verlag, 1936).
25 Neufert taught at the Staatliche Bauhochschule in Weimar, which was founded in 1926. During his teaching experience he formalized 'his own information-centred design model, called "Schnellentwerfen" or "rapid design", [which] specifically involved training students in visualizing and solving any given architectural problem quickly and efficiently.' Nader Vossoughian, 'Standardization Reconsidered: Normierung in and after Ernst Neufert's Bauentwurfslehre (1936),' *Grey Room*, No. 54 (2014), pp. 39–40.
26 Ibid., p. 37.
27 'If the importance of an architect equals the extent to which his work lives on in others, Neufert is the most important of the twentieth century. ... Neufert is everywhere.' Reiner de Graaf, *Four Walls and a Roof: The Complex Nature of a Simple Profession* (Cambridge, London: Harvard University Press, 2017), pp. 55–61.
28 Ibid., p. 43.
29 Ibid., p. 46.
30 'Man shapes his surroundings. In them he moves as a physical being. They must therefore be adapted to his dimensions. The ideal would be to assign each individual an environment adapted to his body. However, this ideal is generally unrealizable for various reasons', 'German Standards Committee, Berlin, March 1936', Neufert, *Bauentwurfslehre* (Berlin: Bauwelt-verlag SW68, 1936), p. 5.
31 Mario Ridolfi, 'Il Manuale dell'Architetto', *Metron* 8 (1946), p. 36.
32 Mario Ridolfi, ibid., p. 36. Regarding Zevi and transatlantic Italy, see Paolo Scrivano, *Building Transatlantic Italy: Architectural Dialogues with Postwar America*, (Burlington: Ashgate Publishing Co., 2013).
33 The 'Irresistible Empire'—the USA—was engaged in 'the struggle for the peaceful [commercial] conquest of the world,' as President Woodrow Wilson claimed as early as 1916. President Woodrow Wilson, Detroit, 10 July 1916 in Victoria de Grazia, *Irresistible Empire: America's Advance Through Twentieth-Century Europe* (Cambridge, MA: Harvard University Press, 2005), p. 1.
34 'James Linen del gruppo Time Inc. plana a Roma, in qualità di "Specialist Assistant to the Director, Office of War Information". Persuaso che "vendere gli Stati Uniti o la democrazia" equivalga a smerciare la Coca-Cola o i settimanali Life e Time, fonda l'United States Information Service. Approccio manageriale. "Cosa divolo bisogna fare in questo paese?".' Bruno Zevi, *Zevi su Zevi Architettura come profezia* (Milano: Magma, 1977), p. 54.
35 The publication's organizing committee consisted of Professor Gustavo Colonnetti (president), the engineer Pier Luigi Nervi, the architect Bruno Zevi, the engineer Biagio Bongioannini (Bongiovannini), and the architect Mario Ridolfi. Three young architects undertook the editing: Cino Calcaprina, Aldo Cardelli, and Mario Fiorentino. Another collaborator was Caterina Corti from CNR. See Ridolfi, op. cit. (note 31), p. 41.
36 Manfredo Tafuri, *Storia dell'Architettura Italiana 1944–1985* (Torino: Einaudi, 1982), p. 19. Muratore emphasizes that Ridolfi was the manual's most significant author. See Giorgio Muratore, 'L'esperienza del manuale', *Controspazio* VI, 1, September 1974, p. 82.
37 Online. Available https: https://www.peanuts.com/ (accessed 9 April 2019).
38 See Lynn Spigel, *Welcome to the Dreamhouse: Popular Media and Postwar Suburbs* (Durham and London: Duke University Press, 2001).
39 Ibid., p.249.
40 Ibid., pp. 222, 224.
41 See De Grazia, op. cit. (note 33).
42 Lynn Spigel, op. cit. (note 38), p. 252.
43 'Cinema provided this "irrational" medium, allowing directors the liberty to portray a form of reality that was distorted, whether for comic effect or due to artistic licence.' Ravi Hensman, 'Oracles of Suburbia: French Cinema and Portrayals of Paris Banlieues, 1958–1998', *Modern & Contemporary France*, 21:4 (2013), p. 447. Online. Available doi: 10.1080/09639489.2013.802681 (accessed 22 August 2024).
44 'Sarcellite': from Sarcelles, a dormitory suburb in Paris. '... an illness equated with the concrete gigantism and poor living conditions of the HLM (*habitat à loyer*

modéré)', Eleonore Kofman, 'Suburb', in: Alexandra Hughes, Alex Hughes, Keith A Reader, Keith Reader (eds.), *Encyclopedia of Contemporary French Culture* (London, New York: Routledge, 1998), p. 512; '... a media-coined term for the social pathology of grand ensemble living', Hensman, op. cit. (note 43), p. 444.

45 See Hensman, op. cit. (note 43), p. 441.
46 Ibid.
47 Godard's *Deux ou Trois Choses que Je Sais d'Elle* has been often credited as the first film to be partially set in the new development of Paris's outer *banlieues*.
48 'Le rôle de Godard', *Internationale Situationniste,* No. 10 (Paris, March 1966). Online. Available http: http://www.bopsecrets.org/SI/10.godard.htm (accessed 8 April 2019).
49 Isabelle Chaise, 'Paris Rediscovering Jacques Tati', *Blueprint*, No. 281 (August 2009), p. 21.

5 Construction: New Materials, Methods, and Systems for Building

Michelangelo Sabatino

Fig. 5.1
Habitat '67 under construction, Montreal (Moshe Safdie with John B. Parkin; engineer: August Komendant, 1964–1967).

> We live in a glass-soaked civilisation, but ... the substance is almost invisible to us. To use a metaphor drawn from glass, it may be revealing for us to re-focus, to stop looking through glass, and let our eyes dwell on it for a moment to contemplate its wonder.
> — Alan Macfarlane and Gerry Martin, *Glass: A World History*[1]

> In short, all the elements of a structure in reinforced concrete have some static or construction suggestion to propose, which can be transformed into a model of expressive aesthetic appearance and shape.
> — Pier Luigi Nervi, *Aesthetics and Technology in Building*[2]

The realization of new building types associated with the increased mobility that contributed to the Global Turn from 1945 to 1989 was supported by an increasingly complex circulation of materials and systems as well as the emergence of new methods of building.

Within this evolving scenario of transnational exchanges in knowhow and products, reinforced concrete and glass (in the form of curtain walls and various other products) played an important role in both aesthetic and technical terms. Prefabricated ('travelling') technologies and the increased capacity to transport (by air, ship, train, or truck) products manufactured in one country to building sites in another led to accelerated building timelines but also infused traditional know-how and reliance upon locally sourced materials with innovative approaches to manufacturing and installation.[3] The new mechanisms by which building elements and systems travelled across various cultural geographies had a substantial impact on architects' working methods as well as on the construction trade and contractors.[4] Understanding the history of construction and the collaboration that developed between architects and engineers from 1945 to 1989 will help us understand the image and substance of modern and contemporary architecture and the city during this period[5] and permit the telling of a complex, multi-disciplinary history of the Global Turn as it relates to the built environment.[6]

→ Figs. 5.1–4

New Materials, Methods, and Systems for Building

Fig. 5.2
Salone B exhibition hall (Pier Luigi Nervi, 1947–1954),
Turin, Italy, 1951.
Fig. 5.3
Pennsylvania Turnpike, newly completed dual carriageway,
1 January 1955.

5 Construction

Fig. 5.4
World Trade Center under construction, New York,
1 Janary 1972.

Fig. 5.5
Canadian government grain elevator at Ogden, Calgary, Alberta (1911; now demolished). Illustration in Le Corbusier's *Vers une architecture* (Paris, 1923).

Fig. 5.6
Installation of prefabricated reinforced-concrete beams at a Soviet-era steel plant in Dunaújváros, Hungary, 1951.

Fig. 5.7
Installation of concrete prefabricated panels for housing in Geuzenveld, Amsterdam, Netherlands, 2 January 1956.

New Materials, Methods, and Systems for Building

Fig. 5.8
Van Nelle Factory, Rotterdam (Leendert van der Vlugt, Johannes Brinkman, Jan Gerko Wiebenga, 1931), 25 March 2017.
Fig. 5.9
Glass curtain wall of workshops, Bauhaus, Dessau (Walter Gropius, 1925–1926).

5 Construction

Fig. 5.10
S. R. Crown Hall (Mies van der Rohe, 1950–1956),
IIT Campus, Chicago, 1969.
Fig. 5.11
860–880 Lake Shore Drive (Ludwig Mies van der Rohe,
1949–1951), Chicago, 1 January 1951.

Fig. 5.12
Lake Point Tower (John Heinrich and George Schipporeit, 1965–1968), Chicago, 1974.

Fig. 5.13
Float glass at Pilkington's glass factory, St Helens, Lancashire, UK, 1944.

Fig. 5.14
Advertisement for Alcoa Aluminium, 1960.

New Materials, Methods, and Systems for Building

Fig. 5.15
Alcoa Building (Harrison & Abramovitz, 1953), Pittsburgh, US, 26 April 2018.

Theorizing Concrete

As 'a child of the age that created the League of Nations' and '[a witness of] transoceanic flights', concrete shared with other media and practices of the Global Turn a ubiquitous role in the twentieth century.[7] From its functional 'noble savagery'[8] in silos, mills, reservoirs, and grain stores — so deeply admired and advocated for by architects such as Walter Gropius and Le Corbusier[9] — to its more emblematic, sculptural resonance in the work of the modernist avant-garde, concrete assumed the role of 'trademark of the new architecture' even before the twentieth century began.[10]

→ Fig. 5.5

Discovered by the Romans and then largely forgotten until it emerged as the material most emblematic of modernity, concrete is 'a material without a history'.[11] Paradoxically, it is both one of 'the oldest of all building methods and, at the same time ... one of the most modern',[12] as highlighted by the French architect Auguste Perret, a pioneer of modern reinforced-concrete buildings.[13] As the British historian Adrian Forty reminds us, this paradox of old material and modern building was addressed for the first time in post-war Italy, where historical reminiscences of the material overlapped with the exigencies of the day in a theoretical continuity of the kind described by the Italian architect and critic Ernesto Nathan Rogers.[14]

Besides this idiosyncratic overlap, reinforced concrete lent itself to a new international construction method and embodied an architectural 'esprit nouveau' which encouraged the development of an international style in contrast with other, regional and local, forms of construction.[15] In fact, as a global standard construction material, concrete fostered adventurous experimentation by the modernist avant-garde in various contexts throughout the globe: the International Style was an umbrella which provided opportunities for hybridization involving different local materials, functions, and uses. 'The power and, with it, the economy of reinforced concrete ...,' wrote the French critic Marie Dormoy in 1923, 'will make it universal and create a universal style.'[16] In the period from 1945 to 1989 the so-called 'International Style' was often conflated with modernism and often challenged. Walter Gropius, like many of the protagonists of this style, understood it not as a static set of principles but as an evolving approach based on a shared understanding of 'universal technical achievements'.[17] A static definition of the International Style was also rejected by the Swiss architect, historian, and critic Sigfried Giedion, who wrote in *A Decade of New Architecture,* published in 1951:

> Since around 1900, when F. L. Wright adapted the free ground plan of early American tradition to modern needs, the single-family house has everywhere provided the greatest range of opportunity for modern architects and has given rise to many of the best examples of contemporary architecture. Even a few examples are enough to show the wide variety of ways in which a common vocabulary has been employed in different regions — extending from Finland to South America, and it is to be hoped that the unfortunate and misleading designation of an 'International Style' will now finally disappear.[18]

The universal spread of reinforced concrete was mainly due to the duality of its essence. Reinforced concrete was a process rather than just a material.[19] As well as possessing weight and corporeal presence, 'concrete is theorized', as the French scholar Cyrille Simonnet has put it.[20]

Its existence is dependent on a conceptual model and a formula which determine its chemical and physical composition and the process which transforms and combines sand, gravel, and cement into concrete and, with the addition of steel, into reinforced concrete.[21] As both a 'theory' and a process, reinforced concrete is a non-natural, ambiguous material whose existence, dimensions, and composition are directly dependent on the synergy between steel and concrete and on theorized formulas that have been calculated beforehand.[22] This '"mongrel" material, neither one thing nor another', as the American architect Frank Lloyd Wright called it in 1928,[23] circulated in the world not as a physical entity but as intellectual property — in the form of technical and commercial patents which obliged contractors worldwide to diligently follow prescribed procedures under a licensed system of concrete construction.[24]

The first registered patent for reinforced concrete came in the late nineteenth century and was the result of pioneering work by the entrepreneur François Hennebique (1842–1921).

A Belgian contractor, Hennebique started experimenting with reinforced concrete in 1879, developing a method in which reinforcement is used for maximum bending moments, which range from the bottom of the midspan of a beam to the top of a beam over a support. The column is rigidly connected to the beams and slab, so no bracing is necessary. After patenting his technique for decks with reinforced-concrete beams in 1897, Hennebique set up his own company. His patent method was used in various types of built structure from bridges to silos, apartment blocks, and industrial buildings. In just a few years the company entered markets and distributed its technique in countries on several continents. In 1905, even though Hennebique was up against competition for patents, he owned one fifth of the world market in construction in reinforced concrete.[25]

Interestingly, Hennebique's work was focused not on contracting but on the design of reinforced-concrete structures, built by licensed dealers.[26] 'Hennebique n'est pas entrepreneur' ('Hennebique is not an entrepreneur') was written under the brand name Hennebique in the 1920s and 1930s,[27] underlining the unconventional role played by the firm, which relied on a complex international organization and a network of entrepreneurs, dealers, and agents. This was a concentrated but distributed organization which underwent rapid worldwide growth: the company's main office — *'le bureau d'etudes'* in Paris — was focused on controlling design of the reinforced-concrete structures, while Hennebique's dealers and affiliated building firms executed and oversaw construction of individual projects.

Hennebique's technical knowledge, which was protected and diffused through a legal patent, was spread through the world using propaganda tools. Hennebique founded the *Congrès Internationaux du béton armé* and edited the journal *Le Béton armé* (1898–1939), which competed with traditional architecture magazines by publishing technical and artistic comments on architecture in concrete structures.[28] *Le Béton armé* was conceived as an open 'mutual teaching body' not only for dealers and agents but also for all who were interested in this construction system.[29] The universal application of the new Hennebique method was promoted through texts and images rather than direct experience. Propelled by its transnational publicity machine, Hennebique activated new forms of collaboration between architects, engineers, and builders within a brand-new system of global circulation of technical knowledge.

Prefab Concrete

Post-war Europe faced an enormous and pressing need for cheap new housing at a time when there was a lack of building materials and skilled labour. In 1950s France construction of new housing units increased from 90,000 in 1952 to 320,000 in 1959.[30] These conditions favoured the rise of innovative methods of construction using *béton*: concrete began to be 'assembled' rather than 'poured'.[31] Instead of being fabricated in the traditional manner directly on site, the concrete architectural elements were prefabricated in a factory before being transported to the construction site and assembled there. In many new buildings the same construction procedure was innovatively employed throughout despite differences in functions, dimensions, and positions. The advantage of this 'heavy prefab' system was reduction of costs and time since it was now possible to condense most of the work in a single factory capable of serving an entire region or city. The standardized elements enabled a building to be erected more rapidly and using a less specialized workforce.[32] This mechanical system relying on standardization and repetition was much influenced by Henry's Ford's methods of mechanized production. As the British historian Nicholas Bullock has pointed out, these influences were fostered and broadcast by journals with strong affinities with the modern movement — e.g. *L'Architecture d'Aujourd'hui* and *Techniques et Architecture*. Here again we see the post-war role of magazines in influencing, directing, and propelling diverse cultural exchange.[33]

One of the pioneers of prefabrication was the French engineer Raymond Camus (1911–1980), who developed and patented in 1948 one of the first and most successful factory-based closed systems of concrete prefabrication and construction. Like Hennebique's technique for use of reinforced concrete, Camus's heavy prefabrication system became well known around the world. By the mid-1960s Camus had opened six factories in France and another 16 in other countries, including Germany, Italy, the United Kingdom, Russia, and Algeria — making his approach's popularity and success truly international.[34] In parallel, other heavy prefab and industrialized building methods were developed in France[35] and other countries — including the UK, Germany, the United States, Scandinavia, and Eastern Europe — with

different compositions of materials, types of contraction joint, dimensions of elements, and so on. In France the pioneering Camus system was first tested on a large scale by the French Ministry of Reconstruction and Urbanism (MRU) in the '4000 logements de la Région Parisienne' ('4000 housing units for the Paris Region') programme, announced in 1952. This programme provided 4000 new dwellings in neighbourhoods of different sizes, including in *grandes ensembles* located in the inner Paris suburbs. The French architect Marcel Lods, a member of CIAM (Congrès Internationaux d'Architecture Moderne) and ASCORAL (Association pour une Rénovation Architecturale), was one of the designers involved, a sign of the widespread interest in, and influence of, the modernist functionalist/technological avant-garde.[36]
→ Figs. 5.6–7

Despite the successes celebrated by Camus — such as a halving of construction times and a 10 per cent reduction in costs — the system had shortcomings which became problematic, as was the case with other systems of prefabrication in Europe in the mid-1960s.[37] Technological issues, such as waterproofing of construction elements, emerged, and maintenance costs turned out to be higher than in traditional construction, while construction costs were rarely lower.[38] More importantly, this repetitive construction system could not respond to the typological and social variety desired by both designers and society — a criticism later expressed by the French film director Jean-Luc Godard in his *Cité des 4000*. Finally, prefabrication posed a challenge to the role of the architect as *genius operandi*: architects now had to subordinate their design knowledge and perspectives to the contingencies and necessities of industrialization: 'we must take into account this imperative or change professions!', Lods himself provocatively claimed.[39]

Circulation of the Façade

The curtain wall, from avant-garde to vernacular
The Crystal Palace, built in London for the Great Exhibition of 1851, may be seen as one of the first pieces of architecture to have driven the extensive circulation of large numbers of goods. The UN Headquarters in New York, meanwhile, is a pivotal example of international collaboration in global transfer of professional knowledge. Both buildings have an important place in the history

of architecture, including in the discourse of technological transfer of knowledge, in particular as regards the use of glass.

Whereas the UN Headquarters (1948–1952) saw the first use of a glass curtain wall in a skyscraper in New York City, the pioneering glass architecture of the Crystal Palace has inspired the architectural imagination ever since.[40] However, the use of glass in both buildings is not enough to give them a common genealogy in the technological progress of the curtain wall. As made clear by David Yeomans, the original meaning of 'curtain wall' is 'a continuous curtain masonry penetrated by windows'.[41] Whereas the Crystal Palace adopted an innovative technology to construct a glazed roof, the curtain wall is instead the child of an innovative extension of the window; it is vertical as opposed to horizontal.[42] Furthermore, although Joseph Paxton's glass palace greatly influenced architects' imaginations in later design of glass buildings, serving as the principal reference for all subsequent expressions of Paul Scheerbart's *Glasarchitektur*, the modern development of the curtain wall is grounded more in technological innovation than conceptual architectural creation. Development of the curtain wall sprang from a *raison d'être* that was more technical and functional than artistic; the principal motivation was to provide better light and increase internal floor space.

This means that the precursors of the modern curtain wall are to be found more in anonymous, 'more prosaic … modern factories' than in architectural icons.[43] The first approaches made by modernist masters to the all-glass curtain were in industrial buildings such as the AEG Turbine Factory (designed by the German architect Peter Behrens, Berlin, 1909) and the Fagus Factory (designed by the German architects Walter Gropius and Adolf Meyer, Alfeld, Germany, 1911). After these first experiments, both of which proposed the use of discontinuous glass elements between the structural elements on their façades, continuous glazing became a mainstream idea in modernist architectural circles, embodying and mirroring the most essential features of the International Style, faith in technology, and the spirit of the age.

In Rotterdam, a city which pioneered glazing of large building surfaces,[44] the Van Nelle Factory (1925–1931), designed by the Dutch architects Johannes Brinkman and Leendert van der Vlugt, has a façade with an innovative continuity of glass. The continuous expanses of glazing sprang from the humanitarian, hygienic, and functionalist concerns shared by the architect and the entrepreneur in their desire to build an ideal 'daylight factory' in which natural illumination would reach all the working spaces, ensuring light, air, and hygiene for all the workers. The technological innovation embodied in the glazed curtain wall would have had a positive effect on social relationships in the working environment, as originally envisaged by the philosopher and artist Kees van der Leeuw, who first conceived the idea for this building.[45] In other words, this icon of modernism was important testimony to both the technological progress represented by the curtain wall and its direct social and humanitarian implications. The dual technological and social innovation in the Van Nelle Factory even marked 'the beginning of a new era in twentieth-century urban planning, as it moved towards [an idea of] the "open city"':[46] the curtain wall was adopted as a tool of democratization and socialization, a threshold between the private interior of the factory and the external public realm of the city.

→ Fig. 5.8

In the Bauhaus building at Dessau (1925–1926) Walter Gropius used an uninterrupted curtain wall over three floors. This building embodies the new idea of unity of art and technology proclaimed at the Bauhaus Exhibition in Weimar in 1923. The use of the glazed wall here emphasized transparency and the mechanical nature of architecture, as professed by the Bauhaus, but was also imbued with a pedagogical purpose, creating a new and ground-breaking relationship between external landscape and interior learning space.

→ Fig. 5.9

Finally, another Bauhaus educator, the German architect Mies van der Rohe, elevated the glazed architecture of the curtain wall to its poetical zenith. The idea of a glazed building at its purest was first revealed in Mies's famous sketches for the Friedrichstrasse skyscraper and for department stores on Alexanderplatz in Berlin in the 1920s. The oneiric and ethereal impression made by the new glazed walls foreshadowed the later aloofness and minimalism of Mies's curtain wall, in particular in his late American period, when the curtain wall became a repetitive, neutralizing skin exuding a sense of institutional engagement in cultivating civility, uniformity, and technology as an expression of human civilization and life. The result was a unified language or vocabulary which in his buildings was continuously refined and often repeated with small but important variations, in the same way that a musical score is subject to continual reinterpretation. Mies' generalized language, the need he felt to impersonalize a building as an expression of the age rather than of individual subjectivity, was thus perfectly embodied by the curtain wall. The latter now gradually started to circulate across the globe, becoming part of common everyday architectural practice. After playing a key role in the avant-garde experiments of the modernist masters, it found its way into 'vernacular architecture', as noted by the British critic Ian McCallum in the late 1950s:

> The pioneers of the modern movement saw the industrialization of architecture as the concomitant of a planned economy, but the curtain wall is the product of industrialization in a free one. It offers the promise — and the problems — of a new architectural vernacular; its mullions, transoms, and spandrels could be the syntax of a common mode of expression that was neither bombastic nor inarticulate, and might occasionally rise to eloquence, as the 'classic' examples already do.[47]
> → Figs. 5.10–12

This global vernacularism of the curtain wall was a development that was made possible not only by the worldwide influence of modernist architecture but also by technological innovations which exploited a revolution in building construction. The centres of these innovations were in Britain and America, where respectively the Pilkington Glass Company pursued walls of smooth glass and the Alcoa Company developed metal-panel walls.[48]

Float glass
The global circulation of the curtain wall was assured by the spread of pioneering inventions and new technologies such as float glass, a new process developed by the British engineer Alastair Pilkington for the glass manufacturer Pilkington Brothers (no relation) in order to produce very large, uniform glass surfaces at an affordable cost.

Float-glass technology replaced the traditional operations of rolling, grinding, and polishing glass that had previously been used in earlier methods for creating crown, cylinder, and finally drawn sheet glass. The new process produced high-quality, inexpensive flat glass, reducing the disadvantages of the previous processes in terms of costs, glass wastage, dimensions, and distortions. The so-called 'Pilkington process' relies on a system by which glass is melted inside a furnace and floated over the surface of an enclosed bath of molten tin inside a chemically controlled atmosphere.[49] After transatlantic collaborations in research, including with the American Ford company,[50] and the spending of 'seven years and four million pounds to make any saleable glass and a total of seven million pounds before the process [could be refined]', the chemical float process was licenced to numerous manufacturers around the world from the 1950s forwards.

'Together they are turning out about 100 square kilometres of glass a year. The Americans are using it, and the Russians are using it,' claimed Alastair Pilkington in 1969 while asserting a global dependence on his system that went behind any Cold War boundaries. He saw an opportunity for the company to attain a global outreach including not only the superpowers of America and the USSR but also countries such as 'Japan, Canada, France, Germany, Belgium, Italy, Spain, Czechoslovakia and Mexico. In fact every major flat glass manufacturer in the world has a licence.'[51]
→ Fig. 5.13

During the 1960s and 1970s the Pilkington Glass Company invested in float-glass plants in 30 countries worldwide. By 1975 float-glass plants would account for 97 per cent of all plate-glass plants worldwide — making Pilkington's float glass one of the greatest and most widely used innovations in the history of the glass industry. Like reinforced concrete, this globally employed technological invention also propelled progress in architectural design and innovation, influencing the development and improvement of architectural typologies. Pilkington's float-glass process contributed to the emergence of new architectural solutions, such as the glass curtain wall, which in turn gave rise to new building typologies, including the glazed office tower.

Mies van der Rohe's Seagram Building (New York, 1958), Arne Jacobsen's SAS Hotel (Copenhagen, 1955–1960), Gio Ponti's Pirelli Building (Milan, 1956), and Arturo Mezzedimi's Africa Hall (Addis Ababa, Ethiopia, 1962) are only a few examples of how float glass as an architectural technology influenced the emergence of the curtain glass wall.

Aluminium

While in Britain Pilkington Brothers was working to improve production of floating glass, opening up new possibilities for use of 'glass walls' in architecture, in the US a new technology was emerging that made it possible to create metal 'panel walls' with inset windows.

The watershed example of this technology was the ALCOA (Aluminium Company of America) headquarters in Pittsburgh (architects: Harrison and Abramovitz; 1951–1953), regarded as the first skyscraper with an all-aluminium façade or a façade that made extensive use of aluminium. The building's 31 floors were completely filled with storey-height panels containing the windows. The panels concealed from sight all the structural vertical and horizontal joints, giving the skyscraper the overall look of an aluminium envelope with a minimalist-repetitive pattern whose effect, according to Ian McCallum, was 'to blur and "soft-focus" the precision-made look' that was typical of the curtain wall.[52] In addition to its architectural effects, at the dawn of the 1950s the ALCOA building served as a highly successful manifesto and advertisement for the uses and marketability of the material that the company was itself trading and producing — aluminium.[53]

→ Figs. 5.14–15

Development of the technology required for large-scale industrial production of aluminium began only at the end of the nineteenth century, when the recently graduated engineer Charles Martin Hall in the USA and, at about the same time, the engineer Paul T. Heroult in France both discovered the electrolytic process for producing aluminium, which in 1889 they secured under patent rights respectively in the USA and in Europe.[54]

Before these patents and the start of modern industrial production that followed, aluminium had been so expensive and so valuable that Napoleon III's most honoured guests had supposedly even been given forks and spoons of aluminium to eat with rather than of gold or silver. Only through mass production did the cost of aluminium steadily fall, opening up new possibilities for the construction sector. The metal's lower production costs and favourable physical characteristics boosted its use in construction in the post-war years. Aluminium became highly appreciated for its truly versatile and adaptable character with many advantages in terms of cost, fabrication, transportation and installation (thanks to its low weight), maintenance (due to its corrosion resistance), and the potential reuse value of windows made from it. After World War II its diffusion was so rapid that while in 1949 only five per cent of all windows were made of aluminium, in 1952 its use in them had increased to 25 per cent. Interestingly, this growth in the use of aluminium derived from its employment as an interfacing material in a wide range of industrial sectors, thanks to its high mechanical performance and reliability in production. In particular, the extensive use of aluminium in experiments and the aircraft industry resulted in a proliferation of scientific-engineering data and know-how which was later transferred to the civil construction sector. Aluminium's use in a broad range of spheres, from airframe solutions to skyscraper curtain walls, showed exceptional inter-sectorial transfer of knowledge. During World War II approximately 80 per cent of the total output of aluminium was used for military aircraft production. Some of the companies that produced American and British aluminium aircraft under licence during the war, such as the Overseas Corporation Aluminium (OCAL) in Australia, became influential in this exceptional cross-transfer of technical knowledge.

Once aluminium had been adopted in the construction industry, a broad range of architectural elements were made with it, including windows and doors, decorative materials, and heating/air conditioning installations. Construction was affected worldwide, especially with the spread of the new 'vernacular' type of curtain wall.

The Circulation of Materials and Technologies

The global transfer of new materials, methods, and systems for building had significant effects on the architect's role and on construction. In some of the most fascinating developments, this transfer of knowledge did not involve the moving of materials but their 'theorization' in the form of intellectual property, technical and commercial patents and licences, conceptual models, and scientific formulae, as was the case with, for instance, Hennebique's reinforced concrete, Camus's prefabrication system, Pilkington's float glass, and Heroult's aluminium. Magazines and journals too played a key role in spreading the new technological knowledge. Hennebique's system was promoted through his own journal *Le Béton armé*; industrialization/prefabrication in architecture was popularized by *L'Architecture d'Aujourd'hui*. The various materials and technological innovations that circulated on a global scale following the end of World War II found their way into everyday practice and urban experience as a contemporary global 'vernacular' and 'a syntax of a common mode of expression'.[55]

1   Alan Macfarlane and Gerry Martin, *Glass: A World History* (Chicago: The University of Chicago Press, 2002), p. 4.
2   Pier Luigi Nervi, *Aesthetics and Technology in Building* (Cambridge, MA: Harvard University Press, 1965; Reprint, Urbana: University of Illinois Press, 2018), Chapter 3, p. 115.
3   David Edgerton, *The Shock of the Old: Technology and Global History Since 1900* (Oxford and New York: Oxford University Press, 2007).
4   On impact in America see Grace Palladino, *Skilled Hands, Strong Spirits: A Century of Building Trades History* (Ithaca, N.Y.: Cornell University Press, 2005). See also George Barnett Johnston, *Assembling the Architect. The History and Theory of Professional Practice* (London: Bloomsbury Visual Arts, 2020); Jelena Dobbels, *Building a Profession: A History of General Contractors in Belgium* (Brussels: VUB Press, 2021).
5   See Ulrich Pfammatter, *Building the Future: Building Technology and Cultural History from the Industrial Revolution Until Today* (Munich and New York: Prestel, 2008); William Addis, *Building: 3000 Years of Design Engineering and Construction* (London and New York: Phaidon, 2007), in particular, Chapter 8, 'Architectural Engineering 1920–1960', and Chapter 9, 'The Computer Age and the Greening of Construction, 1960–present'. See also Cecil D. Elliott, *Technics and Architecture* (Cambridge, MA: The MIT Press, 1992).
6   Eve Darian-Smith and Philip C. McCarty, *The Global Turn: Theories, Research Design, and Methods for Global Studies* (Oakland, California: University of California Press, 2017).
7   'The Ferro-Concrete Style has developed with telegraph and railroad, with motion picture and radio; it is a child of the age that created the League of Nations and witnessed transoceanic flights.' Francis S. Onderdonk, *The Ferro-Concrete Style* (New York: Architectural Book, 1928), p. 255. Quoted in Adrian Forty, *Concrete and Culture: A Material History* (London: Reaktion Books, 2012), p. 13.
8   Reyner Banham, *A Concrete Atlantis* (Cambridge: MIT Press, 1986), p. 15; Forty, op. cit. (note 7), p. 23.
9   See Le Corbusier, *Vers une architecture* (Paris, Éditions Crès, 1923); Walter Gropius, *Jahrbuch Des Deutschen Werkbundes* (Jena: Eugen Diederichs, 1913).
10 Sigfried Giedion, *Space, Time and Architecture: The Growth of a New Tradition* (Cambridge, London: Harvard University Press, 1941; 5th edition, 2009), p. 322.
11 Adrian Forty, 'A Material Without a History', in: Jean-Louis Cohen, Martin Moeller (eds.), *Liquid Stone: New Architecture in Concrete* (Princeton Architectural Press: New York, 2006), pp. 34–45.
12 Ibid., p. 39; Auguste Perret, undated manuscript in the Perret archives; Karla Britton, *Auguste Perret* (London: Phaidon, 2001), p. 244.
13 Peter Collins, *Concrete: The Vision of a New Architecture. A Study of Auguste Perret and His Precursors* (London: Faber & Faber, 1959) (2nd edition, Montreal and Ithaca: McGill-Queens University Press, 2004).
14 'It was only in post-war Italy that the fact that concrete had a past as well as a future was seriously addressed for the first time.' Forty, op. cit. (note 11), p. 39. Ernesto N. Rogers, *Auguste Perret* (Milano: Il Balcone, 1955).
15 'Si tratta esclusivamente in questo caso di costruzioni da realizzare in cemento armato; vengono quindi concepite delle forme che scaturiscono dalla retta, dall'angolo retto, dalla vertical, dall'orizzontale, arte eminentemente ortogonale.' Le Corbusier, 'L'exposition Spéciale d'Arhitecture', *L'Esprit Nouveau*, No. 23, May 1924. Quoted in Réjean Legault, 'Il materiale e la modernità', in: *Cemento armato: ideologie e forme da Hennebique a Hilberseimer, Rassegna* 49/1 (March 1992), pp. 58–65, 60.
16 'La potenza e, con essa, l'economia del cemento armato lo renderà universale e creerà uno stile universale.' Réjean Legault, op. cit. (note 15), p. 61.
17 Walter Gropius, *Scope of Total Architecture* (New York: Collier, 1962), p. 14: 'I want to rip off at least one of the misleading labels that I and others have been decorated with. There is no such thing as an "International Style," unless you want to speak of certain universal technical achievements in our period which belong to the intellectual equipment of every civilized nation, or unless you want to speak of those pale examples of what I call "applied archeology," which you find among the public buildings from Moscow to Madrid to Washington. Steel or concrete skeletons, ribbon windows, slabs cantilevered or wings hovering on stilts are but impersonal contemporary means — the raw stuff, so to speak — with which regionally different architectural manifestations can be created. The constructive achievements of the Gothic period — its vaults, arches, buttresses and pinnacles — similarly became a common international experience. Yet, what a great

18 Sigfried Giedion, *A Decade of New Architecture* (Zurich: Editions Girsberger, 1951), p. 65.
19 At least until the adoption of government standards in 1906, when the new regulations restricted the domination of the patented building systems and 'transformed both the perception and use of reinforced concrete. It is during this period that reinforced concrete became, simply, a new "material".' Réjean Legault, 'Reviewed Work(s): Gwenaël Delhumeau. *L'invention du Béton Armé. Hennebique, 1890–1914'*, *Journal of the Society of Architectural Historians*, Vol. 60, No. 4 (Dec. 2001), pp. 525–528. See Gwenaël Delhumeau, *L'invention du Béton Armé. Hennebique, 1890–1914* (Paris: Éditions Norma, 1999).
20 'Il calcestruzzo è teorizzato.' Cyrille Simonnet, 'Alle origini del cemento armato', *Rassegna* 49/1 (*Cemento armato: ideologie e forme da Hennebique a Hilberseimer*) (March 1992), p. 9.
21 Several researchers have stressed that concrete is a process rather than a material. See Adrian Forty: 'Concrete, let us be clear, is not a material. It is a *process*: concrete is made from sand and gravel and cement — but sand and gravel and cement do not make concrete. It is the ingredient of human labour that produces concrete.' Forty, op. cit. (note 7), pp. 35, 37.
22 See also Forty, ibid., p. 51.
23 Frank Lloyd Wright, 1928. Quoted by Forty; ibid., p. 38.
24 Ernest L. Ransome, *Reinforced Concrete Buildings. A Treatise on the History, Patents, Design and Erection of the Principal Parts Entering into a Modern Reinforced Concrete Building* (New York: McGraw-Hill Book Company, 1912). See also David Segal, *One Hundred Patents That Shaped the Modern World* (Oxford: Oxford University Press, 2019).
25 This estimation derives from data given by Hennebique himself. See Gwenaël Delhumeau, *L'invention du Béton Armé. Hennebique, 1890–1914*, p. 102 and p. 311, note 142. Mentioned also in Forty, op. cit. (note 7), p. 18.
26 Forty, ibid.
27 Cyrille Simonnet, *Le Béton, histoire d'un matériau. Économie, technique, architecture* (Paris: éd. Parenthèses, 2005), p. 194.
28 Online. Available https: https://lib.ugent.be/viewer/collection/BetonArme-001#?c=0&m=0&s=0&cv=0&r=0&xywh=-1285%2C-153%2C4578%2C3025 (accessed 22 August 2024).
29 'Pour Hennebique, le journal est avant tout un "organe d'enseignement mutuel" pour les concessionaires et agents de son système mais aussi, voyons large, "pour tous ceux qui, convaincus de l'excellence de ce système, s'intéressent à son développement".' Delhumeau, op. cit. (note 25), p. 186.
30 Jean-Claude Croizé, 'A Time When France Chose to Use Prefabricated Panel Construction Systems: the "4000 Logements de la Région Parisienne" Programme (1952–1958)', *Proceedings of the Second International Congress on Construction History, Queen's College, Cambridge, March 29 – April 2, 2006 (2ICCH)*, p. 878.
31 Yvan Delemontey, 'Le béton assemblé. Formes et figures de la préfabrication en France, 1947–1952', *Histoire urbaine*, Vol. 20, No. 3 (2007), p. 16. Online. Available https: https://doi.org/10.3917/rhu.020.0015 (accessed 22 August 2024).
32 On 'heavy prefab systems' see Stephanie Van de Voorde, Inge Bertels, Ine Wouters, *Post-war building materials in housing in Brussels, 1945–1975* (Brussels: Vrije Universiteit Brussel, 2015). Online. Available http: http://postwarbuildingmaterials.be/material/heavy-prefab-systems/ (accessed 12 November 2019).
33 Nicholas Bullock, '4000 dwellings from a Paris factory: Le procédé Camus and state sponsorship of industrialised housing in the 1950s', *Architectural Research Quarterly*, 13 (1) (2009), pp. 59–72. Online. Available doi: doi.org.10.1017/S1359135509990108 (accessed 22 August 2024).
34 On 'heavy prefab systems' see Stephanie Van de Voorde, Inge Bertels, Ine Wouters, op. cit. (note 32).
35 By, for instance, Coignet, Barets, Cauvet, Estiot, Tracoba, Balency (Balency et Schuhl), and Porte des Lilas.
36 Other architects were Robert Camelot and Jean de Mailly & Bernard Zehrfuss.
37 See Bullock, op. cit. (note 33), p. 69.
38 Bullock, ibid., p. 70.
39 In French: 'Le point de vue des architectes consiste à dire qu'à partir du moment où le problème de l'industrialisation est posé comme une nécessité, le choix ne nous appartient plus; ... Comme on sait très bien que le bâtiment périra ou ne fera plus face à la demande s'il ne s'industrialise pas, nous n'avons pas le choix: il faut tenir compte de cet impératif ou faire un autre métier!' Raymond Camus, 'Fabrication industrielle de huit logements par jour dans la Région Parisienne', *Annales de l'ITBTP*, No. 101 (May 1956), pp. 427–454. Quoted in Delemontey, op. cit. (note 31), p. 38.
40 David Yeomans, 'The pre-history of the curtain wall', *Construction History*,

Vol. 14 (1998), p. 74. See Docomomo-us, 'United Nations Headquarters Campus Renovation of Facades' (April 27, 2017). Online. Available https: https://docomomo-us.org/news/united-nations-headquarters-campus-renovation-of-facades (accessed 4 November 2019).

41 William Aiken Starrett, *Skyscrapers and the Men who Build Them* (New York and London, 1928), p. 1. Quoted in David Yeomans, op. cit. (note 40), p. 59.

42 David Yeomans, 'The Origins of the Modern Curtain Wall', *APT Bulletin*, Vol. 32, No. 1, *Curtain Walls* (2001), p. 16. Online. Available http: http://www.jstor.org/stable/1504688 (accessed 15 September 2014).

43 Ibid., p. 14.

44 'It is often overlooked that the pioneer work in glazing over really large buildings surfaces was done in and around Rotterdam …' Ian McCallum, 'Syntax: the Contribution of the Curtain Wall to a New Vernacular', *The Architectural Review* 121 (May 1957), p. 306.

45 UNESCO, 'Van Nellefabriek (Netherlands)', Dossier 1441, p. 251. Online. Available https: https://whc.unesco.org/en/list/1441/ (accessed 5 November 2019).

46 Ibid., p. 254.

47 Ian McCallum, op. cit. (note 44), p. 299.

48 See David Yeomans, op. cit. (note 40), p. 59.

49 'A continuous ribbon of glass moves out of the melting furnace and floats along the surface of an enclosed bath of molten tin. The ribbon is held in a chemically controlled atmosphere at a high enough temperature for a long enough time for the irregularities to melt out and for the surfaces to become flat and parallel. Because the surface of the molten tin is dead flat, the glass also becomes flat.' L. A. B. Pilkington, 'Review Lecture. The Float Glass Process', *Proceedings of the Royal Society of London. Series A, Mathematical and Physical Sciences*, Vol. 314, No. 1516 (16 December 1969), p. 8.

50 'The first breakthrough came from Ford in America, where it was shown that glass could be rolled continuously. As a result of Pilkington's cooperation with Ford, this discovery was successfully exploited. And after Ford's initial work the major developments in plate glass manufacture came from Britain. We first developed a process which successfully combined a continuous melting furnace with the continuous rolling of a ribbon of glass. This was then sold back to America.' L.A.B. Pilkington, op. cit. (note 49), pp. 5–6.

51 'The basic float process has now been licensed to 15 overseas glass manufacturers and over 20 plants are in operation or under construction. Together they are turning out about 100 square kilometres of glass a year. The Americans are using it and the Russians are using it. So are Japan, Canada, France, Germany, Belgium, Italy, Spain, Czechoslovakia and Mexico. In fact every major flat glass manufacturer in the world has a licence.' L.A.B. Pilkington, ibid., p. 9.

52 Ian McCallum, op. cit. (note 44), p. 319.

53 See David Yeomans, op. cit. (note 40), p. 71.

54 Paul Weidlinger, *Aluminium in Modern Architecture Volume II, Engineering Design and Details* (New York: Reinhold Publishing Corporation, 1956), p. 15.

55 Ian McCallum, op. cit. (note 44), p. 299.

6 Labour: From *Bidonville* to *Ville Nouvelle*

Tom Avermaete

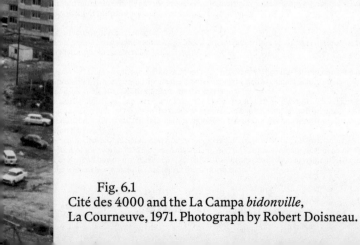

Fig. 6.1
Cité des 4000 and the La Campa *bidonville*,
La Courneuve, 1971. Photograph by Robert Doisneau.

In 1971 the renowned French photographer Robert Doisneau captured a most remarkable image of the municipality of La Courneuve on the periphery of Paris. The background of this photograph shows the new and modern concrete architecture of the 'Cité des 4000', a housing estate that is emblematic of the numerous *grands ensembles* and *villes nouvelles* that were built in France in the 1960s. Initiated by the city of Paris and designed by the architects Clément Tambuté and Henri Delacroix, the Cité des 4000 encompassed four gigantic slabs housing 4000 families that the city centre of Paris was unable to accommodate, including returnees from North Africa.

In the foreground Doisneau exposed another reality equally present on the periphery of Paris: the urban phenomenon of the *bidonville*. Constructed from lightweight materials and without much infrastructure, the *bidonville* known as 'La Campa' was initially built by Roma gypsy families. Originally used as a temporary residence, it soon became a permanent part of the urban landscape, and the municipal authorities closed their eyes to the realities of its daily life. From the mid-1960s onwards, Portuguese people, whether economic immigrants or political exiles, settled *en masse* in La Campa, soon followed by other immigrant labourers coming from Spain, Algeria, Morocco, Tunisia, and Yugoslavia.

In 1966 the *bidonville* of La Campa boasted no fewer than 2600 permanent inhabitants. Doisneau's photograph not only captures the coexistence of two distinct urban realities but also raises the question of urban heritage in the French territory. After all, the *bidonville* of La Campa was not exceptional. On the periphery of Paris, as on the fringes of other major French cities, tens of thousands of immigrant workers lived in *bidonvilles* during the post-war period.[1] Just as at La Courneuve, these *bidonvilles* were often in the direct vicinity of the *villes nouvelles*, the construction sites of the French welfare state where these immigrants worked. Immigrant labourers were key actors in these two urban realities, but the story of their relation to this heritage remains largely untold.

→ Figs. 6.1–2

From *Bidonville* to *Ville Nouvelle*

Fig. 6.2
Gathering of migrant workers in the vicinity of La Défense, Paris. Photograph by Gerald Bloncourt.

Fig. 6.3
North African workers on a construction site in Alsace, France, 1955. Author unknown.

6 Labour

Fig. 6.4
Construction site of the National Centre of Industries and Technologies, near Paris, 17 September 1957.

Fig. 6.5
Bidonville huts in front of the construction site of the Cité du Franc-Moisin, Saint-Denis, early 1970s. Photograph by Pierre Douzenel.

Fig. 6.6
The Nanterre *bidonville* (Rue de La Garenne). Photograph by Jean Pottier.

6 Labour

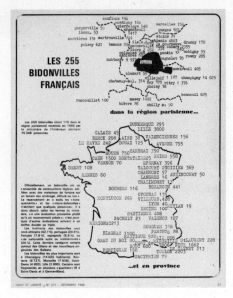

Fig. 6.7
La Campa *bidonville*, La Courneuve, 1967. Photograph by Claude Raimond-Dityvon.

Fig. 6.8
Map of *bidonvilles* surrounding Paris, *Droit & Liberté, Revue mensuelle du Mouvement contre le Racisme, l'Antisémitisme et pour la Paix*, December 1968.

From *Bidonville* to *Ville Nouvelle*

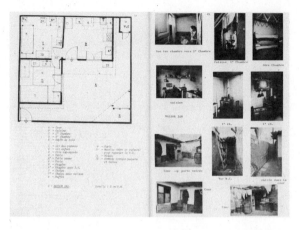

Fig. 6.9
Photographic and drawn survey of the Nanterre *bidonville*, Isabelle Herpin and Serge Santelli, 1968.

Fig. 6.10
Urban plan of the Nanterre *bidonville* with public (black), collective (grey), and private (white) spaces, 1968.

Fig. 6.11
Map of the 'belt' of *bidonvilles* surrounding Paris, *France Soir*, 29 October 1957.

6 Labour

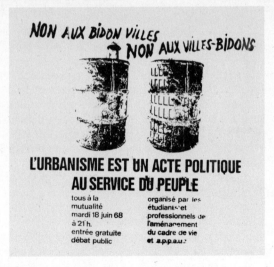

Fig. 6.12
Destruction of a shanty town, La Courneuve
(Seine-Saint-Denis), 1967.
Fig. 6.13
'No to slums, no to slum cities', poster announcing a
debate organized by students and professionals in the field
of urban planning, June 1968.

In order to understand these workers' role in the *ville nouvelle* and the *bidonville*, it is worthwhile considering the novel *Les Boucs* by the Moroccan writer Driss Chraïbi, published in 1955. In this book Chraïbi describes the departure of Yalann Waldik, a Moroccan teenager who 'persuaded his father to sell his last goat, explaining that with the price of this goat he could buy a thousand in ten years. And he sailed for France.'[2] This young man dreamed of starting his adult life as an immigrant worker in the metropole. Like many others, Waldik took the boat from Casablanca to Marseille and travelled by bus to his final destination, where he found himself working on a construction site like La Courneuve on the periphery of Paris and living in a *bidonville* like La Campa on that same periphery.

Yalann Waldik's trajectory was no exception: it is a clear example of how globalization, understood as the circulation of construction labour, intensified during the post-war period. The migration of construction workers and craftsmen to play a key role in the construction industry of a foreign country was, obviously, not a new phenomenon. German immigrants had played a major role in Dutch construction in the second half of the nineteenth century, while Italian masons started to emigrate to France in the 1880s and consolidated their place in the French building sector during the interwar period.[3] However, it seems that the large labour migrations of the late nineteenth and the beginning of the twentieth centuries were tempered in the years between 1914 and 1945.[4] The years after World War II saw a true 'renaissance' of global flows of workers. This was no coincidence.[5]

Fuelled by the atrocities of World War II and supported by the 1951 United Nations Refugee Convention, which became a key tool in international protection of migrants, the post-war period saw an enormous increase in migration of refugees and asylees in Europe.[6] This was accompanied by processes of decolonization, which moved former colonial ruling classes back to their home countries, as well as by international flows of economic labour migrants who became indispensable in bolstering and speeding up the reconstruction of devastated countries.[7] Foreign labour migrants or so-called 'guest workers' — from inside and outside the old continent — were recruited to reconstruct Europe and compensate for the unprecedented shortage of labour caused by World War II.[8]

Construction would repeatedly prove a key sector for immigrants to new countries. Construction sites were places where workers could not only sell their labour but also acculturate. As the sociologist Roger Waldinger has argued, for many labour migrants 'construction represents the quintessential ethnic niche.'[9] Immigrants often gravitate towards construction trades because this is a 'niche' in which they can develop not only their economic capital but also their social and human capital. Working in shifts with co-ethnics provides opportunities for communication in non-official languages. The ties between entrepreneurs and co-ethnic workers are vehicles for not only the distribution of jobs but also the circulation of information on the immigrants' new country of residence. At the same time, construction is a sector where many of the skills that immigrants have acquired before migration are recognized and new skills can be learned on the job.

As a result, from the 1950s and 1960s forwards, labour migrants started to work in large numbers on construction sites in major European cities such as Paris, London, and Brussels. The new housing estates, public buildings, and infrastructure of post-war European welfare states were largely constructed by immigrant labourers. Even when the European welfare state model started to crumble, migrant labour continued to play an important role in the construction of buildings, neighbourhoods, and cities all over Western Europe. In Berlin, for instance, where migrant construction labour dates back to the eighteenth century, almost 100,000 migrant workers were employed in the building sector in 1989; they came mainly from Poland and southern European countries such as Portugal, Spain, Greece, and Italy. This circulation of construction labour during the second half of the twentieth century occurred not only in Europe but also in cities such as New York, where West Indians and Koreans slowly replaced Italians, and Miami, where Latin Americans, especially Cubans, largely predominate.[10] Examples of foreign construction labour playing an important role in the construction industry are countless and extend to Canada, Australia, and South Africa.[11]

Building the French 'Thirty Glorious Years'

To fully grasp the impact of this global circulation of construction labour, it is worth taking a closer look at conditions in post-war France. When the novel *Les Boucs* came out in 1955, France was in the early years of a period that later came to be known as

Les trente glorieuses or 'the 30 glorious years'[12] — a period of economic growth, prosperity, and abrupt social change from 1945 to 1975, or, more precisely, from the liberation of France in 1944 to the economic downturn triggered by the oil crisis of 1973. During this era France experienced substantial increase of its urban population, largely caused by two factors: demographic growth and rural exodus.[13]

This growing urban population was confronted with meagre housing stock, a result of war-time destruction but also of dilapidated buildings. In 1945 dwelling conditions in French cities were little different from those in the nineteenth century. The housing stock was old and lacked modern amenities such as bathrooms, kitchens, and running water.[14] Overcrowding was a major problem. As late as 1962, a census classified one flat in four as overcrowded and recorded that 60 per cent of all housing stock predated 1914. The '30 glorious years' were accordingly marked by a continuous shortage of, and great demand for, new dwellings.

In post-war France *modernisation* was a wide-ranging phrase. The expression represented the vast project — propelled by the state and the market economy — that in the decades after World War II aimed to counter the devastation caused by the war and enemy occupation. This project's priority was the recovery of industrial production, and the key words were *remise en marche* and *redémarrage* (both phrases mean 'restarting' or 'getting things going again'). The injunction was: 'Produce!' (*Produire!*). French modernization was extremely swift and intense, turning the country 'from a rural, empire-oriented, Catholic country into a fully industrialized, decolonized and urban one.'[15] During these '30 glorious years', the building and public works sector was one of the main vectors of job creation in France. The extraordinary demand for manpower that animated the labour market during this era owes much to the near doubling of the construction industry's workforce between 1949 and 1970. In barely 20 years the number of jobs rose from 1,043,800 to 1,992,000.[16]

Migrant Labour

To fill all these jobs, labour from outside the country was needed.[17] Between 1950 and 1970 the metropole attracted large numbers of young men from Africa and the Mediterranean basin to come and work in France with the promise of a better standard of living.[18] These were mostly poor men who were neither trained nor very demanding. Moreover, since their income was very low in their own countries, they were very receptive to France's call. Other factors too stimulated the migratory flows to France. For example, the arrival of Algerians was accelerated due to the freedom of movement allowed after the war, and Morocco in its turn encouraged emigration, having to cope with enormous growth of its population.[19] Taking advantage of the freedom of movement enjoyed by 'French Muslims' after 1962 (the end of the Algerian War), Algerian immigrants constituted a large and growing group. They numbered 210,000 in 1954, 460,000 in 1964, and more than 700,000 in 1975.

In the light of these figures, the French government established a legal framework to regulate and accelerate immigration in the post-war period. The National Immigration Office (Office national d'immigration, ONI), established in 1945, centrally controlled the recruitment of permanent and seasonal foreign workers employed in a number of sectors, including construction, heavy industry, agriculture, and mining. The most-represented national groups were Italian, Spanish, and Portuguese, accounting for 82 per cent of all ONI immigrants to France.[20] In addition to Europeans, France relied heavily on colonial workers. In particular, North Africa became a 'reservoir' of inexpensive extraterritorial workers, who in their turn saw in France a place where they could be safe from the economic agony in their home countries.

→ Fig. 6.3

Propelling the French Construction Industry

Construction was the most common source of work for immigrants to France since the industry required a large manual workforce. Around half of all migrants registered with the ONI worked in the construction trades. Italians formed the largest group of migrant construction workers in 1960, before being overtaken by Spanish, Portuguese, Moroccan, and Algerian workers in the mid-1960s.[21] In 1967 some 47.5 per cent of the 320,000 people employed in infrastructure and building construction in France were non-French nationals.

Recruitment was first and foremost a matter of government initiative, but migrant construction labour was also sought by private parties. In 1963 the large construction company Entreprise Francis Bouygues, for instance, established a special office wholly dedicated to the recruitment of foreign workers. Companies such as Bouygues distributed leaflets among immigrants who were already living in France, but their representatives also travelled abroad to recruit labour directly in these workers' home countries. French construction companies would travel, for instance, to Morocco to hire workers, sometimes selecting large groups of 300 men at a time. The new recruits would be registered, photographed, and checked medically up to five times before they were offered a contract.[22] Mouhammad, a Moroccan man living in the La Folie *bidonville* in the early 1960s, for example, signed a legal work contract with a large public works company that visited his home town before he moved to France.[23] Companies like Entreprise Francis Bouygues largely relied on immigrant labour recruited from rural Algeria, Morocco, and Portugal. In the 1970s 80 per cent of the company's staff were immigrants.[24]

→ Fig. 6.4

In general, construction and civil engineering companies hired more migrant workers than any other industry, but these trades also demanded the longest working week and paid the lowest salaries. Work on a building site was dangerous and insecure. Pierre Bideberry, director of the ONI, argued that French people were unwilling to take up *penible* (hard) and poorly paid jobs and that therefore foreign labour was needed.[25] Some immigrant construction workers reluctantly assimilated this perspective on their role in the building industry. The fitter and welder Lakhdar, for instance, maintained that:

> France needs foreigners when it comes to digging excavations and the like because the lads are paid less, and, anyway, the French would not do that [sort of work] out of pride, you see.[26]

Paris was a migration magnet in post-war France.[27] The massive urban expansion and restoration of the capital absorbed the bulk of labour coming from abroad. In 1968 up to 38 per cent of the 264,000-strong building workforce in the Paris region were non-French. Within the frame of the French welfare state, these migrant workers constructed new housing estates, the so-called *grands ensembles* or *villes nouvelles*, but also new public buildings, such as schools, hospitals, and cultural centres, as well as new infrastructure. All these showpiece French modernization projects depended strongly on importation of construction labour from various parts of Europe and north Africa to the metropole.

Anybody glancing at a construction site in post-war Paris would have seen an ethnic mosaic of workers. This state of affairs was to continue throughout the second half of the twentieth century. Immigrant workers would often constitute the majority on construction sites, although their composition changed over time: the Italians, who dominated during the first half of the twentieth century, were in the post-war period replaced by Algerians, Moroccans, Tunisians, Portuguese, and Poles. This was the case not only in Paris: in other large French cities, such as Marseille and Lyon, the diversity of national origins of the construction workforce would also have been conspicuous.

→ Fig. 6.5

The *Bidonville*, or Housing Global Workers

That the impact of migrant workers on French territory was not limited to construction of beacons of the French welfare state becomes clear from an image of the La Défense area in Paris taken by the photographer Jean Pottier from the Rue de La Garenne in Nanterre. In the background of the photograph is the newly finished Centre National des Industries et des Techniques (CNIT) in La Défense. This was an avant-garde project that was the first gesture in a much more ambitious urban scheme for a business centre on the outskirts of Paris connected by a 'triumphal way' with the Champs-Élysées in the west. The impressive, 22,000-square-metre, concrete shell structure was designed in 1956 by the architects Robert Camelot, Jean de Mailly, and Bernard Zehrfuss as a celebration of French industry and technical knowledge.

The construction of this project demanded not only massive investment but also a large workforce of white-collar experts, such as architects and engineers, and an even larger group of blue-collar labourers. The latter contingent consisted largely of migrant labourers. These global workers not only worked on

French territory but also had to be housed on it. The effects of this 'housing question' can be observed in the foreground of Pottier's photograph, where we see the *bidonville* of Nanterre.
→ Fig. 6.6

The state of affairs captured by Pottier was no exception. On the contrary, all over Paris and France a new urban reality was emerging. It consisted of dense and poorly constructed settlements, often built in the immediate vicinity of their inhabitants' workplaces. In the margins of large-scale heroic construction sites of European welfare states — such as the RER tunnel and the office buildings at La Défense in Paris — numerous prosaic urban settlements sprang up to house labourers working on these same *chantiers* (building sites). As a result, place names such as Saint-Denis, La Courneuve, Aubervilliers, and Montreuil came to stand simultaneously for both shiny modern housing estates and the shabby living environment of the *bidonville*.

Living near or under the walls of a construction site avoided expenditure on commuting, an important motivation for migrants who were accumulating savings for their families back home.[28] Paradoxically, the construction sites of the *villes nouvelles* of the French welfare state also provided the material basis for their counterparts: redundant and discarded materials from the *chantiers* would become the building bricks for huts in the *bidonville*.[29] The *bidonville* thus in many ways became the Janus face of the French welfare state while at the same time maintaining a clear physical and cultural detachment from French society. The living conditions in shantytowns were dreadful, with either inadequate or absent urban infrastructure and poor hygienic conditions, as an Algerian inhabitant of a *bidonville* in Paris protested:

> If I were not ashamed, I would take my five children and my wife — that's six — with me — that makes seven — and I would go to the police station ... Why? Because here there is no light or water. You see, [when] I come home from work, I'm going to line up for water like everyone else, and then I don't come back for an hour, an hour and a half, sometimes two hours.[30]

Living in the *bidonville* meant coping with the poorest dwelling conditions, as Driss Chraïbi explains:

Stretched from wall to wall, tangled up, strings supported everything that the beds could not hold — and it was an art, which could not be learned, but was innate, to get into bed and lie in it. You had to be content with your limited space, with the few air intakes allocated, only snore if the others had been snoring for a long time, and, even then, snore like them, to their measure and at their intensity. If fleas and bugs stung, one should not scratch, because a simple scratch dislocated the whole house of cards; and besides, it was a waste of time and energy to try to kill these parasites which, along with cockroaches and moths, were abundant, tenacious and perennial. Yes, there was a light bulb hanging from the ceiling, with an anti-theft latticework, which the Boss would turn off at will, according to his mood.[31]

For the global workers, these housing conditions were a dehumanizing experience: 'No critical sense would have distinguished them from one other; life had made them prisoners of their anger and equal in misery. Once they had a name.'[32] It was no coincidence that the newspaper *France-Soir* branded the *bidonvilles* 'les îlots d'enfer de la ville lumière' ('the hellish islets of the City of Light').[33] As a socio-spatial antithesis between the local and the global, the formal and the informal, and the rich and the poor, the *bidonville* manifested one of the most prominent urban paradoxes in the post-war period.[34]

That the *bidonvilles* were not an exception but rather the recurrent architectural expression of the presence of global labour in the French territory is clear from the so-called *Carte des bidonvilles* published by the French Ministère de l'Intérieur in 1968.[35] On this map the ministry officially defined the *bidonville* as 'an *ensemble* of light constructions built with makeshift materials on an undeveloped plot of land, fenced or not.'[36] Excluding smaller settlements of shanties or so-called *micro-bidonvilles*, the experts of the Ministère de l'Intérieur counted no fewer than 255 settlements on the territory of the metropole, with more than 90 per cent of the inhabitants being immigrants. 119 of these *bidonvilles* were situated in the Paris region, as portrayed in Robert Bozzi's film *Les Immigrés en France* (1970).[37] In the French capital region up to 35,000 people lived in *bidonvilles* and up to 28,000 lived in less official forms of *micro-bidonvilles*.[38]

→ Figs. 6.7–8

'La Défense' and 'La Folie':
Opposing Socio-spatial Realities in Nanterre

One of the most noteworthy *bidonvilles* in Paris was 'La Folie' in Nanterre, a self-built settlement in the shadow of the Parisian business district of La Défense. La Folie embodied one of the most radical urban spaces of inequality in the French capital, providing a home to 10,000 people as well as to some prominent members of the Algerian National Liberation Front (FLN).[39] In 1962 ten per cent of all the inhabitants of the municipality of Nanterre lived in *bidonvilles*. La Folie was known to house a large ethnic diversity, with North African families in the west, Portuguese families in the east, and single people of diverse origins in the centre. It was the subject of an in-depth investigation conducted by the sociologists Monique Hervo and Marie-Ange Charras between 1967 and 1968.

La Défense and La Folie, meaning literally 'The Defence' and 'The Madness', stand for two socio-spatial systems that confronted one another in Nanterre: one was a fortress of the French values of progress and modernization; the other housed global workers in the wildest of urban conditions. In the 1960s the socio-spatial contrast inside the municipality of Nanterre was made even more acute when a new university campus was constructed next to the La Défense administrative and commercial area and La Folie, as immortalized by the French director Jean-Luc Godard in his 1967 movie *La Chinoise*.[40] Manifesting the educational policies of the French welfare state, the Nanterre University Campus was considered a national symbol of the democratization of higher education. In contradistinction to France's old universities, such as the Sorbonne, the Nanterre university campus was not located in the city centre but on the periphery of Paris. The famous French sociologist Henri Lefebvre described the university as 'a ghetto of students and teachers situated in the midst of other ghettos filled with the "abandoned".'[41] He portrayed Nanterre as a heterotopia of differences, ghettos, and socio-spatial conflicts:

> Within a civilization founded on the city, from the ancient city to the historical city of the European west, wouldn't it be a damned place? Much more than a sad spectacle, the

suburb with its slums looks like a hole. The anomic, the 'social extra-social' is mixed with the image of society. Absence is the place where misfortune takes shape.[42]

Reaction came not only from sociologists such as Lefebvre, Hervo, and Charras but also from architects. Visting the *bidonville* of Nanterre in the spring of 1968, the architecture students Isabelle Herpin and Serge Santelli made precise photographic and drawn surveys of streets, houses, and rooms, producing a complete urban plan. Just as certain CIAM architects had done in the early 1950s with the shanty towns of North Africa, they studied the *bidonville* as a valuable urban environment and argued that it echoed traditional housing patterns in the Maghreb. In their book they maintain:

> The slum always has a negative connotation: it is built of heterogeneous materials, informal and chaotic, with muddy and dirty streets, and its image is one of great poverty and exclusion. No one could imagine that beyond the miserable appearance of the two shanty towns of the Rue des Prés in Nanterre with their density, their dead ends, and their courtyard houses, there is hidden a significant architectural structure stemming from a specific urban and architectural tradition, that of the Maghreb.[43]

Santelli and Herpin tried to illustrate how the global labourers had transposed certain dwelling patterns and forms to Nanterre and, at least in their everyday dwellings, did not conform to French standards and customs but left their own imprint on the territory. The two architecture students maintained that the *bidonville* was also the expression of a certain autonomous agency possessed by the global workers in the built environment: 'The inhabitants had been able to build a specific, ordered, and structured urban and architectural environment. Self-construction had thus made it possible to build, within the regulations and administrative constraints, a physical framework adapted to the needs and culture of the inhabitants.'[44]

→ Figs. 6.9–10

The popular press also paid ample attention to the global construction workers and their dwelling environments. In 1957 the newspaper *France-Soir* thundered in block capitals that

'A belt of *bidonvilles* surrounds Paris' and gave a voice to the shanty towns' neighbours, who often lived in terraced houses and maintained that they 'did not dare go out at night'.[45] Reports in the popular press instilled a sense of fear, discrimination, and anxiety, claiming that immigrant workers 'would remain "encysted" like indigestible foreign bodies in the urban tissue.'[46] While newspapers such as *Le Parisien Libéré* labelled the global workers and their poor settlements 'verrures honteuses pour Paris [shameful eyesores for Paris]' in 1964,[47] policy advisors such as Georges Mauco stressed that the assimilation of African and Asian migrant workers was 'physically and morally undesirable'.[48] These racist viewpoints reached their first climax on 17 October 1961, when one of the most brutal massacres in modern Paris's history took place. A demonstration of Algerians, many of them from the Parisian *bidonvilles*, was cruelly suppressed. The 316 deaths and 73 people missing capture the gravity of the racial conflict.[49]

→ Fig. 6.11

Beyond the popular press, labour unions also reacted to the poor living conditions for global workers. The Confédération générale du travail (CGT) and the more specialized Fédération nationale des travailleurs du bâtiment (FNTB) lamented the poor working circumstances and pitifully low wages of immigrant workers but also their problematic housing in *bidonvilles*. The union's newspaper, *Paris-Construction*, described living conditions in the *bidonvilles* as 'scandalous' and connected them with the 'illegal and racist' attitudes of employers.[50]

Politics and the 'Badlands' of Modernity

In response to all the attention directed at the *bidonville*, in 1964 the French Government promulgated the Debré Law. This was supposed to put an end to the so-called 'badlands of French modernity'.[51] Beginning with an argument about the lack of hygiene and public order but also about the threat to French identity supposedly posed by the global workers, the new law proposed total demolition of the French *bidonvilles*. The 'insalubrious housing' and the expropriated land on which it stood would be replaced with subsidized housing—such as *Habitations*

à loyer modéré (HLMs) — that could absorb the inhabitants of the *bidonvilles*. Employing violent processes of extirpation and harsh operations of destruction, the French police erased the living environments of the global workers from French territory one by one.
→ Fig. 6.12

In 1966 construction of an additional 15,000 HLM housing units was programmed for the city of Paris.[52] This architectural solution seemed to satisfy both sides of the argument about *bidonvilles*: those who wished to treat immigrants like humans and those who feared immigrants' 'malign' influence on French identity. Although they improved the living conditions of many families who had formerly lived in the *bidonvilles*, these huge housing structures paradoxically also persisted in segregating their inhabitants from the rest of the population in France. Replacing informal debris-made shelters with modern concrete constructions and *bidonvilles* with *villes nouvelles*, the architecture of the migrant workers' dwellings continued to deprive them of their right to the city.

This continuing segregation of global labourers became in France a focus of discussion and political dissensus but also a kind of emblem of broader struggles concerning urban space, immigration, and social welfare. A poster of June 1968 announcing a debate organized by 'students and professionals in the field of urban planning' is a typical example. Under the headline 'No to slums, no to slum cities', the poster urges the reader not to allow urban planning to remain the reserved domain of the state and experts but to claim it as a critical terrain where political commitment can be directly expressed. The pair of oil barrels or *bidons* it depicts, one topped by a makeshift chimney and the other divided into a uniform grid of window bays, is in equal parts visual criticism of the poor material living conditions in the *bidonvilles* and of the homogenizing character of the architecture of the *grands ensembles* and *villes nouvelles* which were replacing the shantytowns. This was a visual synthesis of how global labourers had been situated in the French territory.
→ Fig.6.13

'La Campa' ('the Encampment'):
Erasure and Recurrence of Global Labour

Our story on global construction labour ends where it started: at the La Campa *bidonville* in La Courneuve, on the periphery of Paris. The death of five Africans in a *bidonville* in Aubervilliers on 1 January 1970 accelerated the clearance policy, leading to the passing of the Vivien Law on 10 July 1970. This introduced special urban planning procedures to facilitate the removal of slum dwellings. In September 1971 an official survey registered no fewer than 86 *bidonvilles* in the department of Seine-Saint-Denis, including La Campa, which was demolished the same year. A few years later, La Campa was replaced by a large green recreational area: Georges-Valbon Public Park. The families who lived in the *bidonville* were relocated, notably to the large housing estates surrounding the site, such as the 'Cité des 4000'. On 29 June 2013, in the presence of former inhabitants of La Campa, the president of the General Council of Seine-Saint-Denis inaugurated a special plaque in Georges-Valbon Park commemorating the history and memory of the global workers who had inhabited this place.

Patterns of labour migration similar to those in France appeared throughout Western Europe, including in Switzerland, West Germany, and Great Britain. During the boom of the 1950s and 1960s immigrants from Southern Europe, Turkey, North Africa, and, in the case of Britain, from Commonwealth nations flooded into Western Europe to take unskilled and unstable jobs in the construction industry. With the partial exception of Great Britain, these industrial democracies initially treated foreign construction labourers as temporary and controlled their access to the job market. The economic crisis of the 1970s put an abrupt end to this influx of global workers to France and other Western European nations. Immigration policy then aimed at encouraging labour migrants to return home. No longer sought-after agents of modernization and development, global labourers became undesirables blamed for rising unemployment.

1   In 1966 an official census by the French Ministry of Interior Affairs counted 75,346 people living in *bidonvilles* in France. *Droit et Liberté* 277 (1968), p. 21.
2   Driss Chraïbi, *Les boucs* (Paris: Denoël, 1955).
3   Paul Th. van de Laar, *Vier eeuwen migratie: bestemming Rotterdam* (Rotterdam: LomdiTaal, 1998), pp. 146–171 and Dominique Barjot, 'Les Italiens et le BTP français du début des années 1860 à la fin des années 1960: ouvriers et patrons, une contribution multiforme', *Cahier Des Annales De Normandie*. 31 (1), 2001, pp. 69–80.
4   Adam McKeown, 'Global Migration, 1846–1940', *Globalization and Violence* 4, 2006, pp. 32–63.
5   Jeffrey G Williamson, *Globalization and Inequality, Past and Present: the late nineteenth and the late twentieth centuries compared* (Cambridge [Massachusetts]: National Bureau of Economic Research, 1996).
6   Dirk Hoerder, *Migrations and belongings, 1870–1945* (Cambridge, MA: The Belknap Press of Harvard University Press, 2014), p. 581.
7   Hoerder, op. cit. (note 6), p. 579.
8   Hoerder, op. cit. (note 6), p. 584.
9   Roger Waldinger, 'The "other side" of embeddedness: A case study of the interplay of economy and ethnicity,' *Ethnic and Racial Studies* 18, No. 3 (1995), p. 577.
10 Roger Waldinger, *Still the Promized City? African-Americans and New Immigrants in Postindustrial New York* (Cambridge, MA: Harvard University Press, 2000).
11 Jan Rath, 'A quintessential immigrant niche? The non-case of immigrants in the Dutch construction industry', *Entrepreneurship & Regional Development* 14, No. 4 (2002), pp. 355–372.
12 Jean Fourastié, *Les Trente Glorieuses Ou la révolution invisible de 1946 à 1975* (Paris: Fayard, 1979).
13 Colin L. Dyer, *Population and Society in Twentieth Century France* (Toronto: Hodder and Stoughton, 1978).
14 Roger Price, *A Concise History of France* (Cambridge: Cambridge University Press, 2014).
15 Kristin Ross, *Fast Cars, Clean Bodies: Decolonization and the Reordering of French Culture* (Cambridge, MA: MIT Press, 1999).
16 Myriam Campinos-Dubernet, *Emploi et gestion de la main d'œuvre dans le BTP: mutations de l'après-guerre à la crise* (Paris: Documentation française, 1985).
17 James R. McDonald, 'Labor Immigration in France, 1946–1965, *Annals of the Association of American Geographers* 59, No. 1 (1969), pp. 116–134.
18 Charles-Robert Ageron, 'L'immigration Maghrebine en France: Un survol historique', *Vingtième Siècle. Revue D'histoire* 7 (1985), pp. 59–70; Neil MacMaster, *Racism in Europe 1870–2000* (Hampshire: Palgrave, 2013).
19 Yehudit Ronen, 'Moroccan immigration in the Mediterranean region: reflections in Ben Jelloun's literary works', *Journal of North African Studies* 6, No. 4 (2001), pp. 1–14.
20 McDonald, op. cit. (note 17), p. 118.
21 McDonald, op. cit. (note 17), p. 121.
22 Jacob Paskins, *Paris Under Construction: Building Sites and Urban Transformation in the 1960s* (New York: Routledge, Taylor & Francis Group, 2016), p. 79.
23 Monique Hervo and François Maspero, *Chroniques du bidonville: Nanterre en guerre d'Algérie, 1959–1962* (Paris: Seuil, 2001), p. 235.
24 Institut national de l'audiovisuel, 'Francis Bouygues sur les immigrés', 28 July 1983, video. Online. Available https://www.ina.fr/video/I09012135/francis-bouygues-sur-les-immigres-video.html (accessed 28 August 2024).
25 Michel Honorin, 'Ils sont trois millions de travailleurs étrangers en France', 12 June 1964, video. Online. Available https://m.ina.fr/video/CAF89009165/ils-sont-trois-millions-de-travailleurs-etrangers-en-france-video.html (accessed 28 August 2024).
26 Monique Hervo and Marie-Ange Charras, *Bidonvilles l'enlisement: Graphiques et dessins* (Paris: Maspero, 1971), p. 84.
27 McDonald, op. cit. (note 17).
28 Neil MacMaster, *Colonial Migrants and Racism: Algerians in France, 1900–1962* (Basingstoke: Macmillan, 1997), pp. 87–89.
29 Paskins, op. cit. (note 22), p. 100.
30 Hervo and Charras, op. cit. (note 26), p. 1461.
31 Chraïbi, op. cit. (note 2), p. 23.
32 Chraïbi, op. cit. (note 2), p. 45.
33 Maurice Josco, 'Bidonvilles. Le reportage sur les îlots d'enfer de la ville lumière', *France-Soir*, 6 November 1965.
34 Paskins, op. cit. (note 22), pp. 99–100.
35 Mehdi Lallaoui, *Du bidonville aux HLM* (Paris: Syros, 1993), p. 44; see also Jacob Paskins, 'Vague Terrain: Bidonvilles, Run-Down Housing, and the Stigmatization of (Sub)urban Space in and Around Paris in the 1960s', *Moveable Type*, No. 5 (2009), p. 2.
36 See image in *Droit et Liberté* 277 (December 1968), p. 41.
37 Robert Bozzi (dir.), *Les immigrés en France le logement* (Paris: Ciné-archives, 1970), video. Online. Available https://www.cinearchives.org/films-immigr%C3%A9s-en-france-le-logement-les-447-269-0-1.html (accessed 28 August 2024).

38 *Le Parisien Libéré*, 26 March 1966, p. 2. Quoted in Paskins, op. cit. (note 35), p. 2.
39 Léopold Lambert, 'A Colonial History of Nanterre Through Four Commemorative Plates', *The Funambulist* (17 June 2018). Online. Available https: https://thefunambulist.net/history/colonial-history-nanterre-four-commemorative-plates (accessed 28 August 2024).
40 Łukasz Stanek, *Henri Lefebvre on Space: Architecture, Urban Research, and the Production of Theory* (Minneapolis: University of Minnesota Press, 2011), pp. 180–82.
41 Stanek, op. cit. (note 40), p. 186.
42 Lefebre's text reads: 'En attendant, misère, environnement de bidonvilles, de terrils (travaux du métro-express), de HLM prolétariennes, d'entreprises industrielles. Curieux contexte, paysage désolé … Au sein d'une civilization fondée sur la Ville de la Cité antique à la ville historique de l'Occident européen ne serait-ce pas un lieu maudit? Bien plus qu'un spectacle attristant, la banlieue avec ses bidonvilles se présente comme un vide. L'anomique, le "social extra-social" se mêle à l'image de la société. L'absence, c'est le lieu où le malheur prend forme.' Henri Lefebvre, 'L'irruption de Nanterre au sommet', *L'Homme Et La Société* 8, No. 1 (1968), p. 81.
43 Isabelle Herpin and Serge Santelli, *Bidonville à Nanterre: étude architecturale* (Paris: Institut de l'Environnement, Ministère des Affaires, 1973), p. 6.
44 Ibid., p. 6.
45 *France-Soir*, 29 October 1957.
46 MacMaster, op. cit. (note 28), p. 5.
47 *Le Parisien Libéré*, 12 December 1964, quoted in Paskins, *Paris under construction*, p. 4.
48 Quoted and translated in Marcel Maussen, 'Constructing mosques: the governance of Islam in France and the Netherlands' (PhD thesis, Amsterdam School for Social Science Research, 2009), p. 108.
49 Victor Collet, *Nanterre, du bidonville à la cité* (Marseille: Agone éditeur, 2019), p. 66. See also Jean-Luc Einaudi, *Octobre 1961. Un massacre à Paris* (Paris: FAYARD, 2001).
50 Paskins, op. cit. (note 22), p. 174.
51 Mustafa Dikeç, *Badlands of the Republic: Space, Politics, and Urban Policy* (Malden, MA: Blackwell, 2007). Bernardo Secchi, *La ville des riches et la ville des pauvres: urbanisme et inégalités* (Geneva: MētisPresses, 2015).
52 Secchi, op. cit. (note 51), p. 53.

An Incomplete Conclusion:
Towards Other Times and Geographies

Tom Avermaete
Michelangelo Sabatino

At the end of this book it is worth recalling that our six journeys are selective and incomplete explorations whose scope is characterized by inevitable limitations. Two of these limitations, which we may call a 'temporal bias' and a 'geographical bias', are worth mentioning explicitly.

First, we would like to address this book's 'temporal bias'. All of our journeys end in 1989, a year which launched not only the important geopolitical transition brought about by the fall of the Berlin Wall but also the start of an era characterized by a plethora of new developments. Among the many developments that have taken place since the late 1980s, the introduction of the World Wide Web in particular has drastically redirected the processes of globalization.

The internet has been the basis for development of new video conferencing platforms for exchange and collaboration, such as Skype, Zoom, and Teams. These have not only allowed architects and urban planners to work as teams across very different geographical locations but also opened up the possibility of moving building drawings and construction specifications across time zones so that they can be worked upon in a 24/7 cycle.

The World Wide Web has also radically changed the way people travel. Whereas once travel catalogues and guides were the main reference points for travellers and tourists, today online international travel agencies, booking sites, and reservation platforms make it possible not only to buy plane, boat, and train tickets but also to rate and compare hotel rooms and holiday homes. The continual expansion of travel has not only propelled the development of associated infrastructure but also, coupled with the availability of images of buildings and cities online, brought architecture and urban planning to the attention of increasing numbers of people.

The internet has also paved the way for what we today know as platform commerce. Companies that operate over large parts of the world, such as Amazon and Alibaba, have led the way in giving consumers the idea that all goods are available at the touch of a button on a computer or smartphone screen. However, this digital mirage of consumer goods moving effortlessly and rapidly across the globe has been accompanied by the emergence of a vast — but sometimes obscure — physical infrastructure. Large automated distribution centres, regional airport hubs, and armies of countless delivery vans have sprung up in cities and other territories to keep this dream (or should we say nightmare?) of web commerce running. The resulting social and economic disparities, as well as environmental impacts, are well known.

The World Wide Web has also radically changed the acquisition, evaluation, and distribution of architectural knowledge. If the circulation of knowledge from one place to another previously required the shipment of books or magazines, the internet has accelerated and intensified possibilities for knowledge exchange (through platforms such as JSTOR, Artstor, and the Avery Index). While numerous architectural journals used to act as seismographs recording developments in architectural culture, reporting on new buildings, materials, and products as well as new theoretical perspectives, since the 1990s this role has increasingly been played by websites, social media, and blogs. Much of this knowledge is permanently stored on servers and, as 'dark data', represents an enormous environmental burden.

These are just a few examples that illustrate how projecting some of our journeys into eras other than those discussed in this book opens up fresh perspectives on the architecture-globalization nexus.

Second, we want to address this book's 'geographical bias'. Most of our journeys begin with phenomena in Western Europe or the United States, with some excursuses into other geographies. However, the trajectories of our journeys are not limited to these particular geographies. On the contrary: many, if not all, our journeys can be projected onto other conditions and realities.

The global circulation of building materials, for example, is not the exclusive prerogative of North American and European companies. It is now well known that many of the materials and products used in the construction industry are produced in Asia, South America, and Africa and then shipped around the world. Indian-based Tata Steel is a case in point. Founded in 1907, Tata is now one of the most geographically diversified steel producers, with operations in 26 countries, commercial offices in more than 35 countries, and a wide range of products used in the construction industry worldwide.

The same can be said of construction labour, which seems to float ever more fluidly around the globe, independently of old colonial ties such as were formative in post-war France. Examples such as the Great Mosque in Algiers, the capital of Algeria, illustrate the many roads along which construction labour moves nowadays. The Great Mosque of Algiers (2019), at the time of its construction the largest in Africa, was built not by Algerian or North African labourers but by Chinese construction workers imported to the North African capital by the China State Construction Engineering Corporation (CSCEC).

Such examples show that projecting our journeys onto different geographies may reveal many other faces of the relationship between architecture and globalization.

In conclusion, we believe that the above-mentioned temporal and geographical limitations of this book should be understood not so much as shortcomings but as indications of terrains that can be further explored. In this sense our incomplete journeys are invitations to think about the globalization-architecture nexus beyond the time frame of 1945–1989 and beyond the geographies of North America and Western Europe. It is our hope that the readers of this book will be inspired to further explore the trajectories outlined in these journeys toward these other times and geographies.

Coda
The Global Turn:
Perspectives from a Personal Journey

Leonardo Zuccaro Marchi
Assistant Professor of Architecture
and Urban Design, Politecnico di Milano

Globalization has affected our way of working together as well as our daily lives, as is made clear by the six journeys discussed in this book. The pandemic recently sharpened our awareness of the fragility of interrelationships and the global system of which we are all part. Each of us has their own personal direct experience of globalization — experience which remains in our memories as an individual 'journey'. Mine was the twenty-seventh G8 summit held in Genova (Italy) in July 2001,[1] where for the first time members of the 'counter-globalization movement' showed up *en masse* — at least 200,000 of them — to demonstrate. Together with thinkers from multiple disciplines, they rejected a world flattened by the pressure of multinational consumerist brands.[2] The death of one of the young activists during the turmoil in Genova's city centre, the urban destruction wreaked by extremists using 'black bloc' tactics, and the excessive reaction of the police towards the demonstrators was a shock to our generation and all Italy as well. Moreover, for the first time criticism was heard of the contradictions inherent in globalization, which up to that point had generally been perceived by my generation as a natural process necessary to the development of the world.[3]

The G8 meeting in Genova occurred only a couple of months before the attack on the World Trade Center in New York, a moment that is seared into our collective memory. Younger readers may not have personally experienced the global trauma that began on 11 September 2001, yet its impact on our world is undeniable. The fall of the Twin Towers was, as the sociologist Marco Belpoliti has put it, 'opposite and symmetrical' to that of Berlin's wall in 1989.[4] The contrast is stark: in Germany the demolition of the concrete wall, a horizontal line dissecting Berlin, symbolized a new social hope and a geopolitical opening; in New York the fall of the two vertical towers marked the beginning of a new era of global closure and fear. If the coming down of the Berlin Wall brings to an end the time frame of the six journeys in this book, there can be no doubt that the Icarus-like fall of the towers in New York opened new and complex chapters in our global dialogue. It tainted the new millennium and changed the character of mobility, one of this book's key themes. After 9/11 we can no longer fly without undergoing extensive security checks.

Before I eventually visited Ground Zero in person, a piece of the tragedy in New York came to my hometown, Padova, in 2005: a 6-metre-long twisted beam from the WTC that had crossed the Atlantic to be exhibited in the American Pavilion at the Venice Biennale in 2002. A few months later, the fragment was mounted like an *objet trouvè* inside massive glass walls by Daniel Libeskind, who was commissioned to design the first WTC memorial monument in Europe, right in the heart of my city. The monumentality of the tragedy became a physical *memento* of the 'violence of the global', of a tragic setback for globalization itself, which Jean Baudrillard had already portrayed in his 'Requiem for the Twin Towers'.[5] The vulnerabilities inherent in the Global Turn and the virulence of the reaction to it still seem vivid today, in 2024, when we are suddenly faced with an anachronistic dystopia of potential world-war scenarios.

When it comes to education, the importance of travelling and exchanging is now a given. From the Grand Tour to Erasmus programmes, as this book explains, journeys have increasingly become an opportunity for sharing ideas and improving society and the architectural profession. My first international experience occurred before university, on the other side of the world, as a young exchange student in high school in Paeroa, New Zealand. When I was asked to design a new city from scratch for the first time, I felt delighted at being the only European in the room, with a huge urban cultural background at my shoulders. In the end my proposal for a new-medieval-organic Padova was dismissed in favour of more straightforward plans for linear and grid cities drawn by my colleagues, who were used to living in these functionalist settlements. Besides a debate between (post) modern urban design and New Urbanism, awareness of a 'new pattern language' (Christopher Alexander) entailed discovering afresh the different forms of cities and casting off a certain Eurocentric bias. This latter persists today as a topic of debate in our education and research.

The idea of belonging to a network of interconnected countries, such as the EU, certainly shaped my own desire to pursue architecture as a profession and to be part of the academic community in Europe and beyond. One of my most essential experiences of educational exchange was the joint doctorate that I defended in Venice and Delft in 2013 under the guidance of Tom Avermaete and Michiel Riedijk at Technische Universität Delft (TU Delft), Paola Viganò and Bernardo Secchi at Università Iuav di Venezia (IUAV), and Alessandro De Magistris at Politecnico di Milano (PoliMI). This international, interdisciplinary, and transdisciplinary collaboration helped weave a more collaborative idea of Europe. Nowadays, joint doctorates are even more frequent, thanks to European doctoral networks programmes such as Marie Sklodowska-Curie Actions, which foster innovative research and strong collaboration among institutions.

Another pivotal moment in my architectural journey was winning the Europan 14 competition in Germany in 2017 as a member of CoPE (Collective of Projects in Equipoise) with Alice Covatta, Piero Medici, and Annalisa Romani.[6] Our collaboration uses the possibilities of our digital age to transcend geographical boundaries; projects are executed remotely between Italy, France, the Netherlands, and Japan, and now Canada, thereby expanding the horizons of the architectural profession beyond even time-zone boundaries. Founded in 1989, the same year as the fall of the Berlin Wall, Europan is a bi-annual competition which has become an important platform for young architects under 40 years old keen to challenge and redefine approaches to architecture and urban and landscape design across Europe. If the CIAM summer schools and ILAUD pioneered global collaborations after World War II, Europan embodied a new European idea of architectural collaboration at the end of the twentieth century.

New Viewpoints in Education and Research

In education adoption of a global critical perspective remains a challenge for both students and educators, as has been made clear by the research seminar 'The Global Architect' that I currently teach at Politecnico di Milano with Pierre-Alain Croset, Gaia Caramellino, Paolo Scrivano, and Christian Gänshirt.[7] It was Croset who came up with the idea for a research seminar based on the idea of an interdisciplinary 'radical pedagogy' in the Anglo-American mould, with cross-fertilization between the disciplines of architectural design theory and history (thanks to collaboration with the historians Scrivano and Caramellino).[8] This makes it possible to explore the various roles of the contemporary 'global architect', roles which entail multiple transfers of knowledge within a process of hybridization, resistance, or assimilation between local and international aspects, internal references and external stimuli, and old bias and new critical perspectives.

The specific ways in which we organize and conceive the world from multiple local identities are now also a theme for research. Several platforms and research networks have been set up in recent years. GUD—Genealogy of Urban Design,[9] PortCityFutures,[10] and Affirmations,[11] for instance, are but a few of the new-born networks based on web-based technologies that offer unprecedented potential for cross-cultural mobility and interchange. Such networks use international collaboration to explore specific architecture topics that could not be investigated within the scope of a single research group or institution.

In the context of reinterpreting and reiterating the 'Box for the Open Society', praised by Jaap Bakema as early as the 1950s,[12] the Dutch research group led by Dirk van den Heuvel at TU Delft is currently working on types of an 'Architecture Archives of the Future' in collaboration with the Nieuwe Instituut in Rotterdam.[13] Adopting an accessible, Janus-faced research methodology of 'looking back, looking ahead',[14] the group aims to employ new digital tools and technologies to explore ways of preserving, curating, and communicating architectural archives that are usually dispersed (e.g. the National Collection's CIAM archives) while raising urgent societal questions in a global collaboration with other institutions, artists, and researchers.[15]

The collaborative research process tracing the 'Global Turn' in architecture under the supervision of Tom Avermaete and Michelangelo Sabatino was for me a welcome opportunity to discover and understand different viewpoints and thematic conjunctions. This book vividly highlights the shrinking of the world and David Harvey's global 'time-space compression'.[16] The postwar global conditions described in all chapters of the book have in common a rapidly accelerating exchange of global architectural knowledge. This has made critical knowledge of architecture more accessible to a wider audience, bringing a significant shift in the pace of change. Most of the case studies analysed in the book reveal insightful connections and reverberations in different regimes of circulation. With the primary aim of serving as an open intellectual tool, the book is structured to broaden the reader's understanding of the global roots of architecture and urbanism.

The Global Turn: Perspectives from a Personal Journey

1 See Francesco Prisco, 'Da Manu Chao a "Diaz": l'eredità culturale del G8 di Genova', *Il Sole 24 Ore*, 14 July 2021. Online. Available https: https://www.ilsole24ore.com/art/da-manu-chao-diaz-l-eredita-culturale-g8-genova-AEdoAwW (accessed 19 August 2024).
2 See, for instance, Naomi Klein, *No Logo* (Flamingo, 2000); Noam Chomsky, Edward S Herman, *Manufacturing Consent: The Political Economy of the Mass Media* (New York: Pantheon Books, 1988). See also the chapter in this book on the flow of goods.
3 G8 in Genova was also a turning point for political discussion regarding human rights and abuse of power. See *Diaz — Non pulire questo sangue* (film, Daniele Vicari, 2012).
4 Marco Belpoliti, *Crolli* (Torino: Einaudi, 2005), p.3.
5 Jean Baudrillard, 'Requiem for the Twin Towers', 'The Violence of the Global', *The Spirit of Terrorism* (London, New York: Verso, 2003), pp. 35, 85.
6 See online. Available https: https://www.europan-europe.eu/en/exchanges/The-Productive-Heart-of-New-Ulm; https://co-p-e.com/ (accessed 4 September 2024). CoPE's current members are Leonardo Zuccaro Marchi, Alice Covatta, Piero Medici, and Alina Lippiello.
7 The Global Architect, thematic research seminar taught at Politecnico di Milano by Pierre Alain Croset, Gaia Caramellino, Paolo Scrivano, Christian Gänshirt, and Leonardo Zuccaro Marchi. Online. Available https: https://www.theglobalarchitect.polimi.it/?page_id=206 (accessed 5 September 2024).
8 Beatriz Colomina, Ignacio G. Galán, Evangelos Kotsioris, and Anna-Maria Meister (eds.), *Radical Pedagogies* (Cambridge: The MIT Press, 2022).
9 GUD — Genealogy of Urban Design, founded by Heleni Porfyriou in Italy, aims to investigate the history and 'birth' of urban design as a discipline in order to identify best practices that can support proactive undertakings in the future. Online. Available https: https://gudesign.org/ (accessed 19 August 2024).
10 PortCityFutures is led by Professor Carola Hein (TU Delft). 'PortCityFutures explores these particularities and proposes spatial planning and design measures for the use of this limited space so that the port and city (and region) can jointly evolve'. Online. Available https: https://www.portcityfutures.nl/home (accessed 19 August 2024).
11 Founded at GSAPP, Columbia University, Affirmations is curated by Andrés Jaque and Bart-Jan Polman. 'AFFIRMATIONS is intended to align evidence and aspirations. It will summarize and state underrepresented histories and possible futures that emerge from the cracks in the structures of power built on the interdependency of carbonization, extractivism, colonization, racialization, anthropocentrism, inequality, patriarchy, and technocracy.' Online. Available https: https://www.arch.columbia.edu/affirmations (accessed 19 August 2024).
12 See Dirk van den Heuvel (ed.), *Jaap Bakema and the Open Society* (Archis, 2018).
13 Online. Available https: https://www.tudelft.nl/bk/over-faculteit/afdelingen/architecture/organisatie-1/secties-en-groepen-nieuw/building-knowledge/architecture-archives-of-the-future (accessed 19 August 2024).
14 Dirk van den Heuvel, 'Looking Back, Looking Ahead: Ten Years of Jaap Bakema Study Centre', in: D. van den Heuvel, F. Tanis, and W. van de Sande (eds.), *Architecture Archives of the Future* (TUDelft/Het Nieuwe Instituut, 2023), pp. 9–14.
15 As described by van den Heuvel, the first phase of the Virtual CIAM Museum project took the form of interactive visualizations (developed also with Fatma Tanış) and *Alison's Room*, a VR installation by Paula Strunden. Online. Available https: https://nieuweinstituut.nl/en/articles/alisons-room-tijdens-filmfestival (accessed 19 August 2024).
16 David Harvey, *The Condition of Postmodernity: An Enquiry into the Origins of Cultural Change*. (Cambridge, MA: Blackwell, 1990).

Acknowledgements

The beginnings of this book can be traced to a meeting of the Global Architectural History Teaching Collaborative (GAHTC) held at MIT in Cambridge, Massachusetts in the fall of 2014. For that occasion we drew upon our research interests to prepare and deliver a lecture on architecture and the built environment that surveyed the period from the end of World War II to the fall of the Berlin Wall. This lecture eventually became a module of six lectures organized around themes that now reside on the gahtc.org website. These six lectures are the basis of the six journeys in our *The Global Turn*. Excited about the positive feedback we received after delivering our lecture, we decided to extend our collaboration by co-writing a book that from the start we saw as aimed at students of the built environment as well as the general public. We never imagined it would take nearly a decade to complete!

At the time this book project began we were both grappling with the educational and ethical imperative of teaching a survey of architecture and the built environment informed by a global perspective to our students — at TU Delft (in the case of Tom Avermaete) and IIT College of Architecture (in the case of Michelangelo Sabatino, who had arrived in Chicago in 2014 after years spent on the faculty of the University of Houston Gerald D. Hines College of Architecture and Design). Tom eventually moved to ETH Zürich's Institute for the History and Theory of Architecture (gta), where he continues to implement what we learned from our GAHTC collaboration in a different environment. During the decade it has taken us to complete *The Global Turn* various studies have been published to support and stimulate survey teaching at both undergraduate and graduate levels, a field in which Mark Jarzombek and Vikramāditya Prakāsh's *A Global History of Architecture* (2006) led the way. We hope our book will make a useful if modest addition to the growing body of survey books concerning the built environment from a global perspective.

One of the best parts of a book project that has taken longer to finish than initially intended is that it has allowed us to meet and work and enjoy each other's company in different cities. Our research and writing trajectory for *The Global Turn* reflects at least three of the themes that structure this book:

collaboration, mobility, and knowledge. Whether in Houston or Delft, Chicago or Zurich, it was always a great pleasure to collaborate and learn from each other along the way. The global pandemic momentarily interrupted our cross-Atlantic exchanges and forced us to move to the virtual world of Zoom.

We received a subsidy from the Andrew W. Mellon Foundation and MIT's Global Architecture History Teaching Collaborative to support the publication of this book. We are especially grateful to Professor Mark Jarzombek at MIT for his encouragement throughout the process and are pleased that he agreed to write the foreword. Our thanks also go to Eliana Abu-Hamdi (former GAHTC project manager) for helping with logistics throughout the process. Additional financial support for this book was provided by Michelangelo Sabatino thanks to the John Vinci Distinguished Research Fellowship at IIT College of Architecture and, in the case of Tom Avermaete, by ETH Zürich.

We wish to acknowledge the contribution made by Leonardo Zuccaro Marchi, Avermaete's former PhD student and currently a faculty member at the Politecnico di Milano, to the initial phase of research for the book and to thank him for writing the coda. We would like to thank Fatma Tanis for her enthusiastic help in teaching a joint seminar at TU Delft based on an early version of our research and Pierre Eichmeyer (ETH Zurich) for kindly assisting with the image research for some of the chapters. In the final phases of the book John Nicolson played a key role in the editing process. We are especially grateful to our publisher, Marcel Witvoet, and his team at nai010 in Rotterdam for their patient support of our book over the years and to the talented Studio Joost Grootens in Amsterdam for their understated yet engaging design. We wanted the informal visual character of our black and white paperback book to reflect the fact that we make no claim to producing a 'definitive' study. Our intention from the start has been to identify the most important themes that that we believe have come to define the Global Turn in the built environment while providing a sampling of examples to illustrate the themes.

Finally, we dedicate this book to our fellow GAHTC colleagues, whose contributions we continue to appreciate (the initiative originally funded by the Andrew W. Mellon Foundation lives on at https://gahtc.org/). And we dedicate this book to our graduate and doctoral students (past, present, and future), who come to Chicago and Zurich from all over the world. Their personal and educational trajectories have been shaped by the same global historical events that are outlined in the pages of this book. Having ourselves been students and faculty in very different contexts and countries, we are especially sympathetic to the challenges and rewards of transnational classrooms.

Authors and Contributors

Tom Avermaete

trained as an architect and historian in Belgium and Denmark. He is Professor for the History and Theory of Urban Design at the Institute for the History and Theory of Architecture at ETH Zürich, Switzerland. Avermaete has a special research interest in the architecture of the city in western and non-western contexts. His research focuses on the changing roles, approaches, and tools of architects and urban designers, especially within cross-cultural perspectives. Avermaete is the author of *Another Modern: the Post-War Architecture and Urbanism of Candilis-Josic-Woods* (2005), *The Balcony* (with Rem Koolhaas, 2014) and *Casablanca-Chandigarh: Reports on Modernity* (with Maristella Casciato, 2014). He is a co-editor of *Architectural Positions* (with Klaske Havik and Hans Teerds, 2009), *Colonial Modern* (with Marion von Osten and Serhat Karakayali, 2010), *Structuralism Reloaded* (with Tomás Valena and Georg Vrachliotis, 2011), *Making a New World* (with Rajesh Heynickx, 2012), *Architecture and the Welfare State* (with Mark Swenarton and Dirk van den Heuvel, 2015), *Shopping Towns Europe* (with Janina Gosseye, 2017) *Acculturating the Shopping Centre* (with Janina Gosseye, 2018), *The New Urban Condition* (with Leandro Medrano and Luiz Recaman, 2021), *Urban Design in the 20th Century: A History* (with Janina Gosseye; gta Verlag, 2021, 2023) and *Agadir. Building the Modern Afropolis* (with Maxime Zaugg, 2022). He is a member of the editorial board of the peer-reviewed journal *OASE Architectural Journal* and a co-editor of the series *Bloomsbury Studies in Modern Architecture* (with Janina Gosseye). Avermaete has curated several exhibitions, including *In The Desert of Modernity* (Berlin, 2008; Casablanca 2009), *SESC Stories: A Social Archive* (Biennale Sao Paulo, 2019), and *Unspoken Knowledge* (Zurich, 2023).

Michelangelo Sabatino

trained as an architect, preservationist, and historian in Canada, Italy, and the US. He is Professor of Architectural History and Heritage at IIT's College of Architecture, where he directs the PhD programme and is the inaugural John Vinci Distinguished Research Fellow. Sabatino's interdisciplinary research explores the cultural, material, political, and social histories of twentieth-century built environments in the Americas and Europe. His first book, *Pride in Modesty: Modernist Architecture and the Vernacular Tradition in Italy* (2011), won multiple awards, including the Society of Architectural Historians' Alice Davis Hitchcock Award. Since arriving at IIT in Chicago Sabatino has co-authored *Modern in the Middle: Chicago Houses 1929–1975*; this won the Modernism in America Award from Docomomo US. Sabatino's co-edited book *Modern Architecture and the Mediterranean: Vernacular Dialogues and Contested Identities* (with Jean-Francois Lejeune, 2010) received a commendation from the UIA's International Committee of Architectural Critics. His recent books include *Canada: Modern Architectures in History* (with Rhodri Windsor Liscombe, 2016), *Avant-Garde in the Cornfields: Architecture, Landscape, and Preservation in New Harmony* (with Ben Nicholson, 2019), *Making Houston Modern: The Life and Architecture of Howard Barnstone* (with Barrie Scardino Bradley and Stephen Fox, 2020), and *Carlo Mollino: Architect and Storyteller* (with Napoleone Ferrari, 2021). New books include *MIES in His Own Words: Complete Writings, Speeches, and Interviews* (with Vittorio Pizzigoni, 2024) and *The Edith Farnsworth House. Architecture, Preservation, Culture* (2024). His forthcoming book is *Building, Breaking, Rebuilding. The Illinois Institute of Technology Campus and Chicago's South Side* (with Kevin Harrington, 2025).

→ www.michelangelo-sabatino.com

Leonardo Zuccaro Marchi

is Assistant Professor (ricercatore RTDA) of Architecture and Urban Design at the Politecnico di Milano. He is an Italian architect whose research addresses the ambiguous complexity and different ambassadorial roles and practices of architecture. He graduated from the Politecnico di Milano and from the Politecnico di Torino (A.S.P. Alta Scuola Politecnica). He received his PhD at the IUAV and TU Delft (joint doctorate programme) with research on 'The Heart of the City' (published by Routledge in 2018). After completing his PhD, he developed his research in various international post-doctoral research projects and fellowships in collaboration with renowned academic institutions (CCA-Montreal, TU Delft, KTH Stockholm, ETH-Zurich). He has taught at TU Delft, PoliMi, UDEM, and IUAV. He has collaborated in urban design/landscape projects and theoretical research with international firms such as CZA-Cino Zucchi Architetti, MECANOO architecten, and LAND. He was awarded the Europe 40 Under 40 Award and was runner-up at Europan 11 in Leeuwarden. He is co-founder of {Co-P-E} — Collective of Projects in Equipoise — which won Europan 14 in Neu Ulm.

Mark Jarzombek
is Professor of the History and Theory of Architecture. He received his diploma of architecture at ETH Zurich in 1980 and his PhD at MIT in 1986. He teaches in the History Theory Criticism Section (HTC) of the Department of Architecture at MIT. He works on a wide range of topics, both historical and theoretical, is one of the country's leading advocates for global history, and has published several books and articles on this topic. His most recent book, *Architecture Constructed: Notes on a Discipline* (Bloomsbury, 2023), studies the frictions between architects and contractors as seen from an awareness of the problem of Eurocentrism. Together with Vikramāditya Prakāsh (University of Washington, Seattle), Jarzombek created the Global Architecture History Teaching Collaborative (GAHTC), funded by the Andrew W. Mellon Foundation. Promoting the development and exchange of teaching materials for architectural history education across the globe, GAHTC provides awards to members and their teams for developing new lecture material from global perspectives.

SJG
is a graphic design studio based in Amsterdam (NL) and Biel/Bienne (CH), focusing on books, maps, typefaces, spatial installations, and digital information environments for publishers such as Lars Müller Publishers, nai010 publishers, and Phaidon Press; educational and research institutes like ETH Zürich, Future Cities Laboratory Singapore, and TU Munich; and museums like Astrup Fearnley Museet Oslo, Serpentine Galleries London, and Van Abbemuseum Eindhoven. Joost Grootens established SJG in 1995. He is also a professor of artistic research in visual design at the Royal Danish Academy and teaches at the Master in Editorial Design program at ISIA Urbino. Dimitri Jeannottat joined SJG in 2013 and also teaches graphic design and typography at the École d'arts appliqués de La Chaux-de-Fonds.

Index

Note: Page numbers *in italics* refer to illustrations.

Abraj Al Bait shopping centre (Mecca), 89–90
AEG Turbine Factory, 181
Africa Hall (Addis Ababa), 184
airports, 120–124, 217
Albini, Franco, 62
Alcoa Aluminum Company, *174*, 183
 – headquarters, *175*, 185
Alexander, Christopher, 222
aluminium, *174*, *175*, 185–186
Andreu, Paul, 123–124
architectural manuals, *144–145*, 151–154
architectural periodicals, 29, 63, *141*, *142–143*, 148–151, 186
Association pour une Rénovation Architecturale (ASCORAL), 180
Augé, Marc, 89

Bakema, Jaap, 63, 224
Barlow, William Henry, 115
Bauhaus building, *171*, 182
Behrens, Peter, 181
Belluschi, Pietro, 128
Ben Barka, Mehdi, 91
Berg, Maxine, 23
Berlage, Hendrick Petrus, 53
Berlin Wall, 11, *11*, 31, 52, 94, 223, 227
Berners-Lee, Tim, 94
Bianchi, Salvatore, 118
Bideberry, Pierre, 205
bidonvilles, 30, *192*, 193–194, *197–200*, 201, 205–213

 – Aubervilliers, 207, 213
 – La Courneuve 'La Campa,' *190–191*, 193–194, *198*, *200*, 201, 207, 213
 – Montreuil, 207
 – Nanterre 'La Folie,' *199*, 205, 209
 – Saint-Denis, *197*, 207
Bloc, André, 149
Briand, Aristide, 54
Brinkman, Johannes, *171*, 181
Broggi, Carlo, 55
Bullock, Nicholas, 179
Burke, Ralph H., 122
Burnet, John J., 53

Cahen, Marcel Eugène, 149
Calini, Leo, 119
Camelot, Robert, 206
Camus, Raymond, 179, 180, 186
Canal City Hakata (Fukuoka), 90
Candilis, George, 63
Caproni, P. P., and Brother, 148
Castellazzi, Massimo, 119
Castells, Manuel, 24
Centre National des Industries et des Techniques (CNIT), *196*, 206
Chehab, Fuad, 92
China State Construction Engineering Corporation (CSCEC), 219
Chraïbi, Driss, 201, 207–208
Chyrosz, Jacek, *81*, 93
Cité des 4000, *190–191*, 193, 213
collaboration, 27–28, 36–38, 49–65
colonialism, 24
concrete, 176–180

Congrès International
 d'Architecture Moderne
 (CIAM), 17–18, *17*, 28, 50,
 54, 59, 149, 180
– Athens Charter, 89
– Centre for Fine Arts
 (Brussels), *41*
– Summer School, *47*, 60–62
Congress for the New
 Urbanism, 50
Cornell University (Ithaca), 147
Crawford, Margaret, 88, 89
Crinson, Mark, 49
Cuff, Dana, 21–22

Dallas/Fort Worth
 Airport, 123
De Carlo, Giancarlo, 18, *47*,
 48, 50, 62–63
de Mailly, Jean, 206
decolonization, 30, 154
Delacroix, Henri, 193
Delos Conferences, 18
Doisneau, Robert, *192*,
 193–194
Dormoy, Marie, 176
Doxiadis, Constantinos, 18
Drew, Jane, 93
Durand, Jean-Nicolas
 Louis, 151

Ecochard, Michel, 92
École des Beaux Arts
 (Paris), 147
Eiermann, Egon, 28, *75*, 84, 85
Eisenman, Peter, 18
Erasmus Programme, 64
Erskine, Ralph, 63
European Union, 64, 65

façade, 180–186
Fadigati, Vasco, 119

Fagus Factory, 181
Flegenheimer, Julien, 55
Fletcher, Banister, 25, *26*
float glass, *174*, 183–184, 186
Ford, Henry, 179
Ford company, 184
Forty, Adrian, 176
Foster, Norman, 86
Foster Associates, *77*
Fourastié, Jean, 74
Frampton, Kenneth, 21–22,
 24, 58
Franklin D. Roosevelt Four
 Freedoms Park, *46*, 58
Fraser, Murray, 25
Friberger, Eric, *144*
Friedrichstrasse skyscraper,
 182
Fry, Maxwell, 93
Fundació Mies van der Rohe,
 65

Gardella, Ignazio, 62
Gato, Carlos, 53
Gatwick Airport, *111*, 122
Georges-Valbon Public Park,
 213
Ghana National Construction
 Corporation (GNCC), 93
Giddens, Anthony, 15
Giedion, Sigfried, 54–55, 58,
 82, 88, 178
Global Architectural History
 Teaching Collaborative, 8,
 12, 14
Global Village, *136*
Godard, Jean-Luc, *146*,
 156–157, 181
Gordon, Alastair, 124
Graaf, Reinier de, 152
grain elevator
 (Ogden, Calgary), *169*

Index

Grand Tour, 113, *139*, 147, 222
Great Mosque (Algiers), 118–119
Gregotti, Vittorio, 60, 61
Gropius, Walter, 128, *171*, 176, 181, 182
Gruen, Victor, 28, *78*, *79*, 86–87, 89, 90
Guggenheim Museum (Bilbao), 22, *22*
Gutkind, Erwin Anton, 23

Habitat '67, *162–163*
Hall, Charles Martin, 185
Hämer, Hardt Waltherr, 52
Harrison, Wallace, 57
Harrison & Abramovitz, *176*, 186
Heinrich, John, *173*
Hénard, Eugène, 120
Hennebique, François, 177–178, 179, 186
Herpin, Isabelle, *199*, 210, 213
Hertzberger, Herman, 63
Hilton, Conrad, 20, *108*, 125, 126
Hilton Hotels Corporation, 125–128
 – Amsterdam, 127–128
 – Cairo, *108*
 – Istanbul, *20*, 126, 129
Hoffmann, Josef, 53
Horta, Victor, 53
hotels and motels, 125–128

Ingersoll, Richard, 25
Institute for Architecture and Urban Studies (IAUS), 18
International Building Exhibition Berlin (IBA), 52
international competitions, 51–52

International Fair of Casablanca, *80*, 91–92
International Fairground, *81*, 92
International Laboratory of Architecture and Urban Design (ILAUD), 18, 28, *47*, *48*, 50, 59–60, 62–65
International Style, 177–178
International Trade Fair, *81*, 93–94
International Union of Architects (UIA), 50, 149
Isler, Heinz, 85

Jackman, Alonzo, 138
Jacobsen, Arne, 184
Jahn, Helmut, 122
James-Chakraborty, Kathleen, 24
Jarzombek, Mark, 24
Jerde, John, 90
Joedicke, Jürgen, 23

Kahn, Louis, 58
Katona, George, 73
Keynes, Milton, 28
Kleihues, Josef Paul, 52
Klein, Norman M., 90
Koenigsberger, Otto, 18
Koolhaas, Rem, 19–20
Kostof, Spiro, 24
Kultermann, Udo, 23

Lapasso, Frank J., *108*
Le Corbusier, *45*, 54, 56, 58, 121, 124, *139*, *169*, 176
Le Havre, *11*
League of Nations, 53, 54, 55, 57, 177
Lefaivre, Liane, 24
Lefèvre, Camille, 55

Lemaresquier, Charles, 53, 54
Lenzi, Luigi, 152
Linen, James, 153
Lods, Marcel, 180
London Bridge Terminus Hotel, 116
Lucaud, Raymond, *80*, 92

Maddalena, Robert, *80*, 92
Maki, Fumihiko, 117, 118
Marlin, Camille, 54
Marshall Plan, *12*, 127
Marxism, 24
mass distribution, 83–86, 219–220
Mauco, Georges, 211
Mayer, Adolf, 182
Mazzoni, Angelo, 119
McCallum, Ian, 128, 183, 185
McLuhan, Marshall, *134–135*, 137, 158
Metropolitan Museum of Art, 147
Meyer, Hannes, 54
Mezzedimi, Arturo, 184
Middleton, Robin, 150–151
Midland Grand Hotel, 116
Mies van der Rohe, *172*, 182–183, 184
Mies van der Rohe Award, 65
migrant labour, 204–213, 218–219
Moffet, Marian, 25
Moholy-Nagy, Sybil, 23
Montuori, Eugenio, 119
Moser, Karl, 53
Muggia, Attilio, 53
Mumford, Lewis, 123
Musée du Louvre (Paris), 148

National Interstate and Defense Highway Act, 82, 88

Neckermann Distribution Centre, *75*, 84–85
Nénot, Henri-Paul, 55
Nervi, Pier Luigi, 152, *167*
Neufert, Ernst, *142–143*, 151
Niemeyer, Oscar, *45*, 56, 58, *81*, 92
Nkrumah, Kwame, 93
Norberg-Schulz, Christian, 59

Obata, Gyo, 123
Olivetti Technical Centre and Distribution Centre, *76*, 86
Osawa, Masato, 117
Overseas Corporation Aluminum (OCAL), 187

Palace of Nations, *43*, 52–55, 56, 58
Pan American, *109*, 128
Parkin, John B. (& Associates), *34–35*, *164*
Paxton, Joseph, 182
Peanuts, *146*, 155
Peck, Bradford, 89
Pennsylvania Turnpike, *167*
Pietilä, Reima, 61, 63
Pilat, Maurice, 156
Pilkington, Alastair, 183–184, 186
Pilkington's Glass Company, *174*, 183–184
Pintonello, Achille, 119
Ponti, Gio, 184
popular media, *146*, 154–157
Portoghesi, Paolo, 65
Pottier, Jean, *197*, 206–207
Prakash, Vikramaditya, 24

railway stations, 115–120

REITs (Real Estate Investment Trusts), 88
Renault Parts Distribution Centre, 77, 86
Rencountres Internationales des Architectes (RIA), 149
Revell, Viljo, 52
Ridolfi, Mario, 152, 154
Robertson, Roland, 15
Rogers, Ernesto Nathan, 59, 62
Rostow, Walt Whitman, 74
Roth, Emery, *31*
Roth, Richard, 128
Rudofsky, Bernard, 23
Rymaszewski, Stanisław, *81*, 93

Samonà, Giuseppe, 62
San Francisco International Airport, *107*
Sant'Elia, Antonio, 120
Santelli, Serge, 210
SAS Hotel (Copenhagen), 184
Sassen, Saskia, 24
Schengen Agreement, 64
Schiphol (Amsterdam), 122
Schipporeit, George, *173*
Schulz, Charles M., 155
Scott, George Gilbert, 116
Scott Brown, Denise, 61
Scott-Brown, Robert, 61
Sears Company, *70–71*, 73, 84
Sert, Josep Lluís, 88
Servian Wall, 119, 129
Shinjuku Terminal, 117–119
shopping malls, 86–90, 94–95, 124
Silk Road(s), 14–15, *14*
Simonnet, Cyrille, 178
Skidmore, Owings & Merrill, 127

Smith, Larry, 78
Society of Architectural Historians (SAH), 50
Society of Architectural Historians of Great Britain (SAHGB), 50
Southdale Shopping Centre, 79, 87–88
St Pancras Station, 115–116
Stazione Termini (film), *104*
steel plant (Hungary), *170*
Stirling, James, 28
suburbs, 112, *146*, 154–155
Swiss Coop supermarkets, 85
Sydney Opera House, 52

Tafuri, Manfredo, 24, 60
Tambuté, Clément, 195
Tange, Kenzo, *76*, 86
Tata Steel, 220
Tati, Jacques, 156, 157
Team 10, 50, 59–60, 62, 63, 64
Temple of Angkor Wat, 148
Tengbom, Ivar, 53
Termini Station (Rome), 118–119
'The Strip' (Las Vegas), *103*
Thonet brothers, 84
Toronto City Hall, *42*, 52
tourism, 113–114
trade fairs, 90–94
Turner, John, 61
Tyrwhitt, Jacqueline, 18
Tzonis, Alexander, 24

UNESCO headquarters, 55
United Airlines, *110*
United Nations, *39*
– Geneva office, *42*
– Headquarters, *40*, *44*, 49, 52, 55, 56–58, 180–181
– Refugee Convention, 201

United States Information
  Service (USIS), 153–154
Utzon, Jørn, 52

Vágó, József, 55
van der Leeuw, Kees, 182
van der Vlugt, Leendert,
  181–182
van Eyck, Aldo, 63
van Gool, Frans, 122
Van Nelle Factory, *171*,
  181–182
Veblen, Thorstein, 117
Venice Biennale, 18, 65
Victoria and Albert
  Museum, 147
Vitellozzi, Annibale, 119

Wachsmann, Konrad, *145*
Waldinger, Roger, 202
Waters, Malcolm, 16
Weismann, Ernest, 18
Wharton, Annabel, 127
Wilson, Woodrow, 126
World Trade Center, *31*, *168*
World Wide Web, 94, 158,
  217–218
Wright, Frank Lloyd, 177

Yamasaki, Minoru, *31*

Zeebrugge Sea Terminal, 122
Zehrfuss, Bernard, 208
Zevaco, Jean-François, *80*, 92
Zevi, Bruno, 152, 153, 154

Image Credits

p. 11 (top) © Bibliothèque municipale du Havre • p. 11 (bottom) © Alamy Stock Photo • p. 12 © Interfoto/Alamy Stock Photo • p. 14 © Alamy Stock Photo • p. 17 (top) © gta Archive/ETH Zurich, CIAM • p. 17 (bottom) © Het Nieuwe Instituut • p. 19 © Granger-Historical Picture Archive/Alamy Stock Photo • p. 20 © Interfoto/Alamy Stock Photo • p. 22 © Nadia Isakova/Alamy Stock Photo • p. 26 © Banister Fletcher, *A History of Architecture on the Comparative Method for Students, Craftsmen, and Amateurs*, 6th ed. (London: B. T. Batsford, 1921). • p. 31 (left) © Università Iuav di Venezia, Archivio Progetti • p. 31 (right) © Alamy Stock Photo.

Fig. 1.1 © Canadian Architectural Archives, University of Calgary (Panda Associates fonds) • Fig. 1.2 © UN Geospatial Information Section [Map A000/10/2011]. New York: Dept. of Field Support, Cartographic Section, May 2010 • Fig. 1.3 © Acacia Card Company, 258 Broadway, New York 7. N. Y. • Fig. 1.4 © LEGO Group and United Nations, 2013 • Fig. 1.5 © gta Archive/ETH Zurich, CIAM • Fig. 1.6 © Canadian Architectural Archives, University of Calgary (Panda Associates fonds) • Fig. 1.7 © Photo Edition C. Sartori, Geneva • Fig. 1.8 © gta Archive/ETH Zurich, Karl Moser • Fig. 1.9 © United Nations Department of Global Communications, UN 7770807 © Fig. 1.10 © United Nations Department of Global Communications • Fig. 1.11 © United Nations Department of Global Communications • Fig. 1.12 © Iwan Baan Photography B.V. • Fig. 1.13 © Het Nieuwe Instituut (Jaap Bakema) • Fig. 1.14 © Università Iuav di Venezia, Archivio Progetti • Fig. 1.15 © ILAUD (Milano) • Fig. 1.16 • © Spazio e Società (Sansoni Editore, Firenze)

Fig. 2.1 Neil Baylis/© Alamy Stock Photo • Fig. 2.2 © Aero Exploration • Fig. 2.3 Horstheinz Neuendorf/saai/© Archiv für Architektur und Ingenieurbau, Karlsruher Institut für Technologie, Werkarchiv Egon Eiermann • Fig. 2.4 © Associazione archivio storico Olivetti, Società Olivetti • Fig. 2.5 © Associazione archivio storico Olivetti, Società Olivetti • Fig. 2.6 Martin Charles/© Architectural Press Archive/RIBA Collections • Fig. 2.7 Victor Gruen and Larry Smith, *Shopping Towns USA: The Planning of Shopping Centers* (New York: Reinhold publishing corporation, 1960), p. 119 • Fig. 2.8 © Gruen Architects • Fig. 2.9 © Alamy Stock Photo • Fig. 2.10 © Travaux Publics et Batiments • Fig. 2.11 © Alexandre Guirkinger • Fig. 2.12 © Commonswift

Fig. 3.1 © Curt Teich Color, Newberry Library, Chicago • Fig. 3.2 © Università Iuav di Venezia, Archivio Progetti • Fig. 3.3 © Alamy Stock Photo • Fig. 3.4 © Underwood Archives, Inc/Alamy Stock Photo • Fig. 3.5 © Curt Teich Color, Newberry Library, Chicago/Alamy Stock Photo • Fig. 3.6 © Chicago Transit Authority • Fig. 3.7 © Underwood Archives, Inc/Alamy Stock Photo • Fig. 3.8 © Freeman Studios, Berrien Springs, Michigan • Fig. 3.9 © Conrad N. Hilton Foundation • Fig. 3.10 © Ads R/Alamy Stock Photo • Fig. 3.11 © Alamy Stock Photo • Fig. 3.12 © Courtesy of Special Collections, University of Miami Libraries, Coral Gables, Florida • Fig. 3.13 © United Airlines Archives • Fig. 3.14 © Hum Historical/Alamy Stock Photo • Fig. 3.15 © Jusitn Kase z12z/Alamy Stock Photo

Fig. 4.1 © CBC Still Photo Collection • Fig. 4.2 © F.L.C./2024, ProLitteris, Zurich • Fig. 4.3 © Architekturmuseum der TUM, thie-79-4 • Figs. 4.4–6 © *L'Architecture d'Aujourd'hui* • Figs. 4.7–8 © Ernst Neufert, *Bauentwurfslehre* (Berlin: Bauwelt-Verlag, 1936) • Figs. 4.9–10 Mario Ridolfi, *Manuale dell'architetto, compilato a cura del Consiglio nazionale delle ricerche* (Rome: Ufficio informazioni Stati Uniti, 1946) • Fig. 4.11 © Alamy Stock Photo • Fig. 4.12 © Commons

Fig. 5.1 © Safdie Architects • Fig. 5.2 © Università Iuav di Venezia, Archivio Progetti • Figs. 5.3–4 © ClassicStock/Alamy Stock Photo • Fig. 5.5 © Provincial Archives of Alberta, Edmonton (Harry Pollard fonds) • Fig. 5.6 © colaimages/Alamy Stock Photo • Fig. 5.7 © Penta Spring Limited/Alamy Stock Photo • Fig. 5.8 © Photopat/Alamy Stock Photo • Fig. 5.9 © Tolo Balaquer/Alamy Stock Photo • Fig. 5.10 © Università Iuav di Venezia, Archivio Progetti • Fig. 5.11 © SuperStock/Alamy Stock Photo • Fig. 5.12 © Università Iuav di Venezia, Archivio Progetti • Fig. 5.13 © piemags/ww2archive/Alamy Stock Photo • Fig. 5.14 © adsR/Alamy Stock Photo • Fig. 5.15 © Amy Cicconi/Alamy Stock Photo

Fig. 6.1 © Robert Doisneau/GAMMA RAPHO • Fig. 6.2 © Estate of Gerald Bloncourt. All rights reserved, 2024/Bridgeman Images • Fig. 6.3 © Coll. Part/DR • Fig. 6.4 © AGIP/Bridgeman Images • Fig. 6.5 © Archives municipales de Saint-Denis, 3 Fi • 42/15, Pierre Douzenel • Fig. 6.6 © Jean Pottier • Fig. 6.7 © Claude Raymond-Dityvon/Université d'Angers/Archives départementales de la Seine-Saint-Denis • Fig. 6.8 © Archives du Mouvement contre le Racisme et pour l'Amitié entre les Peuples (http://archives.mrap.fr) • Figs. 6.9–10 Isabelle Herpin et Serge Santelli, *Bidonville à Nanterre: étude architecturale* (Paris: Institut de l'Environnement, Ministère des Affaires, 1973) • Fig. 6.11 © France Soir • Fig. 6.12 © Georges Azenstarck/Roger-Viollet • Fig. 6.13 © BnF ou Bibliothèque nationale de France

Colophon

Texts: Tom Avermaete, Michelangelo Sabatino
Foreword: Mark Jarzombek
Coda: Leonardo Zuccaro Marchi
Research assistance: Pierre Eichmeyer, Leonardo Zuccaro Marchi
Copy editing: John Nicolson
Indexer: Meridith Murray

Design: SJG / Joost Grootens, Dimitri Jeannottat
Lithography, printing and binding: Wilco Art Books
Publisher: Marcel Witvoet, nai010 publishers

This publication was made possible by financial support from:
Global Architectural History Teaching Collaborative (GAHTC)
Department of Architecture (D-ARCH), ETH Zurich
PhD Program in Architecture, College of Architecture, IIT

Printed and bound in Europe

ISBN 978-94-6208-583-1

NUR 648
BISAC ARC005080, ARC013000
THEMA AM

The Global Turn is also available as an e-book:
ISBN 978-94-6208-584-8 (e-book, pdf)

© 2025 nai010 publishers, Rotterdam
All rights reserved. No part of this publication may be reproduced, stored in a retrieval system, or transmitted in any form or by any means, electronic, mechanical, photocopying, recording or otherwise, without the prior written permission of the publisher.

© 2025, c/o Pictoright Amsterdam
For works of visual artists affiliated with a CISAC-organization the copyrights have been settled with Pictoright in Amsterdam.

Although every effort was made to find the copyright holders for the illustrations used, it has not been possible to trace them all. Interested parties are requested to contact nai010 publishers, Korte Hoogstraat 31, 3011 GK Rotterdam, the Netherlands.
    nai010 publishers is an internationally orientated publisher specialized in developing, producing and distributing books in the fields of architecture, urbanism, art and design.
    nai010 books are available internationally at selected bookstores and from the following distribution partners:
 • North, Central and South America: Artbook | D.A.P., New York, USA, dap@dapinc.com
 • Rest of the world: Idea Books, Amsterdam, the Netherlands, idea@ideabooks.nl
    For general questions, please contact nai010 publishers directly at sales@nai010.com or visit our website www.nai010.com for further information.